*Dedicated to the memory of my husband, John Bird, for his
infinite encouragement in the writing of this book,
and to that of my friend Josette Ahuir, whose unquenchable
enthusiasm made researching it such fun*

The
Vendée

ANGELA BIRD

Malnoue Publications
LONDON

With thanks to
Carole and David, Sue and Nick, Doreen, David and Daniel,
to the Hulf family, to keen-eyed Jonathan, Miranda and Sue,
to all my long-suffering visitors
and finally—of course—to my own family

Design and cartography Adrian Hulf

Cover picture: **Saint-Gilles-Croix-de-Vie**
© Angela Bird.

*While every care has been taken in the compiling of this book, neither the author nor the publisher can accept responsibility
for any inaccuracies, and visitors are advised to check details in advance before making a special journey.
Prices, usually based on 2003 rates, are given as a guide only and do not constitute a guaranteed admission charge.
The author welcomes any comments, corrections or suggestions to: angelabird@the-vendee.co.uk*

British Library Cataloguing in Publication Data:
a catalogue record for this book is available from the British Library.

*First published as "The English Family Guide to the Vendée" 1994; reprinted 1996, 1997, 1998;
second edition published as "The Vendée: An English Family Guide" 2000; reprinted 2000, 2002;
by Éditions Hécate, Luçon, France*

*This edition published 2004
Malnoue Publications
London
malnouepublications@the-vendee.co.uk*

Contents

Names in bold indicate main towns.

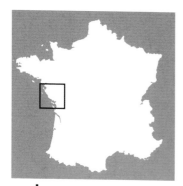

The Vendée

This guide is divided into six areas. Below are the various symbols used on maps and other pages.

NANTES   major town
Challans   smaller town
Apremont   village
★   Top 20 site (see p 34)
≈   road
≡   motorway
≈   motorway under construction
⌐   river
▬   lake
▦   woodland
⋮   marshland
▨   county boundary
- - -   ferry service
⌘   golf course
ⓘ   tourist office
✚   hospital
🅿   car park
⌑   church
♿   disabled access
●   long season
◐   medium season
○   short season

Maps are for guidance only, and do not show all roads and villages. They should be used in conjunction with current Michelin or IGN maps.

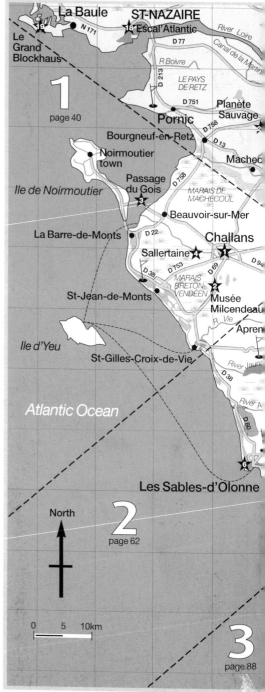

La Baule
ST-NAZAIRE
Le Grand Blockhaus
☆ Escal'Atlantic
N 171
River Loire
Canal de la Martin
D 77
R Boivre
D 213
LE PAYS DE RETZ
D 751
Planète Sauvage

1 page 40

Pornic
D 758
Bourgneuf-en-Retz
D 13
Noirmoutier town
Machec
Passage du Gois
D 758
MARAIS DE MACHECOUL
Ile de Noirmoutier
Beauvoir-sur-Mer
La Barre-de-Monts
D 22
Challans ★
Sallertaine ☆
D 753
D 69
D 9
MARAIS BRETON-VENDÉEN ☆
Musée Milcendeau
St-Jean-de-Monts
R. Vie
Apren
Ile d'Yeu
St-Gilles-Croix-de-Vie
River Jaun
D 38

Atlantic Ocean

River A
D 80
☆
Les Sables-d'Olonne

North

2 page 62

0   5   10km

3 page 88

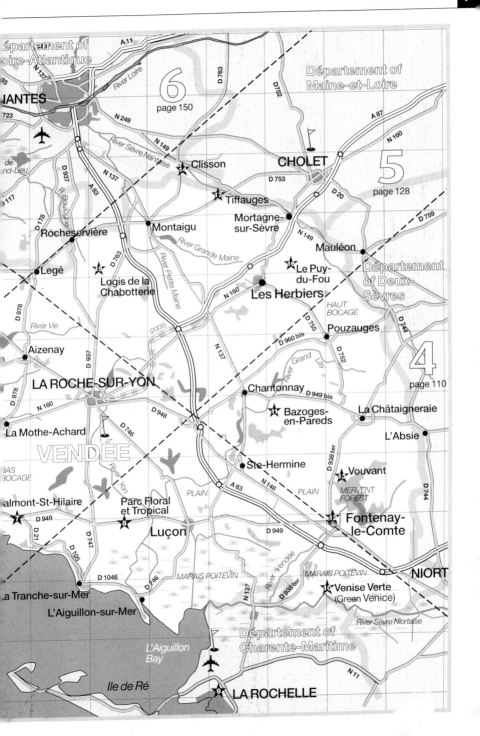

Département of
Loire-Atlantique

A 11

N 137

River Loire

6
page 150

D 763

D 752

Département of
Maine-et-Loire

A 87

NANTES

N 249

N 149

723

River Sèvre Nantaise

CHOLET

N 160

de
nd-Lieu

D 937

N 137

A 83

Clisson

D 753

5
page 128

117

D 178

R. Boulogne

Tiffauges

D 20

D 759

Rocheservière

Montaigu

Mortagne-
sur-Sèvre

N 149

Mauléon

Legé

D 763

River Grande Maine

River Petite Maine

Le Puy-
du-Fou

Département
of Deux-
Sèvres

Logis de la
Chabotterie

N 160

Les Herbiers

HAUT
BOCAGE

D 978

River Vie

(2005)

D 937

N 137

D 755

D 960 bis

Pouzauges

D 752

D 744

Aizenay

River Grand Lay

4
page 110

LA ROCHE-SUR-YON

D 948

Chantonnay

D 949 bis

La Châtaigneraie

D 978

N 160

Bazoges-
en-Pareds

L'Absie

La Mothe-Achard

D 746

D 938 ter

Vouvant

VENDÉE

River Yon

Ste-Hermine

N 148

MERVENT
FOREST

D 744

BAS
BOCAGE

PLAIN

A 83

PLAIN

Fontenay-
le-Comte

almont-St-Hilaire

Parc Floral
et Tropical

D 949

D 949

D 21

8

Luçon

NIORT

D 747

D 105

D 1046

D 746

MARAIS POITEVIN

N 137

River Vendée

D 938 ter

MARAIS POITEVIN

La Tranche-sur-Mer

Venise Verte
(Green Venice)

L'Aiguillon-sur-Mer

River Sèvre Niortaise

L'Aiguillon
Bay

Département of
Charente-Maritime

Ile de Ré

LA ROCHELLE

N 11

Introduction

Nobody needs advice on how to soak up the 2,500 annual hours of sunshine that beam down on the 140km of beaches lining the coast of the Vendée. Yet inland the scenery changes. Green fields, shady forests and gentle rivers make up a land of legend and troubled history.

I have been in love with the Vendée for 35 years, slowly uncovering the mysteries of this large French *département* (or county) the size of Devon, and finding offbeat outings for family and friends. I aim to share my enjoyment and give you a taste of the towns, villages, waterways and countryside that lie beyond the seaside campsite or the rural *gîte*. I have left aside any discussion of camping establishments, hotels or B&Bs—which are well covered in other, specialist, guides. In response to requests (though with a good deal of trepidation!) I am including a small number of restaurant suggestions—a selection based on my own experience or that of friends. It is varied, but by no means exhaustive; serious gastronomes should check more expert opinions in the Michelin and *GaultMillau* guides.

This guidebook will concern itself with culture and fun, and will lead you into lesser-known corners—and even slightly beyond the Vendée's boundaries to other places within easy reach: the Pays de Retz and Nantes to the north; Muscadet country to the north-east; west, to Cholet, and the state-of-the-art cinema park of Futuroscope at Poitiers; and south to historic La Rochelle.

Although the Vendée is known to most holidaymakers for its coast, generations of French schoolchildren have learnt that it is composed of *marais*, *plaine* and *bocage*—fens, plain, and wooded hills. If you are staying near the seaside you will almost certainly be familiar with the *marais*, the marshland dredged out of the sea by 12th-century monks and 16th-century Dutch engineers. You may have already

crossed the Marais Breton (famed for salt production and duck-breeding), a patchwork of fields divided by watery ditches and canals that stretches from Bourgneuf-en-Retz and Machecoul southwards to St-Gilles-Croix-de-Vie. Perhaps you have glimpsed the salt-marshes north of Les Sables-d'Olonne, or the oyster-rich marshland that lies between Talmont-St-Hilaire and Jard-sur-Mer. Or maybe you know the Marais Poitevin, consisting of the flat, treeless *marais desséché* (dry marsh) east of Longeville and La Tranche and south of Luçon, and the idyllic *marais mouillé* (wet marsh), a network of poplar-lined, duckweed-covered waterways south of Fontenay, nicknamed the "Venise Verte", or "Green Venice".

The *bocage* covers most of the rest—the *haut-bocage* being the hilly, wooded region down the eastern fringe of the *département*, and the *bas-bocage* the gently undulating land that surrounds La Roche-sur-Yon and continues towards the coast. This area is dotted with small farmhouses and cottages—their doorways often outlined in white and topped by a painted cross to keep witches and ill-fortune at bay. Here, neolithic man built dolmens and raised the enormous standing-stones known as menhirs; more than 4,000 years later—after the French Revolution—18th-century guerrillas hid in the forests to escape the flames and the bayonets of Republican troops.

Blending into the Marais Poitevin and the *bocage* is the *plaine*, a series of vast, rolling prairies that stretch between Ste-Hermine and Fontenay-le-Comte and provide crops of sunflowers, maize and wheat. The red-roofed houses here exude prosperity. Tall and substantial, they are built of fine, white stone, unlike the more primitive, ground-hugging cottages of the windswept marshes.

On the coast, I shall suggest some alternative attractions to the beach, and recommend

LOCAL FUN AND FESTIVITIES

Heavily advertised on local posters and banners, **village festivals**, are great fun. Usually low-key affairs held on a Sunday, they tend to promote different, often food-related local traditions, from oyster-fishing to the baking of brioche. Youngsters bowl for a pig, older men drink steadily at long trestle bars, and groups of folk-dancers swirl through the hot summer afternoons. Tossing a hoop over a duck can mean just that; if you succeed, you get to take the bewildered bird home. Events are usually rounded off with a *bal populaire* where you can find yourself dancing a conga with the butcher, baker and local clog-maker.

Look out for the **Fête de la Cuisine** in late May, a day when many restaurants put on half-price menus—you'll need to book in advance as it's understandably popular!

June is full of unusual delights. On the **Journées du Patrimoine du Pays** craftsmen demonstrate time-honoured skills of thatching, brick-making

and so on. The date usually coincides with the **Journée des Moulins** (French National Mills Day) when windmills and watermills, many of them privately-owned, open their doors to show off their restoration work. Around 24 June bonfires are often lit to celebrate the **Feast of St John the Baptist**; unmarried girls who managed to jump over three different bonfires on this night were supposed to meet the man of their dreams. During the week-long **Fête de la Musique**, in late June, concerts are held indoors and out. The month is also the focus for a **Fête des Jardins**, when some unusual private gardens may be open for visits.

The **Fête Nationale** (Bastille Day) is marked by parades and fireworks on the evening of either 13 or 14 July, though events are sometimes low-key in this region, which was decidedly anti-Republican after the 1789 French Revolution. The **circus** remains a much-loved tradition in France, and

travelling companies large and small still pitch their colourful big tops in holiday towns and villages.

In mid-September a weekend of **Journées du Patrimoine** (Heritage Days) gives you a chance to visit historic properties at reduced rates—including some that are normally closed to the public. You can pick up a brochure from tourist offices during the few weeks beforehand.

From mid-September to mid-January is the eagerly-awaited season for **la chasse** (shooting). On Sundays and on one weekday, which varies from village to village, trigger-happy locals lurk among the hedgerows from dawn to dusk, firing at anything from rabbits to wild boar. If you take a country walk, wear something brightly-coloured to make sure you're noticed.

December brings some wonderfully rustic **Christmas cribs** that often remain on display until February. Drop into any country church you pass in winter—just in case.

serious seaside-lovers to obtain tide-tables (*horaires des marées*), free from tourist offices. To enjoy the maximum personal space, aim for the period around low tide (*basse mer*, or *marée basse*). In July and August the sands are often crowded, and smarter town beaches like those of Les Sables-d'Olonne and St-Gilles-Croix-de-Vie can become unbearably congested at high

tide (*pleine mer*, or *marée haute*). A little research pays off, here, if you want to avoid the crush.

For a bit of variety, get out a good map and head inland. There you can walk in the forests, rent a mountain-bike and canoe through the marshes, or admire the Vendée's rich legacy of Romanesque architecture, ride on a steam train, go bird-watching or visit a vineyard. And, if you are unfortunate enough to wake up to a spot of rain, you can dip into this book to find museums, castles, aquariums and *brocante* (junk) shops in which to spend the time until the sun comes out again. I have included at-a-glance symbols as an indication of opening periods, which I hope will help out-of-season visitors home in easily on what to do in autumn, winter and spring, as well as high summer.

Sports-lovers and night-owls will have no difficulty discovering riding establishments, casinos and discos, which are well documented in tourist offices. The Vendée's other resources include unusual museums, rural events and market-days. I have sprinkled in a seasoning of things that I find irresistible on holiday, from flea markets and crafts fairs to details of local customs and food. You haven't lived until you've tried the region's ham and *mogettes* (white haricot beans), barbecued quail, grilled sardines, or eels cooked over cowpat fires.

The heritage has its melancholy side, too. Western France was torn by the Hundred Years War (against the English) and the Wars of Religion (which pitched Catholics against Protestants). But the area suffered most cruelly during the bitter civil war waged immediately after the French Revolution of 1789 by the strongly Catholic Vendean peasants—who supported the deposed French monarchy—against the Republicans' new ideas and well-armed forces. To understand the soul of the region you should skim through the section on the Vendée Wars (page 31), which outlines the savage events that are indelibly stamped on collective memory. In just three years from March 1793 the uprising cost more than 250,000 lives. Almost every village was destroyed, castles and manor houses were reduced to ruins, and a ruthless extermination policy cut the population by one third—in some villages by up to a half. So it is no surprise that most pre-19th-century castles, houses and churches are in various stages of ruination—the miracle is that any are left at all. Since those days the Vendean emblem has featured two

intertwined hearts topped with a cross and a crown to symbolise the region's twin loyalties to church and king, though—in keeping with republican sentiment—with every redesign of the logo the crown is becoming less apparent.

As befits a *département* whose major industry is now tourism, the Vendée has begun to rescue its heritage of crumbling Romanesque churches, feudal strongholds, Renaissance castles and industrial relics from layers of ivy and centuries of neglect. Houses connected with local celebrities, such as politician Georges Clemenceau, painter Charles Milcendeau and military hero Marshal Jean de Lattre de Tassigny, give fascinating insights into provincial French life. No less intriguing are museums that have evolved from private passions such as collecting kitchen utensils, tractors, perfume-bottles or sewing-machines.

I have usually given titles of museums and events in French, since this is how you will see them advertised or signposted. Most smaller establishments have tours and details only in French, so I have tried to explain enough historical background to give non-French speakers a little understanding of displays or events.

Keep an eye open for *passeport* cards or leaflets, which give reductions on admission to designated sites in an area once you have visited a first one. Many attractions are beginning to offer family tickets and to have all-day opening in summer. The cut-off point for children's admission rates varies between about 12 and 16 years. However there are very few reductions offered for senior citizens. Opening details may be varied on public holidays (see page 22).

Oh, and if your children are taking a turn on a roundabout, tell them to keep a look-out for the monkey's tail. The operator often releases a soft toy towards the end of the ride, dangling it above the children until one of them grabs the tail and pulls it off—winning a second, free ride.

I wish you a wonderful, interest-filled holiday, though I am certain you will find—as I have, even after 35 years of Vendée summers—that it will not be long enough.

Planning Your Trip

WHEN TO GO

The Vendée's climate is generally considerably warmer than that of southern England, with hot summers and mild, damp winters. Peak French holiday times are 14 July to 15 August. Apart from seaside and purely child-orientated activities, there is still plenty to visit between May and October. Main museums and cultural sites are open—at weekends at least—almost all year.

HOW TO GET THERE

Most holidaymakers opt to take their car across the Channel but, with ever-higher ferry fares, it's also worth considering air and rail travel.

By sea

Brittany Ferries: Portsmouth to St-Malo, to Caen and to Cherbourg; Poole to Cherbourg; Plymouth to Roscoff; Cork to Roscoff.
Condor Ferries: Poole to St-Malo (via Jersey) and to Cherbourg.
Hoverspeed: Dover to Calais, to Newhaven, and to Dieppe.
Irish Ferries: Rosslare to Cherbourg and to Roscoff.
P&O: Portsmouth to Cherbourg, to Caen and to Le Havre; Dover to Calais; Dublin to Cherbourg; Rosslare to Cherbourg; Hull to Zeebrugge.
SeaFrance: Dover to Calais.
Superfast Ferries: Rosyth to Zeebrugge.
Transmanche Ferries: Newhaven to Dieppe.

By air

British Airways and Air France: London (Gatwick) to Nantes-Atlantique.
Ryanair: London (Stansted) to La Rochelle and to Poitiers.

By rail

Eurotunnel: Folkestone to Coquelles (Calais), for cars and their passengers.
Eurostar: London (Waterloo) to Lille-Europe, foot passengers only. Then TGV (high-speed train) service from Lille-Europe to Nantes; local trains onward to Challans and St-Gilles-Croix-de-Vie, or to La Roche-sur-Yon and Les Sables.
London (Waterloo) to Paris (Gare du Nord); then Paris (Gare du Montparnasse) by TGV to Nantes, La Roche-sur-Yon and Les Sables-d'Olonne.

WHERE TO STAY

Camping

The Vendée has almost 400 classified camp sites, plus *campings à la ferme* (small sites on working farms). Specialist British tour-operators offer luxury camping in tents or mobile homes, while the Caravan Club, or the Camping & Caravanning Club can advise independent travellers.

Holiday cottages

Houses can be rented through Brittany Ferries, Bonnes Vacances and Chez Nous catalogues. French-owned cottages in the area can be found through Gîtes de France, 124 Boulevard Aristide-Briand, BP735, 85018 La Roche-sur-Yon Cédex (tel: 02 51 37 87 87; fax: 02 51 62 15 19; www.gites-de-france-vendee.com); or from Clévacances, 8 Place Napoléon, 85018 La Roche-sur-Yon Cédex (tel: 02 51 47 71 07; fax: 02 51 47 88 27; www.clevacances-85.com).

Hotels and Bed-&-Breakfasts

For hotel information, see page 16. Gîtes de France (see above) also categorises B&Bs. A list of hotels under the Logis de France banner is available from 65 Rue d'Ulm, 85000 La Roche-sur-Yon (tel: 02 51 62 27 52; fax: 02 51 36 30 07; www.logis-de-vendee.com).

FURTHER INFORMATION

Vendée Tourist Board: BP 233, 85006 La Roche-sur-Yon Cédex (tel: 02 51 47 88 22; fax: 02 51 05 37 01; www.vendee-tourisme.com).
Sud Vendée Tourisme (for south-east of the *département*): 51 Route de Fontenay, 85570 Pouillé (tel: 02 51 87 69 07; fax: 02 51 87 69 08; email: sudvendeetourisme@wanadoo.fr).
Western Loire Regional Tourist Board: 2 Rue de la Loire, BP 20411, 44204 Nantes Cédex 2 (tel: 02 40 48 24 20; fax: 02 40 08 07 10; www.westernloire.com).

Useful Information

ACCESSIBILITY

Things in France are improving for people with limited mobility (*à mobilité réduite*, or *handi-capé*), and the Vendée is no exception. The traditional single-storey construction of many Vendean buildings means that museums are often on ground level only—though, unfortunately, those that are not sometimes have no lift (*ascenseur*). Special parking spaces are provided at tourist attractions and at supermarkets. Obviously all new establishments are designed with accessibility in mind, and feature such facilities as toilets for the disabled. I have indicated wherever a venue specifically claims to have easy access (though absence of a logo does not necessarily mean entry is impossible). For others, I have tried to mention in the text any particular obstacles that might pose problems. If in doubt, contact the venue itself or the local tourist office for up-to-date information. "*Est-ce que c'est accessible aux fauteuils roulants?*" or "*Y a-t-il des toilettes pour handi-capés?*" are useful phrases if you ever need to check wheelchair access or the existence of toilets for the disabled.

Most beaches now have wooden or concrete ramps leading down to them, and sometimes continuing a little way onto the sand. Several seaside resorts provide at one of their lifeguard stations, during July and August, a specially adapted beach-buggy-style wheelchair called a "Tiralo" on which a bather can be assisted down to the water's edge and right into the sea for a swim. At the time of writing these beaches include Noirmoutier (L'Épine), Notre-Dame-de-Monts, St-Jean-de-Monts, St-Gilles-Croix-de-Vie, Brétignolles (La Normandelière) and Longeville (Plage du Rocher), but it is as well to check with the relevant tourist office.

A karting circuit near La Roche-sur-Yon has one vehicle specially equipped with controls on the steering-wheel. Wheelchair-bound fishing enthusiasts are particularly well served, with many riverbanks and lakesides having specially designed pontoons jutting out into the water.

The Vendée Tourist Board (see page 11) produces an excellent booklet, called *La Vendée Accessible*, suggesting wheelchair-friendly holiday cottages, bed-and-breakfasts, restaurants and activities—even including vineyards to visit. The Gîtes de France website (see page 11) also has a section on suitable accommodation.

BEACHES

Many of the beaches—including those of St-Brévin, Tharon, La Bernerie (all in the neighbouring *département* of Loire-Atlantique), La Barre-de-Monts, Notre-Dame, St-Jean, St-Hilaire-de-Riez, Talmont, Longeville, La Tranche and L'Aiguillon—receive regular European Blue Flag accolades for their cleanliness and for their water quality. You can check out these and others on the French Blue Flag website: www.pavillonbleu.org/

Best surfing beaches are reckoned to lie between St-Gilles and Les Sables (Plage de Tanchet) and between Longeville and La Tranche, with surf shops at St-Jean, St-Gilles, Brétignolles, Les Sables and La Tranche.

BIRD-WATCHING

Ornithologists are spoilt for choice. The Vendée is on migratory routes for many species, so large numbers of birds are seen in spring and autumn. The region is a popular nesting area for avocets, terns and lapwings and, between April and September, for storks, which favour sites in the open marshland around Châteauneuf and Velluire.

The mudflats of the Bay of Bourgneuf provide an incredible wintertime spectacle at high tide when thousands of wading birds advance with the rising water, probing the mud for food. Herons, egrets and other marshland birds are often seen on the salt-meadows, and brent geese arrive in large numbers during

December on the Marais Breton. Other areas that attract migrant species include the large lake of Grand-Lieu, and L'Aiguillon Bay.

If you have brought your own binoculars, you can use them in observatories at La Barre-de-Monts (at the Écomusée), Châteauneuf, Ile-d'Olonne, Les Landes-Génusson, St-Denis-du-Payré (which also provides high-quality viewing equipment) and Velluire.

You will find details of ornithological outings with the Vendée branch of the Ligue pour la Protection des Oiseaux listed on the organisation's website: vendee.lpo.fr/

■ Boating: plenty of opportunity to sail, windsurf or canoe on coast, inland lakes and canals.

BOATING

Canoes

Guided tours are available through the open marshland at Sallertaine and at Bois-de-Céné. Canoes may also be rented on many of the Vendée's lakes, rivers and canals, including the open waterways of the western side of the Marais Poitevin.

Traditional craft

You can be taken out on a punt-like *yole* at Le Perrier, paddle a flat-bottomed *plate* along tree-lined waterways in the Marais Poitevin's "Venise Verte", or enjoy guided tours by traditional *chaland* in the Grande Brière national park.

Pedalos, windsurfers, rowing boats and sailing dinghies

The above may be rented on inland lakes such as those of Apremont, Jaunay, Moulin-Papon, Mervent-Vouvant, La Tricherie and Rochereau. Sailing and windsurfing are also possible at St-Gilles, Les Sables and other seaside resorts.

CASINOS

French seaside resorts are, by tradition, well-endowed with casinos. Far less exclusive than in the UK, they are welcoming establishments with a casual atmosphere, pleasant restaurants and bars open to non-players, and occasional evenings of cabaret entertainment by well-known names. The fruit machines are usually in operation all day for over-18s. A rather more serious approach is necessary for the gaming rooms (open from around 10pm to about 4am); potential black-jack or roulette players must pay the equivalent of several pounds to gain admission (which usually includes a free drink), and produce a valid passport or some other satisfactory means of identification (*pièce d'identité*). You will find casinos at St-Jean-de-Monts, St-Gilles-Croix-de-Vie, Les Sables-d'Olonne (two), La Faute-sur-Mer, and also at Pornic and at St-Brévin-les-Pins.

CHURCH-GOING

Worshippers are always welcome to attend Mass at local Catholic churches—weekly services are held on Saturday evenings or Sunday mornings. Protestant churches, or *églises réformées*, hold weekly services (in French), known as *cultes*, at Mouchamps, Fontenay-le-Comte, and La Roche-sur-Yon.

There is now a Vendée Fellowship of the Anglican Chaplaincy of Poitou-Charentes, with a permanent resident Anglican vicar, Brian Davies (tel: 02 51 62 96 32). He takes regular services at La Merlatière church (16km north-east of La Roche-sur-Yon) and at Le Puy-de-Serre (12km south-east of La Châtaigneraie).

Also, from mid-July to the end of August, a temporarily-resident Anglican chaplain conducts Sunday services in English at seaside campsites or churches. For details, look for an information slip usually available from tourist offices, or contact the Intercontinental Church Society in Warwick (UK tel: 01926 430347).

if you have brought an adaptor to convert your plug to fit a French socket. These are widely available in British shops, on ferries and at airports, but you are unlikely to find them once you are in France. A couple of warnings: power supplies may be interrupted during storms; and the voltage in many holiday cottages often does not allow you to run several major appliances—e.g. oven and dishwasher—at once.

ENTERTAINMENT

Concerts

One of the most accessible forms of entertainment for non-French speakers is music. A free quarterly brochure, *Musique Danse* (available from *mairies*, tourist offices and the Conseil General office in La Roche), lists fixtures—from jazz and rock to classical and gospel—in concert halls, churches and other venues. The Logis de la Chabotterie organises a baroque music festival in June and July; a festival of romantic music is held at Luçon in July; and a colourful festival of world music takes place annually in late August at Cugand, near Clisson.

Theatres

Theatrical performances in France tend to rely heavily on words, and anyone with limited command of French may find them difficult to follow. There are traditional theatres at La Roche-sur-Yon, Luçon and Fontenay-le-Comte, and modern performance spaces at Les Sables-d'Olonne (within the tourist office complex), Challans, Les Herbiers and elsewhere. Outside the *département* you will find theatres at La Rochelle and Nantes (where opera performances are also given between October and June at the Théâtre Graslin).

The best thing is to go for spectacle, and for this the night-time, open-air Cinéscénie at the Puy-du-Fou (see page 143) cannot be beaten. Other good *son-et-lumière* productions are performed at Olonne-sur-Mer and at Machecoul; newer ones appear from time to time. They all tend to be popular, so book in advance

CYCLING

■ **Freewheeling: 150km of coastal cycleway, and many other routes, wait to be explored.**

Many local cycle trails (*pistes cyclables*) are signposted; details of them, as well as of bike hire (*location de vélos*), are obtainable from tourist offices. Most sections of a 150km Atlantic cycleway running the whole length of the Vendée's coastline, from Bouin to L'Aiguillon-sur-Mer, are now in place. Among other popular paths are a super-smooth cycle track along the route of an old railway from La Roche-sur-Yon, via Aizenay to Coëx, joining a route to St-Gilles-Croix-de-Vie, and a canalside trail linking La Tranche with Maillezais and the picturesque "Venise Verte" ("Green Venice") area. Rather more hilly will be the forthcoming 250km cycle route along the eastern edge of the Vendée, meandering through the beautiful scenery of the *haut bocage* and due for completion in 2006.

The most unusual form of cycling is unquestionably the *vélo draisine*, a flat-bed wagon that runs along disused railway tracks from Commequiers, carrying four or five people, two pedalling and three "resting".

DIVING

If you have an internationally-recognised diving certificate, you can join local groups exploring wrecks off Noirmoutier or the Ile d'Yeu. Enquire about *la plongée* at tourist offices.

ELECTRICITY

The electric current is usually 220 volts, so British equipment should function successfully through local tourist offices. In July and August, at seaside towns, some highly original street-theatre artistes are often engaged to give free open-air evening performances.

Cinemas

The French are great movie-goers and most towns, even quite small ones, have cinemas, including an increasing number of new multi-plexes. However, with the exception of show-ings in a few Nantes cinemas such as the Katorza, near the Théâtre Graslin, and occa-sionally at the Concorde in La Roche-sur-Yon, films will always be in French (English-language ones being dubbed rather than subtitled), so entertainment value for non-French-speakers is restricted. The letters "V.O." (*version origi-nale*) indicate that a movie is being shown in its original language, with French subtitles—not much help, of course, if a film was in Russian or Japanese in the first place.

In July and August a programme of free open-air film shows, known as Cinésites, is usually organised at castles and other venues. These are often selected to provide an appropri-ate backdrop—for example a tale of medieval swashbuckling might be projected alongside a ruined château of the period. Details are given in local newspapers. (Be sure you pick up the appropriate edition—a copy bought at some distance from your base may cover different towns from the one you are interested in.)

FISHING

Sea fishing

Boat trips may be taken from Les Sables-d'Olonne or from St-Gilles-Croix-de-Vie to fish for sea-bass and mackerel.

Shrimping and shellfish-collecting

At low water, it's fun to push a shrimping net through the shallows and the rock-pools or to join the locals digging for cockles, clams and other shellfish. You need to consult tide-tables to find the days with the highest figure in the column marked "*coefficient*" (a method of indi-cating extra-low and -high tides). *Coefficients* of more than 90 are best, giving the opportunity to

dig on some of the more rarely-uncovered sandbanks. The Pont d'Yeu, south of Notre-Dame-de-Monts, or the mudflats alongside the causeway leading to Noirmoutier island are popular spots, but keep an eye on the time, and stay away from any dubious outflow pipes as well as from commercial oyster-beds or mussel-posts. Official rules stress that you should not collect anything too tiny, nor harvest more shellfish than you can eat at a sitting.

Freshwater fishing

The Vendée's inland lakes and rivers yield bream, black-bass, perch, roach, tench, pike, zander and carp. In some areas of the *haut-bocage* around Pouzauges, on the eastern side of the county, are some trout rivers; marsh-land canals may harbour eels; while the slug-gish lower reaches of rivers like the Vie contain more than their fair share of small catfish.

A holiday licence (*Carte Pêche-Vacances*), from many tackle shops, allows you to fish in all non-private waters in the Vendée and sur-rounding *départements*. These include rivers, and also areas on them where lakes have been created by dams. It is valid on 15 consecutive days between 1 June and 30 September, and costs 30€. Charente-Maritime, to the south, requires a separate permit—something to bear in mind if you are fishing in the Marais Poitevin's "Green Venice" area, where you might stray over the county boundary.

"*Pêche Interdite*" means No Fishing; ask if in any doubt about whether a stretch of water is included in the pass. Tackle and bait are on sale in sports and watersports shops and hypermarkets.

Information is obtainable from tourist offices, or from La Fédération de Pêche de Vendée, 10 bis Rue Haxo, BP 673, 85016 La Roche-sur-Yon Cédex (tel: 02 51 37 19 05; fax: 02 51 05 34 13; www.unpf.fr/85; e-mail: federation.peche.vendee@wanadoo.fr), which produces an informative free booklet each year called *Le Guide du Pêcheur*. Another brochure, *Séjour Pêche*, is available from Sud Vendée Tourisme (see page 11) suggesting waterside holiday

cottages in the south Vendée, from L'Aiguillon-sur-Mer, on the coast, to La Châtaigneraie, in the east, including the marshlands of the Marais Poitevin.

Of special interest to anglers are the tourist office at Chaillé-les-Marais (tel: 02 51 56 71 17), full of fishing information, and Pescalis, a huge fishing centre at Moncoutant (see page 118). There is a growing number of fisheries where you can rent a rod, and fish in a lake all day; ask at the nearest tourist office about "*pêche à la ligne*" or "*pêche à la journée*".

Traditional fishing

Each year, on 15 August and the Sunday following, visitors can accompany the fishermen of Passay (see page 162) as they cast their nets in the Lac de Grand-Lieu. This is a rare opportunity to see the centre of the large and mysterious lake that is now a nature reserve.

GOLF

The Vendée has no fewer than five golf courses. These are located at St-Jean-de-Monts, Nesmy (near La Roche-sur-Yon), L'Aiguillon-sur-Vie (near Coëx), Olonne-sur-Mer (near Les Sables-d'Olonne), and Port-Bourgenay (near Talmont). There are more in the surrounding area, too, at Pornic, Nantes, Cholet, Niort and La Rochelle. Golf clubs may be hired on the spot. Between May and September it is advisable to book in advance for more popular courses such as those of St-Jean-de-Monts and Port-Bourgenay. Green fees for 18 holes range from around 25€ (low season) to 50€ (high season).

■ **Angling: carp and other fish are keen to nibble the bait in the Vendée's lakes and rivers.**

Formule Golf pass

A season ticket is available that covers four of the Vendée's five 18-hole, par-72 courses. Allowing you unlimited use within a certain number of days—three days out of six, for instance, or four days out of eight—it costs from 92€ (1 July-31 August, 116€) for three days. Details on www.formule-golf.com/

Swin-Golf

This is not a misprint, but a family golfing game over special nine- or 18-hole courses, using just one club with three different faces in place of a normal bagful. Swin-golf locations include St-Jean-de-Monts and St-Philbert-de-Grand-Lieu.

Mini-Golf

Also known as "crazy golf", and great fun for all ages, these nine- or 18-hole circuits with their jokey hazards will entertain everyone from six-year-olds to grandparents.

HOTELS AND RESTAURANTS

Good reference books are the Michelin red guide or the Logis de France handbook (see page 11) for both hotels and restaurants. Those who read French will find the *Guide du Routard* series of regional books a reliable source of information on where to eat and sleep; its chatty style is guaranteed to brush up your grasp of current colloquialisms, too. The Gîtes de France brochure (see page 11) lists B&Bs (*chambres d'hôte*), graded with *épis*, or ears of wheat; *Bienvenue au Château*, free from the French Government Tourist Office, 178 Piccadilly, London W1J 9AL, gives details of stylish private B&B accommodation, often in historic settings. A quick mention also for *The Rough Guide to French Hotels and Restaurants* and for Alastair Sawday's excellent *Special Places to Stay: French Bed and Breakfast.*

Restaurant guides include the Michelin red guide, again, which awards up to three rosettes for gastronomic excellence, and the upmarket *GaultMillau* (which accords marks out of 20). From Monday to Friday, even many of the top restaurants offer good-value fixed-price menus at lunchtimes, so this is a good opportunity to sample gastronomic output at affordable rates. You can often eat well and cheaply at small, family-run establishments—look around a market-square, for example, for somewhere that looks popular, or ask the locals for advice—and most hypermarkets have good, reasonably-priced self-service restaurants.

For true local flavour, it's worth trying a *ferme-auberge*. These are real restaurants, rather than farmhouse kitchens, where at least half the produce served has to be home-produced—so you're guaranteed fresh duck, lamb, *foie gras*, vegetables, or whatever is the farm's speciality. The owners always prefer you to book in advance, so that they have an idea of how many diners they will be catering for.

Vegetarian eating

In spite of the fantastic displays of vegetables in French greengrocers' shops and markets, vegetarians are poorly catered for in rural France. Those who eat fish have no problem, of course; those who don't might find restaurants a little stunned to be asked about vegetarian dishes, and that they are too easily fobbed off with the offer of an omelette. So far, there is little feeling that restaurants should provide such food as a matter of course—though some may be willing to concoct something suitable with 24 hours' notice. Unless you are lucky enough to spot a vegetarian dish on the menu, you will mostly have to resort to eating in pizzerias or *crêperies*.

INTERNET

France has at last embraced the internet, so many of the attractions listed can now be found on-line. However, the "addresses" of their sites quite often change, so I shall try to provide an up-to-date selected list on www.the-vendee.co.uk/

Keeping up with e-mail while on holiday is becoming easier, especially if your service-provider allows for collection elsewhere. The alternative is to forward your e-mail temporarily to a web-based account, such as Hotmail, so that you can pick it up anywhere. Cybercafés are opening all the time; many campsites now provide their clients with internet access; and most small towns have a *médiathèque*, where visitors can pick up e-mails and do their surfing.

MAPS

You need good maps to get the most out of a holiday. With new motorways and bypasses opening every year, it is a false economy to use out-of-date ones, so always scrutinise the date printed on a new map before purchase.

The familiar, yellow-backed Michelin series at 1:200,000 (1cm=2km) is still excellent, and good value. Most useful of these will be No 67 (Nantes/Les Sables-d'Olonne) and No 71 (La Rochelle/Bordeaux). From the same company, there is now a slightly blown-up version with an orange cover (Michelin No 316 Local, 1cm=1.75km) for Loire-Atlantique and the Vendée, plus a blue-backed "*départementale*" map (Michelin No 4085, 1cm=1.5km) covering the Vendée and its near periphery, with gazetteer and some town plans. These last two are widely available once in the area.

Much more detailed—though a bit more expensive—are the maps in the IGN (Institut Géographique National) green series on the scale of 1:100,000 (1cm=1km)—either No 32 (Nantes/Les Sables-d'Olonne) or No 33 (Cholet/Niort), depending on where you are based. For even more detail on an area that you want to walk or to explore in depth, nothing beats the 1:25,000 IGN blue series where 4cm=1km. IGN also produces a red series at 1:250,000 (1cm=2.5km); map No 107 covers Poitou-Charentes, from St-Nazaire down to Royan, and from Tours, south as far as Limoges, its scope making it handy if you are going to be touring by car over a wide area. All are widely available in the Vendée. Michelin and IGN green series can also be found in good UK bookshops, while maps in the blue and red IGN series may be purchased from the specialist map dealer Stanfords, 12-14 Long Acre, London WC2E 9LP (UK tel: 020 7836 0189).

MARKETS

Most markets are morning-only events. Some may have lost the importance they had in pre-supermarket days, but the central food market of Les Sables is always a delight, and the street markets of Challans on Tuesday and Vallet on Sunday are famous. Below is a selection of market days. Check main entries for the respective towns, though, as some are held only during summer.

> ■ **Markets: the best source of delicious locally-grown fruit and vegetables and tasty cheeses.**

Monday
L'Herbaudière (Noirmoutier island); Jard-sur-Mer; Longeville-sur-Mer; Merlin-Plage (St-Hilaire-de-Riez); La Roche-sur-Yon (second Mon of month); Les Sables-d'Olonne.

Tuesday
L'Aiguillon-sur-Mer; Brem-sur-Mer; Challans; Chantonnay (second and fourth Tues); La Chaume (Les Sables); Clisson; Mortagne-sur-Sèvre; Port-Joinville (Yeu island); La Roche; Les Sables; St-Gilles; Sion; La Tranche-sur-Mer.

Wednesday
Angles; Commequiers; Croix-de-Vie (St-Gilles); Les Essarts (third Wed); Luçon; Machecoul; Merlin-Plage (St-Hilaire-de-Riez); Mouilleron-en-Pareds (first Wed); La Roche; Les Sables; St-Jean-de-Monts; La Tranche (La Grière).

Thursday
Avrillé (second Thurs); Beauvoir; Brétignolles; Chaillé-les-Marais; La Chaume; La Faute; La Guérinière (Noirmoutier island); Les Herbiers; Mareuil (last Thurs); La Mothe-Achard (first Thurs); Le Poiré-sur-Vie (first and third Thurs); Pouzauges (first and third Thurs); La Roche; Les Sables; St-Gilles; St-Hilaire-de-Riez; St-Michel-en-l'Herm; Talmont-St-Hilaire (third Thurs).

Friday
L'Aiguillon-sur-Mer; Brem; Challans; Clisson; Coulon; Longeville; Maillezais; La Mothe-Achard (third and fourth Fri); Noirmoutier town; La Roche-sur-Yon; Les Sables-d'Olonne; Ste-Hermine (last Fri); Sion.

Saturday
Challans; Chantonnay; Cholet; Coëx; Croix-de-Vie (St-Gilles); La Faute-sur-Mer; Fontenay; Fromentine; Les Herbiers; Luçon; Marans; Merlin-Plage (St-Hilaire-de-Riez); Montaigu; Port-Joinville (Yeu island); La Roche-sur-Yon; Les Sables-d'Olonne; St-Jean-de-Monts; Talmont; La Tranche-sur-Mer.

Sunday
Beauvoir; Brétignolles; La Chaume; La Faute; La Guérinière (Noirmoutier island); Maillé; Noirmoutier town; Notre-Dame-de-Monts; Olonne; Les Sables; St-Florent-des-Bois (first Sun); St-Gilles; St-Hilaire-de-Riez; St-Philbert-de-Grand-Lieu; St-Vincent-sur-Jard; Vallet.

MEASUREMENTS

All indications of distance, area and weight in this guide are metric. Imperial equivalents are:

1kg = 2.2lb

500g (also often called *une livre*) = 1.1lb

1litre = 1.75pt (1 gallon = 4.54 litres)

1km = 0.6 miles (1 mile = 1.6km)

1 hectare = 2.47 acres

(1 square mile = 260 hectares)

MEDICAL TREATMENT

Obviously it is best to take out comprehensive travel insurance for your annual holiday. But if you hold a form E111 (obtainable free from UK post offices on quotation of your National Insurance number), you can claim some reimbursement of medical expenses under the reciprocal arrangement between Britain and other European countries. However, although the E111 is valid indefinitely, French authorities like to see one that is less than 12 months old. So even if you already have an E111, it's best to ask for an up-to-date one for visiting France.

After consulting and paying the doctor (20€) take the *feuille de soins* (medical treatment form) that you are given and hand it to the chemist with your *ordonnance* (prescription) form. The chemist dispenses the drugs (it is most important to keep any sticky labels attached to the boxes), and adds their details to the form.

Gather together the form and sticky labels, your E111 and the passport (or a photocopy of its important pages, if you are posting it) relating to the person in whose name the E111 is issued. Take or send these to the nearest Caisse Primaire Assurance Maladie (CPAM), which are located at La Roche-sur-Yon, Les Herbiers, Challans, Fontenay-le-Comte and Les Sables-d'Olonne. You should get quite a large percentage of your costs reimbursed. The offices at La Roche and Les Sables can arrange to hand over the cash, or at least a cheque you can cash locally; otherwise the system operates by sending a cheque to your home address in around six weeks.

Chemists are often consulted about minor ailments and discuss them with doctor-like gravity, binding up sprained ankles and dishing out reasonably strong medicines without the need for getting into the intricacies of the French health system. You do not, however, get reimbursed for this treatment.

There are casualty departments (*urgences*) at the Vendée's main hospitals: Challans (on Boulevard de l'Est, at the north-east corner of the inner ring road); La Roche-sur-Yon (signposted "CHD" on the Cholet road at Les Oudairies, on the north-east side of town); Fontenay-le-Comte (Rue Rabelais, the La Roche road, west of Place Viète); Les Sables-d'Olonne (Route de Talmont); and at smaller hospitals in Luçon and Montaigu—as well as outside the Vendée in the cities of St-Nazaire, Nantes, Cholet, Niort and La Rochelle.

MONEY

Since France joined the euro in January 2002, the French-franc coins and notes remaining from long-ago holidays can no longer be used or exchanged. The euro, made up of 100 centimes (or *centièmes d'euro*), is worth between 66 and 70 UK pence, depending on currency fluctuations. For a rough conversion of euro prices to pounds, knock off one-third, making 30€ equivalent to a little over £20.

In towns and large villages, banks are usually open from Tuesday to Saturday, from 9am to noon, and 2pm till 6pm. Since the euro arrived, they have wound down their foreign-exchange desks, so do not count on being able to change foreign cash, or anything other than euro-denomination travellers' cheques, over the counter. Ask your own bank for its most up-to-date recommendation, or whether it has negotiated commission-free deals for its clients with any particular French bank.

Banks close for public holidays (see page 22) from lunch-time the previous day. This can catch you unawares, as also can the fact that if the holiday falls on a Tuesday or a Thursday there is a tendency to join the day up to the nearest weekend (*faire le pont*) and close for several days at a stretch. However, if you have the sort of bank card that extracts cash from a "hole in the wall" in Britain, the chances are it will work in France, as long as it bears a similar logo to one of those displayed on the French cashpoint machine (*distributeur de billets*, or *guichet automatique*). On-screen instructions are usually automatically given in English as well as French. If you have more than one cashpoint card in the family it is a wise precaution to take both away with you, in case you lose or damage the main one.

You may often be asked for your passport during banking transactions, and even when paying by credit card in hypermarkets and large stores, so it is as well to carry it with you.

Credit cards such as MasterCard, Visa, American Express and Diner's Club (particularly the first two, which are known as *cartes bancaires*) are widely accepted at petrol stations, supermarkets, hotels, restaurants and stores (except, of course, in the smallest village shops and cafés). The microchip incorporated into French credit cards allows the cardholder to tap a secret authorisation code onto a special little keypad. If you use a British card you will, instead, have to sign for the goods you buy, and you may need to remind the shopkeeper of this if he/she offers you the keypad to use. Cards without the microchip (i.e. most UK-issued ones at the time of writing) will *not* operate unmanned petrol pumps marked "24/24", so never let the fuel tank run low at lunchtimes, late at night, or on Sundays.

■ **Motoring: taking your car to France gives you freedom to explore out-of-the-way places.**

MOTORING

You should always have the originals of the car's documents—the registration document (plus a letter of authorisation from the owner if the vehicle is not registered in your name), and insurance certificate (or green card, if your insurer still provides one)—plus your driving licence and passport, in the vehicle when you are on the road. You can be stopped at any time for a random check, and it is an offence to be without these papers. (Major roads are particularly heavily policed around 5pm each day, and on Sunday afternoons.)

On-the-spot fines are common: penalties for using a mobile phone (even a hands-free one), or for failure to wear a seat belt, start at 135€; speeding fines go from around 200€ to more than 800€, with immediate confiscation of driving licence in the more serious cases. Drink/drive limits, at 50mg/100ml are actually lower than those operating in England, and random breath tests are carried out. The police can withdraw your licence on the spot if your test is positive, as they also can if they catch a

motorist driving at excessively high speed. You should carry a warning triangle for use in case your car breaks down, and a spare set of bulbs for your lights as it is an offence to drive with any light out of order. Seat belts must be worn by all front- and rear-seat passengers. No child under 10 may travel in the front seat. Motorists are not allowed to stop on the open road (see Parking).

Although the old *priorité à droite* rule (by which any vehicle arriving from your right-hand side had the right of way) has faded, there can still be some instances when it applies, particularly in larger towns. So if you are not sure from the road signs and markings whether the priority is yours, it's wise to give way. Note that if a French driver flashes headlights at you he is *not* giving you the right of way: he is announcing that he is taking it for himself.

UK credit cards can be used at manned and automatic motorway toll boths, but not in 24-hour petrol pumps. (See Money, above.)

Speed limits

130kph/81mph on motorways (reduced to 110kph/68mph in bad weather conditions).

110kph/68mph on dual carriageways (100kph/62mph in bad weather conditions).

90kph/56mph on other roads (80kph/50mph in bad weather conditions).

(Where visibility is reduced to 50 metres, limits on all open roads are 50kph/31mph.)

50kph/31mph in towns and villages, unless

marked otherwise, from the moment you have passed the village's welcoming name-board, until you pass the crossed-out name on the way out—even if no speed limit is marked. 30kph/19mph in some town centres.

Parking

In villages and small towns, as well as at non-resort beaches and for major events, parking is usually ample and free. You are not allowed to stop on the open road without pulling right off it onto a verge or pavement, or into a lay-by. Where parking meters are installed, there is not much need for explanation—except to say, look closely at the times and days. A free period often covers protracted French lunchtimes in inland towns; while, at seaside resorts, even Sundays and public holidays still require payment. If you're visiting out of season, though, read the instructions carefully as there may be no charge at all. In streets and car parks the system is often one of pay-and-display (*horodateur* or *distributeur*)—again, look at just what hours and days require payment. The third, and oldest-established, method of parking regulation is by cardboard parking disc in areas designated as *zones bleues*, indicated by street signs or by painted blue marks on the road. If you do not already own a parking disc (*disque de contrôle de stationnement*), you can usually pick one up at the nearest tourist office or *tabac* (tobacconist's) for about 2€.

NATURISM

Nudism is permitted on certain secluded beaches: Luzéronde on Noirmoutier island, south-east of L'Herbaudière; Les Lays, at La Barre-de-Monts; Merlin-Plage, at St-Jean-de-Monts; Petit Pont-Jaunay, south of St-Gilles; La Grande Pointe, near Les Granges and Sauveterre, north of Les Sables; between Les Conches and La Terrière, near La Tranche; and the Pointe d'Arçay beach at La Faute.

There are two specialised naturist holiday centres: Cap Natur' at St-Hilaire-de-Riez, on the coast; and Le Colombier, at St-Martin-Lars, in the countryside around Ste-Hermine.

NEWSPAPERS

One-day-old English newspapers are readily available—though without their magazine sections—throughout the holiday season in good newsagents/bookshops like Maisons de la Presse and, increasingly, in small village shops in the most tourist-friendly areas. The main local daily newspapers are the broadsheets *Ouest-France* and *Vendée-Matin*, both of which carry a certain amount of national and international news. In addition, each has invaluable pages of local snippets to interest the French-reading holidaymaker, such as cinema and exhibition listings, weather maps, the day's tides, details of local fêtes, accidents, domestic scandals and other indispensable trivia. However, *Ouest-France*—which enjoys the larger circulation—has several local editions, so if you are looking for ideas for outings it's best to buy a copy near to your base. Both papers produce useful supplements in July and August listing events and places to visit. You can usually pick these up free in tourist offices.

PETS

It's a relatively new concept to be able to take one's pets abroad on holiday, and it still needs a good deal of planning in advance—not least because the animal must be microchipped and vaccinated against rabies six months before your trip. It is imperative to understand the Pets Travel Scheme thoroughly and to follow it to the letter, as the slightest mistake could mean delaying your return crossing while required veterinary treatment takes effect. Contact the Department for Environment, Food and Rural Affairs (UK tel: 0870 241 1710) for the most up-to-date information, or visit the DEFRA website, www.defra.gov.uk/

Other important considerations are that you have checked with the place you are intending staying that animals are welcome, and that you have not chosen a time of year when temperatures might be too high for the comfort of your pet—who may be used to a cooler climate. On many beaches, dogs are prohibited between

7am and 9pm between June and September; double-check with the local tourist office, however, as this rule can vary from one town or village to another.

Once you arrive in the Vendée, contact a local veterinary surgery well in advance, to make sure they will be able to do the necessary microchip scan, worming treatment and paperwork for you on the day before you return.

POST OFFICES

Main offices are open Monday to Friday, 8am-7pm; Saturday 8am until noon. However, outside La Roche-sur-Yon and large cities like Nantes they close from noon until 2pm for lunch. You can send faxes (*télécopies*) from the larger post offices (and also from coin-operated machines in some supermarkets), and consult phone books or Minitel terminals (computerised telephone directories).

Letter-rate postage to the UK is the same as that within France, so you might want to invest in a book of 10 stamps (*un carnet de timbres*) for your postcards. Stamps can also be bought at any tobacconist's shop (*tabac*).

PUBLIC HOLIDAYS

Public holidays (*jours fériés*) are: 1 January; Easter Monday (*lundi de Pâques*); 1 May; 8 May (Armistice 1945, or VE Day); Ascension Day; Whit Monday (*lundi de Pentecôte*); 14 July (*Fête Nationale*, or Bastille Day); 15 August (*l'Assomption*); 1 November (*la Toussaint*); 11 November (Armistice 1918); and 25 December.

PUBLIC TRANSPORT

There are not too many bus routes outside the main towns (information from local tourist offices), but the train can be useful if you want to visit cities like Nantes or La Rochelle without the hassle of driving round a strange town, or of parking a car. From St-Gilles-Croix-de-Vie and St-Hilaire-de-Riez you can go to Nantes via Challans and Machecoul (sometimes the service is by coach instead of by train). From Les Sables you can reach Nantes via La Roche-sur-Yon and Montaigu; from La Roche you can also head south to Luçon and La Rochelle.

Before you board any train, it is *essential* to validate your rail ticket by punching a corner of it in one of the yellow machines located near the entrance to the platform—a process with the unlikely name of *compostage*.

RIDING

There are many equestrian centres (*centres équestres*) in the region—enquire through local tourist offices. Style is often a bit more casual and "wild western" than the British are used to. Most establishments seem to provide hard hats (*bombes*), but it is as well to check this point first when booking a *promenade*, or ride.

SAFETY

Safety norms at tourist attractions are improving, though do not always seem to be as stringently adhered to as they are in Britain. You are usually routinely issued with lifejackets or hardhats before canoeing, riding or karting jaunts, but safety arrangements at zoos, wildlife parks, lofty viewpoints and some amusement parks can still occasionally seem a bit casual.

As regards personal safety, street crime rates are mercifully low; upgrade your vigilance, though, in crowded hypermarkets. Seaside towns have their share of unruly summer visitors, but if you avoid dodgy nightspots and dark back streets you should be unaware of them. As in major cities anywhere, it pays to be street-wise about money and valuables when visiting larger towns such as Nantes or St-Nazaire.

SHOPPING

Markets usually operate mornings only, up to about noon (see page 18). The lunch hour is sacrosanct in France, and most shops, apart from large supermarkets and hypermarkets, close between noon and 2pm. Consequently, the lie-a-bed holidaymaker will find the mornings extremely short for shopping but, in contrast, the afternoons deliciously long as shops generally stay open until around 7pm. The smaller local food shops are usually open on Sunday mornings—as are some of the super-markets in holiday areas—though almost everything is closed on Sunday afternoons. Factory shops, or *magasins d'usine*, are becoming popular; some of the best are included in entries for the relevant towns and villages.

Look out for *marchés aux puces* (flea markets), for brocante fairs or for *vide-greniers* (car-boot sales) where you can often pick up some unusual holiday souvenirs.

STAR-GAZING

If you are staying somewhere far from street-lighting, under night skies that are really dark, the Milky Way, the constellations, the stars and the planets stand out wonderfully, especially on out-of-the-way beaches or under the wide, unpolluted skies of open marshland. Around mid-August, don't forget to look out for shooting-stars, which are always particularly prolific at that time.

■ **Bargain-hunting: shopping for souvenirs is fun, especially in the local flea markets.**

TELEPHONING

As in the UK, telephone cabins come in two varieties—those that take cash (very few now) and those that take cards, for which *télécartes* can be purchased from post offices and tobacconists (*tabacs*). If you want to make a transfer-charge call (*une communication en PCV*, pronounced "pay-say-vay") or to have somebody call you back in a call-box, look around first to find the number, printed somewhere on the wall inside the cabin. (French numbers are quoted in pairs: 01 23 45 67 89 would be "*zéro-un, vingt-trois, quarante-cinq, soixante-sept, quatre-vingt-neuf*". You may need to practise that first before telling the operator.) To make a transfer-charge call to the UK, you can dial 0800 99 0044 for an English-speaking operator.

To call within France, simply dial the 10 digits of the number. To call a number in Britain direct, dial 00 44, followed by the British number (but omitting its initial zero). Cheap-rate time for calls to the UK is Monday to Friday from 7pm to 8am, Saturdays from 2pm, Sundays and French public holidays all day.

Although all Vendée telephone subscribers' numbers fit into a single telephone directory, you have to know in which town or village someone lives before you can look them up, as entries are listed under localities. This can be a problem if the person you are calling lives in an isolated house or a small hamlet, as you need the name of the *commune* (the larger village under which it falls administratively) to be able to find the entry.

Mobile phones

If you intend to use your UK mobile phone in France, check with your service-provider to see if you need to make any special arrangements for overseas use. Once in France, to call a French number you just dial the 10 digits. To dial a UK number from within France (including a UK-based mobile—even if you know it, too, is in France), you must treat it as a foreign one, i.e. dial 00 44 followed by the UK number without the initial zero. (This may require amendment of numbers stored in your mobile's memory.) A caller ringing you from within France must treat yours as a foreign (i.e. a UK) number, dialling 00 44 and dropping the initial zero. Anyone calling your mobile from the UK, however, just dials your normal number (as if you were in the UK).

Don't forget that, at the time of writing, you are charged to *receive* calls while using your

UK mobile abroad, as well as to make them, so you may want to ask friends to text you (reception of texts is free) rather than to telephone.

Emergency and other useful numbers

Europe-wide number, covering all three emergency services, and which should be used from all mobiles 112

If calling from a fixed phone, the individual ones for France are:

Fire (pompiers, who also deal with medical emergencies) 18

Police (police in towns; gendarmerie in rural areas)...17

Ambulance (SAMU, or paramedics) 15

Operator (opérateur) 13

Directory enquiries (renseignements) 12

International directory enquiries...............3212

TENNIS

Most villages have a municipal tennis court or two, which can be booked by the hour, for a modest fee. Ask at tourist office or mairie.

TIPPING

Strictly speaking, service is now included in the bill for bars, hotels and restaurants, and indicated by the words prix nets. However, people often leave something extra—even if it is just the bits of loose change on the plate—if service was particularly good or if they are likely to return. It is still customary to tip hairdressers and taxi-drivers about 10 per cent of the bill; and to press a euro or two into the hand of a guide after a particularly interesting tour.

WALKING

Long-distance walks

The IGN map 903 shows all the Grande-Randonnée (long-distance footpath) routes in France; topo-guides (special large-scale maps) describing individual walks in detail are obtainable from good bookshops in France. Grande-Randonnée footpaths in the Vendée, waymarked with red-and-yellow signs, include GR36, GR364, GR Pays Entre Vie et Yon and GR Pays de la Côte de Lumière.

Local walks

You can, of course, walk shorter sections of any Grande-Randonnée route. In addition, almost every village has a network of signposted footpaths leading to its main beauty spots and places of interest. Maps are usually sited on large panels in village car parks, or are available from local tourist offices and mairies.

WEATHER

The Vendée claims a summer sunshine record similar to that of the South of France—though obviously there can be exceptions. If you're staying in a house in high summer, you'll find it a great help to close curtains or shutters before the sun gets too strong; if you're in a tent or a mobile home, then the best advice when the temperature climbs is to head for somewhere air-conditioned—the latest museums, hypermarkets or shopping malls. Coolest museums to date are the Musée Milcendeau at Soullans and the Mémorial building at Les Lucs; or chill out at Les Flâneries—the large shopping centre north of La Roche.

The same advice holds good for rainy days, a good time to head inland to museums, junk shops, restaurants and shopping centres that might be less overwhelmed with other dripping holidaymakers than those nearer the coast.

WILDLIFE

Among bird-life, hoopoes and buzzards are not uncommon. (See Bird-watching, page 12.) Swallow-tail butterflies are a more usual sight than in Britain, and at twilight you may sense bats swooping in the darkness, or spy glow-worms as pinpricks of bright neon in hedgerows. In some weather conditions mosquitoes may be a problem: plug-in insect repellants are effective, as is citronelle oil, from chemists, rubbed on the skin. Most menacing insects are the wasp-like frelons (hornets), which can give a nasty sting.

As in Britain, the only poisonous snake you are likely to come across, basking on sunny heathland, is the vipère or adder, a shy creature that will retreat rapidly if it senses you coming.

Vendée Food and Wine

Traditional local specialities are hearty, peasant food like cabbage, and the white haricot beans known as *mogettes*—that would be set to simmer slowly in the embers of the kitchen fire while a family toiled in the fields. With such a long coastline and active fishing industry, fish and shellfish are an important part of the repertoire, especially oysters from the Bay of Bourgneuf, sardines from St-Gilles-Croix-de-Vie, sole from Les Sables and mussels from L'Aiguillon.

■ Vintage sardines: the pride of St-Gilles-Croix-de-Vie.

HEALTHY SHOPPING

The idea of buying organic foods is slowly starting to take hold in the region. Look for the words *bio* or *agriculture biologique*, sometimes showing a special green-and-white "AB" logo, indicating foodstuffs that conform to similar "organic" regulations to those in the UK. It's also worth knowing that there's a "*Label Rouge*" (Red Label) designation, indicating produce—from meat to melons—that has been farmed subject to stringent rules governing natural conditions and feeding. The phrase "*sans OGM*" on an item means the product contains no genetically-modified organisms.

For people with allergies, the French are beginning to mark products that might contain peanuts (*arachides*), though you have to read the small print carefully. "*Traces éventuelles d'arachide et autres noix*" means "May contain traces of peanuts and other nuts". Biscuits and other items containing *huile végétale* or *matière grasse végétale* may also contain peanut oil. However, some manufacturers now specify whether the oil used is the more acceptable *tournesol* (sunflower seed), *palme* (palm), *colza* (oilseed rape) or *olive* (olive).

SHELLFISH

When you buy fish and shellfish in a shop, don't hesitate to ask for advice on cooking. Shrimps and prawns are usually sold ready-cooked (the little brown shrimps

known as *crevettes grises* have much more flavour than their pretty pink cousins). Be careful when buying *langoustines* (salt-water crayfish), that you notice whether they are being sold ready-cooked (*cuites*) or raw (*crues*), as it's difficult to tell at a glance. If uncooked, they should be plunged into a large saucepan of well-salted boiling water flavoured with pepper and a little vinegar, brought back to the boil and then cooked briskly for just three minutes, before being cooled rapidly under cold water.

Crabs can be bought cooked, but most often are still clambering over one another, blowing bubbles, in the fishmonger's tray. The non-squeamish can steel themselves to place the creature in a large saucepan of cold water, heavily salted and flavoured with pepper and a *bouquet garni* of available herbs, bringing it to the boil and cooking for 12 minutes per kilo (about six minutes per pound). Plunge the crab into cold water immediately it is cooked. The only parts you should not eat are the fleshy, grey, finger-shaped gills and the stringy intestine. A pair of nutcrackers (or pliers, hammer, or even—at a pinch—a couple of good, flat stones) is invaluable for cracking your way into the better-protected parts—try to buy some pointed metal shellfish-picks in a supermarket to

dig out the best bits. Spider crabs (*araignées*) should be put into boiling water flavoured with a little cayenne pepper and cooked for 20 minutes per kilo (about 10 minutes per pound), then allowed to cool in the cooking water. If you can't face this, you can order cooked crabs or lobsters from a fishmonger at a day's notice.

Mussels and other shellfish are always sold alive, and need to be well scrubbed and scraped, using a sharp knife to remove barnacles and any whiskery bits of "beard". Discard any that are not tightly closed. You can often buy ready-scraped mussels (*moules grattées*) which saves a bit of work, but you should still look them over carefully.

■ **Vendée specials: hearty fish soup, and the nourishing white beans known as mogettes.**

To cook a kilo of mussels, heat 125ml of Muscadet, Gros-Plant or other dry white wine with a chopped onion, a chopped clove of garlic, two teaspoonful of chopped parsley, and some seasoning. When it is boiling, add mussels, cover, and steam for five to 10 minutes until they open (throw out any that remain closed). Remove mussels, and stir a little butter or cream into the juice before pouring it over them.

Oysters—usually the long, knobbly *portugaise* variety—are in season all year and are, to British minds, incredibly inexpensive. To open, attack the hinged end of the creature using one of the cheap, stubby blades with a special shield around the handle (available in supermarkets), avoiding getting flakes of shell mingled with the delicate flesh. Wrap your other hand in a tea-towel for protection! If you are going to open many, you may want to treat yourself to an electric, vibrating oyster-knife.

FISH

A wonderful fish soup in large glass jars, sold under the label of "La Vendéenne", can be eaten with a little spicy *rouille* sauce stirred in, and then sprinkled with *croûtons* and grated gruyère cheese. It's almost a meal in itself. Fresh sardines are a real, yet inexpensive, treat. Gut and wash them well. For barbecuing it is easiest to cook them in a metal contraption

resembling a double tennis-racquet, if you can lay your hands on one. Sprinkle them with olive oil and some coarse Noirmoutier sea-salt and grill for about three minutes each side (depending on thickness), then eat with something plain, like boiled potatoes or crusty bread, and butter. You can also barbecue steaks of fresh tuna (*thon*). The red-tinged meat is very filling, and particularly delicious with a horseradish and cream sauce—if you have thought to bring the horseradish with you, that is.

VEGETABLES

Mogettes (haricot beans), introduced to the area by monks in the 16th century, need to be soaked overnight before cooking, then simmered for an hour or two in water with no salt, just a bouquet garni. Salt them only *after* they are cooked. You can stir in some *crème fraîche* (slightly soured cream) after draining them. If this sounds too much trouble, there are excellent, home-cooked versions bottled in glass jars, either plain or "*à l'ancienne*" (with tasty bits of bacon and carrot included), available in supermarkets. The beans—also called *lingots*—are traditionally served with ham (*jambon*), another Vendée speciality, cured using a mixture of sea-salt, spices and *eau-de-vie*. In late summer you sometimes see the new season's beans, called *demi-secs*, on sale still in their withered pods; these need no pre-soaking, and are supposed to be more digestible.

If you find strange mushrooms irresistible, you can take any that you gather in forests and hedgerows to a chemist for identification and advice on whether they can be eaten. On the whole it is probably safer to stick with those you can buy in the markets around October: chanterelles, ceps and horns of plenty (*trompettes de la mort*) look quite adventurous enough for most people.

The island of Noirmoutier enjoys a micro-climate that enables it to produce the first French new potatoes of the year—rather like Jersey Royals on the British market—as early as February. The sweet, fresh taste in early spring compensates for the slightly sorry sight of the island's fields shrouded in plastic wraps throughout the winter.

Sea-salt—grey and chunky, known as *sel de mer* or *gros-sel*, and the finer, white *fleur de sel* that forms the first sparkling crystals on the surface of the salt-pans—made the fortunes of the monasteries in the Middle Ages. In those days salt was in constant demand everywhere for the preservation of food. At the time of Richard III, the Bay of Bourgneuf supplied 80 per cent of the salt used in London. Today it is still made, on a smaller scale, with the same techniques in the salt-marshes of Guérande, Bouin, Noirmoutier, St-Hilaire-de-Riez, Olonne and Talmont, and makes interesting, and comparatively cheap, presents for foodie friends at home. Grown in the same marshes—though looked on by the salt-makers as a weed—is the red, fleshy-leaved samphire (*salicorne*) that turns green when cooked and is sold, pickled, as a condiment, or fresh for brief cooking and use as a vegetable or in a salad.

■ **Vendée brioche: the fluffy, yellow, fragrantly-scented loaf is a favourite at local weddings.**

POULTRY AND MEAT

One of the region's most important agricultural products today is poultry. Chicken (*poulet*) and duck (*canard*, or *canette*) are familiar enough; guinea-fowl (*pintade*) can be cooked as chicken; quail (*caille*)—of which you need one or two per person—may be roasted or casseroled for about 20 minutes, and needs extra flavour from added bits of bacon, grapes, Muscadet wine etc. Beautiful, speckled quail's eggs make an attractive starter when hard-boiled (place in cold water, bring to the boil, simmer for about four minutes, and then cool rapidly under the tap) and served with salt or mayonnaise. You can also barbecue quail: split the birds down the backbone, open them out, and marinate for a few hours in a tasty combination of herbs, oil, onions and other flavourings.

Meat is often sold in boned and rolled joints that make carving a real pleasure—just indicate to the butcher the length you want, or tell him how many people it's for. If you have a barbecue with a battery-operated spit, try doing a piece of beef (*rôti de boeuf*), studded with a few cloves of garlic. It doesn't take long to cook—about 20 to 30 minutes, depending on thickness—and, though it is not cheap, there is no waste. In the unlikely event of any being left over, it is even better cold.

CHEESE, BUTTER AND MILK

Many craftsman-made cheeses can be found in the market-halls of Vendean towns and villages. Even if you don't usually like goat's cheese, it's worth trying one of the very fresh, white ones, whose characteristic flavour is less pronounced. Among local cow's-milk cheeses are Halbran, fairly hard and tasty, and the slightly blander Mizotte. Look out for dairy stalls selling butter cut from towering yellow slabs—you can buy it by the pound (*une livre* is the equivalent of 500g) or by the kilogram, and can choose from unsalted (*doux*), slightly salted (*demi-sel*) or salty (*salé*). Fresh milk is

strangely hard to find, as the French are fond of the UHT or sterilised varieties. You will find fresh milk in the chiller cabinets, usually near creams and yoghurts. Red-top is whole milk, blue-top semi-skimmed, yellow-top is unpasteurised farm milk, and green-top a slightly-fermented Breton favourite, *lait ribot*, rather similar to drinking-yoghurt. Cream is almost always the slightly sharp *crème fraîche*, For pouring, use the small cartons of *crème fleurette entière*; this will whip fairly satisfactorily when chilled. There is no equivalent of British double cream.

DESSERTS

For the sweet-toothed, there is quite a choice. The Vendée is known for its loaves of impossibly light, fluffy brioche (a sweet bread made of eggs, flour, sugar, yeast, salt, butter and milk, plus a dash of rum or orange-flower water). Though traditionally an Easter speciality, at local weddings brioche is always served at midnight, with coffee. Every baker has his own version, though it is said to originate in Vendrennes, near Les Herbiers. Other treats include *flan maraîchin* (a pastry case holding an egg custard), *tourteau au fromage* (a zingy, black-domed cheesecake made from goat's cheese, nestling in a shallow pastry case and tasting rather better than it looks), *fouace* or *fouasse* (a cross between cake and bread, firmer than brioche), and "*R'tournez'y*" (a delicious vanilla, hazelnut and wild-strawberry ice-cream confection bearing the Vendée's hearts-and-crown logo, and sold in the best pâtisseries).

WINES

Besides the celebrated dry white Muscadet made from a Burgundy grape variety called Melon, the Vendée is known for the even drier, white Gros-Plant, derived from the Folle-Blanche grape—both grown on the northern limits of the *département*. The Vendée's other wine-growing areas produce some unpretentious reds, whites and rosés which have earned VDQS status (see below). These wines, produced at Brem-sur-Mer, Mareuil-sur-Lay, Chantonnay, Vix, and Pissotte and marketed under the Fiefs Vendéens label, have a long history. Known to the Romans, they were quaffed by the 16th-century writer François Rabelais and served at the table of Cardinal Richelieu when he was bishop of Luçon.

The main categories of wine quality, in descending order, are: AOC (Appellation d'Origine Contrôlée), bestowed on the region's three types of Muscadet: Muscadet de Sèvre-et-Maine, Muscadet des Coteaux de la Loire, and the standard Muscadet; VDQS (Vin Délimité de Qualité Supérieure), that is accorded to Gros-Plant and Fiefs Vendéens wines, and also to the reds, rosés and whites produced in the Coteaux d'Ancenis area alongside the Loire to the east of Nantes; Vin de Pays, denoting a rougher table wine; and Vin de Table, covering the rest.

The finest of the local wines is Muscadet de Sèvre-et-Maine (produced to the south-east of Nantes), particularly that which is bottled *sur lie*—left in the barrel on the lees, or sediment, to acquire a near-sparkling quality. In the heart of the Muscadet region you will find museums of wine at Le Pallet and at St-Hilaire-de-Loulay.

Among stronger local products are Pineau des Charentes, a fortified wine made from grape juice blended with cognac and drunk, chilled, as an apéritif; Troussepinette, a red apéritif flavoured with hedgerow fruits; and Kamok, a coffee-based liqueur distilled in Luçon.

■ **Wines: the region produces simple reds, whites and rosés, plus many fine Muscadets.**

A Little French History

You will probably decide that the last thing you want on holiday is a history lesson. Nevertheless, there may come a moment when you want to understand more of the Vendée Wars, for example, or to work out which British historical periods coincided with which French ones. Here are some historical landmarks with, in italics, a few notes about architectural styles, followed by a potted history of events in the Vendée.

DATE	FRENCH HISTORY	CORRESPONDING BRITISH HISTORY
EARLY TIMES		
7500-2500BC	Neolithic period (*dolmens, menhirs*).	Neolithic period.
4th century AD	Christianity reaches Poitou.	Christianity in Britain.
MIDDLE AGES		
AD486	Beginning of Merovingian period.	Anglo-Saxon.
751	Beginning of Carolingian period.	Saxon kingdoms.
987	Beginning of Capetian period.	Ethelred II (Saxon),
	(Romanesque architecture;	then Danes,
	10th-12th centuries)	Saxons and Normans.
1152	Henri Plantagenêt (Henry II of England)	From 1154
	marries Eleanor of Aquitaine.	Henry II (Plantagenet).
	(Gothic architecture, 12th-15th centuries.)	
1189-1199		Richard Coeur-de-Lion (Plantagenet).
1337-1453	**Hundred Years War**	Edward III (Plantagenet).
	between France and England.	
1431	Death of Joan of Arc.	Henry VI (Lancaster).
MODERN TIMES		
1515	Accession of François I (d 1547).	Henry VIII (Tudor).
	(Renaissance architecture.)	
1562-98	**Wars of Religion in France**;	Elizabeth I (Tudor).
	destruction of many churches.	
1589	Accession of Henri IV of France (d 1610).	Elizabeth I.
	(Classical architecture 1589-1789.)	
1598	Edict of Nantes, allowing Protestants freedom to worship.	Elizabeth I.
1610	Accession of Louis XIII (d 1643)	James I (Stuart).
	(1622 king fights Protestants near St-Gilles).	
1624-42	Richelieu prime minister	Charles I (Stuart).
	(1627-28 siege of La Rochelle).	

DATE	FRENCH HISTORY	CORRESPONDING BRITISH HISTORY
1643	Louis XIV, "the Sun King" (d 1715).	Charles I.
1685	Revocation of Edict of Nantes by Louis XIV; 400,000 Huguenots (French Protestants) flee abroad, many to England.	James II (Stuart).
1774	Accession of Louis XVI.	George III (Hanover).
1789	**FRENCH REVOLUTION**.	George III.
1792-1804	**First Republic**.	George III.
1793	Louis XVI guillotined 21 January.	George III.
1793-96	**WARS OF THE VENDÉE**.	George III.
1804-14	**First Empire**: Napoleon I (Bonaparte). (1814 Napoleon exiled to Elba.) *(Classical-style architecture and furniture, resembling Britain's Regency style.)*	George III.
1814-15	**First Restoration**: Louis XVIII.	George III.
1815	**Napoleon returns to power for 100 days** (April-June), then banished to St Helena.	George III.
1815	Louis de la Rochejaquelein attempts unsuccessfully to reignite the royalist cause in the Vendée.	George III.
1815-48	**Second Restoration**: Louis XVIII (d 1824).	George III.
1824	Charles X (exiled 1830).	George IV (Hanover).
1830	Louis-Philippe I (abdicates 1848 in favour of his grandson, the Comte de Paris).	William IV (Hanover).
1832	The Duchesse de Berry, daughter-in-law of Charles X, attempts a rebellion in the Vendée to place her son, the Duke of Bordeaux, on the French throne.	William IV.
1848-52	**Second Republic**.	Victoria (Hanover).
1852-70	**Second Empire**: Napoleon III (Louis-Napoleon). *(Opulent architecture with wrought-iron features; heavy, Victorian-style furniture.)*	Victoria.
1870-1940	**Third Republic**.	Victoria.
1914-18	**World War I** 20,000 Vendean troops die at Verdun.	George V (Windsor).
1939-45	**World War II**	George VI (Windsor).
1940-44	France (including Vendée) under German occupation.	George VI (Windsor).
1947-59	**Fourth Republic**.	George VI / Elizabeth II (Windsor).
1959-date	**Fifth Republic**.	Elizabeth II.

FRENCH AND VENDEAN HISTORY

The region was inhabited from prehistoric times—evidence in the shape of menhirs and dolmens, dating from 2500BC and earlier, is scattered all around, particularly near Avrillé and Le Bernard. From the end of the 10th century AD, after the collapse of Charlemagne's empire, feudal castles began to appear, at St-Mesmin, Ardelay, Noirmoutier, Tiffauges and Talmont. From the 11th century much of France, including the area now known as the Vendée, saw the passage of pilgrims making their way from northern countries towards the shrine of St James the Elder at Santiago de Compostela, in north-west Spain. During the next 200 years abbeys, churches, convents, almshouses and hospitals sprang up along the most popular routes to shelter the 500,000 people who made the long journey, though in the Vendée these Romanesque buildings received heavy damage during the succession of later wars.

The marriage, in 1152, of Eleanor of Aquitaine to Henri Plantagenêt, Duke of Normandy (who, two years later, became King Henry II of England) combined her dowry of western France with his existing lands in the north to bring half of France into English hands. Their son Richard the Lionheart (Richard I of England) enjoyed hunting, and often stayed at Talmont, atoning for his foreign warmongering by providing funds for several abbeys, including that of Lieu-Dieu, at Jard.

More than a century later, after his accession to the throne of England in 1327, Edward III made a claim through his mother's line to the French crown. The resulting Hundred Years War, sustained by Richard II, Henry IV and Henry V, made much of northern France into a battleground until 1453, when the French had won back all but the town of Calais.

Since the Vendée held many influential Protestants (les Réformés) the

36-year-long Wars of Religion that broke out in 1562 between Catholics and Protestants raged fiercely throughout the region and brought fresh devastation to religious buildings. Eventually Henri IV, who had been brought up a Protestant and converted to Catholicism on his accession, granted freedom of worship to the Protestants in 1598, through the Edict of Nantes, and the conflict came to an end. (The Edict was revoked a century later by Louis XIV.) Cardinal Richelieu, one-time bishop of Luçon, and chief minister to Louis XIII between 1624 and 1642, saw the need to unite the whole of France—Catholic and Protestant—under one crown. To prevent strategic strongholds falling into Protestant hands, and to reduce the power of provincial dukes and princes, he ordered the destruction of many castles, including those of Apremont, La Garnache and Les Essarts.

THE WARS OF THE VENDÉE

After the Storming of the Bastille in 1789 and the Declaration of the First Republic in 1792 the new régime established by the French Revolution was total. The nobility was abolished. Priests who refused to swear allegiance to the Republican government (rather than to the king, the previous head of the Church) were deported and replaced with "loyal" ones. The names of towns and villages were changed from any with religious overtones (St-Gilles-sur-Vie, for example, becoming Port-Fidèle). The calendar was altered: Year I began on 22 September 1793; 12 months (composed of three 10-day weeks) were renamed Vendémiaire, Frimaire, Brumaire..." etc, and the days were re-baptised "Primidi, Duodi, Tridi, Quartidi ...". Even the then-familiar measurements of *pieds* and *pouces* (feet and inches) were superseded by a new metric system.

■ The Vendée Wars: farmers improvised lethal weapons from their scythes and their billhooks.

After having endured the absolute power of the monarch, many of the urban middle class embraced the new philosophies and ideas of a world of greater justice. The labouring classes, too, welcomed the Declaration of the Rights of Man, and looked forward to the abolition of the taxes that they had to pay to the Crown.

However, new ideas permeated only slowly to the Vendée—then known as Bas-Poitou—more than 350km from Paris. In this rural region there was less social inequality than elsewhere: aristocrats were not as rich; tenant farmers were less poor; and priests were more revered in a religion that combined elements of local superstition with orthodox Catholicism.

The Vendean peasants were appalled to find that the Revolution removed their king (Louis XVI was executed in January 1793), forced on them new priests loyal to the changed order, and required payment to the Republican government of even higher taxes than had been due under the monarchy. Worse, the confiscated goods of the old Church

■ **Vendée building styles (right):** neolithic dolmen; thatched bourrines; the elegant, slate-roofed Logis de la Chabotterie; a pair of typical red-tiled farmhouses.

and deported clergy were thought to be lining the pockets of the *bourgeoisie*, or middle classes, who had engineered for themselves top administrative posts. Ignoring the new priests assigned to their churches, the Vendeans attended clandestine open-air Masses led by rebellious, pre-Revolutionary clergy.

The spark that ignited three years of horrific civil warfare, was the Republican government's decision in February 1793 to raise a 300,000-strong army to defend France's borders against threatened invasion by neighbouring countries. The people of Bas-Poitou and surrounding *départements* refused to submit to formal conscription, so Republican soldiers were sent in to draw names at random. Riots ensued. In March, the town of Machecoul saw the massacre of its Republican sympathisers; other villages followed suit.

The event generally considered the start of the wars was the mass refusal of conscription, on 11 March 1793, by the people of St-Florent-le-Vieil on the river ⫸➜ *page 37*

FAMOUS AND INFAMOUS FIGURES IN VENDÉE HISTORY

Memorable names connected with the Vendée include **Gilles de Rais** (1404-40), companion-in-arms of Joan of Arc and notorious in legend as the murderous Bluebeard; **Pierre Garcie-Ferrande** (c1430-c1520), intrepid navigator from St-Gilles-sur-Vie, praised by King François I for his charting of Europe's coastline; **François Rabelais** (c1494-1553), Renaissance writer, monk, and father of good living, who spent time at Fontenay-le-

Comte and Maillezais; **François Viète** (1540-1603), inventor of modern algebra, born at Fontenay-le-Comte; **Cardinal Richelieu** (1585-1642), prime minister to Louis XIII, and bishop of Luçon from 1606 to 1622; **Nau l'Olonnois** (c1630-71), bloodthirsty pirate from Olonne-sur-Mer who was chopped up and eaten by cannibals; painter **Paul Baudry** (1824-86), a native of La Roche-sur-Yon, commissioned to decorate the foyer of the Paris Opéra;

statesman **Georges Clemenceau** (1841-1929), twice prime minister, who drew up the Treaty of Versailles after World War I, born at Mouilleron-en-Pareds and buried near Mouchamps; artist **Benjamin Rabier** (1864-1939) of La Roche-sur-Yon, creator of the cheery Vache-qui-Rit (Laughing Cow) logo; and the distinguished World War II soldier **Jean de Lattre de Tassigny** (1889-1952), born, and buried, at Mouilleron-en-Pareds.

A Vendée Top 20

Among my favourite sites in and around the Vendée I hope you, too, will find a few unexpected delights. Grouped under the area numbers you will find later in the book, my list includes subjects that are historic, artistic, unusual—or just plain fun.

AREA 3 Around La Tranche

⭐8 **Parc Floral et Tropical** Marvel at the exquisite pink lotus flowers growing in the lakes at St-Cyr-en-Talmondais (page 102).

⭐9 **La Rochelle** Walk through the streets of this historic town, climb its ancient towers and visit its modern aquarium (page 99).

⭐10 **"La Venise Verte"** Paddle the tree-lined waterways of "Green Venice", a picturesque corner of the Marais Poitevin (page 105).

AREA 4 Around Fontenay

⭐11 **Bazoges-en-Pareds** Enjoy a bird's-eye view of this attractive village from the top of the castle keep (page 112).

⭐12 **Fontenay-le-Comte** Follow in the footsteps of Rabelais and Simenon among the mellow buildings of this Renaissance town, once the Vendée's capital (page 115).

⭐13 **Vouvant** Wander through the ancient hilltop village, and admire the Romanesque carvings on the church porch (page 127).

AREA 5 Around Les Herbiers

⭐14 **Clisson** Savour the Italianate architecture of this tranquil riverside town (page 133).

⭐15 **Le Logis de la Chabotterie** Experience the style of 18th-century living at an elegant country mansion (page 147; picture page 33).

⭐16 **Le Puy-du-Fou** Take the family to the entertaining daytime historical Grand Parc; or to the Cinéscénie—the dazzling night-time *son-et-lumière* show (page 142).

⭐17 **Tiffauges Castle** Watch demonstrations of medieval siege machinery at the ruined castle of the infamous Gilles de Rais, model for the character of Bluebeard (page 149).

AREA 6 Around the Pays de Retz

⭐18 **Escal'Atlantic** Tour a real submarine, or take a virtual cruise on board an ocean liner, ingeniously recreated inside the German submarine base at St-Nazaire (page 166).

⭐19 **Le Grand Blockhaus** Step inside an impregnable German gun emplacement, built during World War II at Batz (page 152).

⭐20 **Planète Sauvage** Set off on safari with the family at an entertaining wildlife park (page 163).

Loire, midway between Nantes and Angers. The populace routed the *"Bleus"* ("Blues", or Republican troops, sometimes referred to as *patriots*), and captured their cannon. The villagers called upon a humble carter, Jacques Cathelineau, to lead them and the others who joined the cause. He and former gamekeeper Jean-Nicolas Stofflet were working-class generals; for the rest, the Vendean peasantry prevailed on trusted local aristocrats to take command—François Athanase Charette de la Contrie, Louis de Lescure, Henri de la Rochejaquelein, the Duc d'Elbée—whose names have passed into local folklore.

After spectacular Vendean victories in the early days at Bressuire, Thouars, Fontenay-le-Comte and Saumur, and then at Angers in June 1793, the *"Blancs"* ("Whites" or royalist Vendeans, also sometimes referred to by their opponents as *brigands*) seemed invincible. Their success was partly due to the fact that they would disperse immediately after a battle, leaving no "army" for the Blues to seek out and destroy. The initially ill-prepared Republicans were, however, soon reinforced by General Kléber's crack troops known as the "Mayençais" who had been fighting on the German front, and victory turned to

■ The Vendée Wars (left): dashing Vendean leader Charette; Vendeans worship in secret; windmill used as a semaphore. Below: Napoleon calmed the troubled region.

defeat at Nantes (where Cathelineau received mortal wounds). The Whites lost Cholet, where Lescure was severely injured, and then, in search of hoped-for reinforcements from England, the Vendée army made a seemingly-impossible dash north across the river Loire. Here, before his death from wounds also sustained at Cholet, another leader, the Marquis de Bonchamps, earned his place in history by refusing to allow his Vendean troops to massacre their 4,000-5,000 Republican prisoners.

This exodus known as the "Virée de Galerne" has, ever since, evoked a kind of Dunkirk spirit in the region. Harried by the Blues, on 18 October 1793 the Vendeans ferried between 60,000 and 100,000 men, women and children north across the wide and treacherous river. Their aim was to capture a suitable port—Granville, on the Cherbourg peninsula, or St-Malo—ready to receive the expected English aid. During the epic journey the hungry, cold Vendeans marched some 200km north, where they were joined by Breton guerrillas known as "Chouans".

In November, they laid siege unsuccessfully to Granville. After a fruitless wait for help from England (in 1795 William Pitt did eventually send forces, who were cut down during an attempt to land on the Quiberon peninsula on the south coast of Brittany), the Vendeans set off back towards the Loire. At Le Mans, 10,000 were slain by the town's heavily-armed Republicans. Tens of thousands more died in further combats, or from sickness and hunger. In December 1793 a few thousand managed to re-cross the Loire; many others, prevented from doing the same, fled west where 6,000 fell victim to Republican troops in the forest of Savenay, west of Nantes.

Determined such insurrection should never happen again, the Republican General Turreau gave orders that *colonnes infernales* ("fiery columns" of troops) should be sent to lay waste every village and kill every remaining person in

the *département* of Bas-Poitou—that would henceforth be renamed "Vendée". From early 1794 these death squads passed from village to village burning, pillaging and massacring. At Les Lucs-sur-Boulogne 563 people—women, children and old men—were shot as they knelt in church. At Les Sables-d'Olonne, blood from the guillotine ran thickly onto the town's golden sands; at Nantes, where even the 90 seconds required for this method of execution proved too slow, General Carrier instituted a more efficient system by drowning entire boatloads of prisoners in the river Loire.

The few surviving Vendeans returned home to find ruined houses, murdered families, and a reign of terror. They continued their guerrilla

---

INTERESTING VENDÉE WAR SITES, MUSEUMS AND BOOKS

TO VISIT

Logis de la Chabotterie Country house where General Charette was captured. Atmospheric 18th-century-style interior and garden; exhibitions on Vendée themes; multi-media Vendée Wars experience (see page 33 and 147).

Les Lucs-sur-Boulogne Scene of a terrible massacre. Memorial chapel built on the site; modern Chemin de la Mémoire building; stained-glass windows in village church (see page 139). New museum, L'Historial de Vendée, opens in 2005.

Noirmoutier Castle Bullet-ridden chair on display in which injured Vendean general d'Elbée was shot on the square outside; a painting of this scene, and other souvenirs (see page 51).

Mont des Alouettes Windmills on this ridge were used to pass coded messages to the Vendean guerrillas. Three mills remain, one restored to working order (see page 137).

Grasla Forest Woodland in which 2,500 Vendeans hid

out in 1794. Reconstruction of encampment; video explaining Vendée Wars; living-history sessions in summer (see page 130).

Musée d'Art et d'Histoire, Cholet Modern museum, with portraits of Vendean leaders, and a good English explanation of uprising (see page 132).

Panthéon de la Vendée Cemetery where General Sapinaud and many other Vendean combatants are buried (see page 136).

Sur les Pas de Charette A signposted route around 13 places associated with the Vendean general; leaflet from tourist offices and from the Logis de la Chabotterie.

TO READ

In English

La Vendée by Anthony Trollope. Historical novel, based closely on the memoirs of Madame de la Rochejaquelein, which first appeared in 1850. It paints a vivid picture of the early part of the war and of its principal characters. (Penguin, 1993.)

Citizens, by Simon Schama.

Highly readable history of the French Revolution, with a substantial section on the Wars of the Vendée. (Viking, 1989.)

In French

Blancs et Bleus dans la Vendée Déchirée by Jean-Clément Martin. Pocket-sized, information-packed book, alive with evocative paintings and drawings. (Découvertes Gallimard, 2001.)

Plein Ciel sur les Châteaux de Vendée by Joseph Rouillé. Aerial views and history of Vendean castles and their fates during the wars. (Editions du Vieux Chouan, 1989.)

L'Accent de Ma Mère by Michel Ragon. A moving autobiography by a present-day writer and critic, who interweaves memories of his Vendean childhood with accounts of the wars 150 years earlier. (Livre de Poche, 1983.)

Les Mouchoirs Rouges de Cholet by Michel Ragon (see above). Historical novel about the Vendée Wars. (Livre de Poche, 1986.)

warfare for many months among the gorse and bracken of the *bocage*. Charette and Stofflet signed peace treaties with the Republicans in 1795, though Charette continued to lead skirmishes against the Blues until his capture at La Chabotterie in March 1796 and subsequent execution, a few weeks after that of Stofflet.

Under a treaty drawn up by the Republican General Hoche in 1799, freedom of worship returned to France. Napoleon Bonaparte made supervision of the unruly region less difficult by transferring the capital from Fontenay-le-Comte to La Roche-sur-Yon, in the geographical heart of the Vendée. Here, he created a new town of straight, broad avenues, allowing rapid deployment of troops to quell future uprisings.

Although, with Charette's death, the wars reached an end, some further attempts were made to rekindle them. During Napoleon's brief return to power in 1815, Louis de la Rochejaquelein (brother of Henri) carried out an unsuccessful invasion near Croix-de-Vie. Seventeen years later the Duchesse de Berry tried to seize the French throne for her son, the Duke of Bordeaux—grandson of Charles X.

Debate still rages as to whether the uprising that cost so many lives was truly spontaneous or was engineered by landowners and priests reluctant to lose their power and fortunes. Atrocities were, no doubt, perpetrated by both Vendean and Republican forces but, in the area where memories live on, a certain bias in the retelling of the stories is inevitable.

RECENT TIMES

Vast areas of pine and *chêne vert* (holm oak) were planted from the mid-19th century to anchor the shifting sands along the coast around St-Jean-de-Monts and north of Les Sables-d'Olonne. The coming of the railways in the 1860s helped to develop tourism around the ports of Les Sables and Croix-de-Vie, where fine examples of Victorian-period seaside architecture remain. Railways also provided a means of escape for many of the inhabitants of marshland farms, leading to a rural exodus around the end of the 19th century as young people found more lucrative work in towns. From the late 18th until the mid-20th century there were coal-mining and glass-making industries at Faymoreau-les-Mines, north-east of Fontenay-le-Comte.

The brooding silhouette of the occasional blockhouse reminds you that for more than four years of World War II the Vendée was occupied by German forces. A Commonwealth War Graves Commission sign on the wall of a country cemetery usually indicates that it contains the graves of an Allied aircrew shot down over the Vendée or—particularly around the Loire estuary—of some of the 3,000 who drowned when the merchant ship *Lancastria* was sunk by enemy action in 1940.

After tourism, the wealth of the *département* today is based on agriculture (beef and dairy cattle, pigs and poultry in the *bocage*, cereal-growing in the plain, sheep and cattle in the marshes, and early vegetables on the island of Noirmoutier), fishing (sardines, tuna, sole, langoustines, oysters and mussels), manufacture of clothes and shoes, boat-building (Bénéteau and Jeanneau), food-canning, and construction of agricultural machinery.

Typical architecture of the region (see photographs on page 33) includes the low, thatched cottages with whitewashed, mud-built walls, called *bourrines*; examples are dotted about the Marais Breton, from La Barre-de-Monts down to St-Hilaire-de-Riez. Rather more grand are the elegant stone manor houses, known as *logis*, such as that of La Chabotterie.

■ **Premier Georges Clemenceau: the Vendean politician shaped the Treaty of Versailles in 1918.**

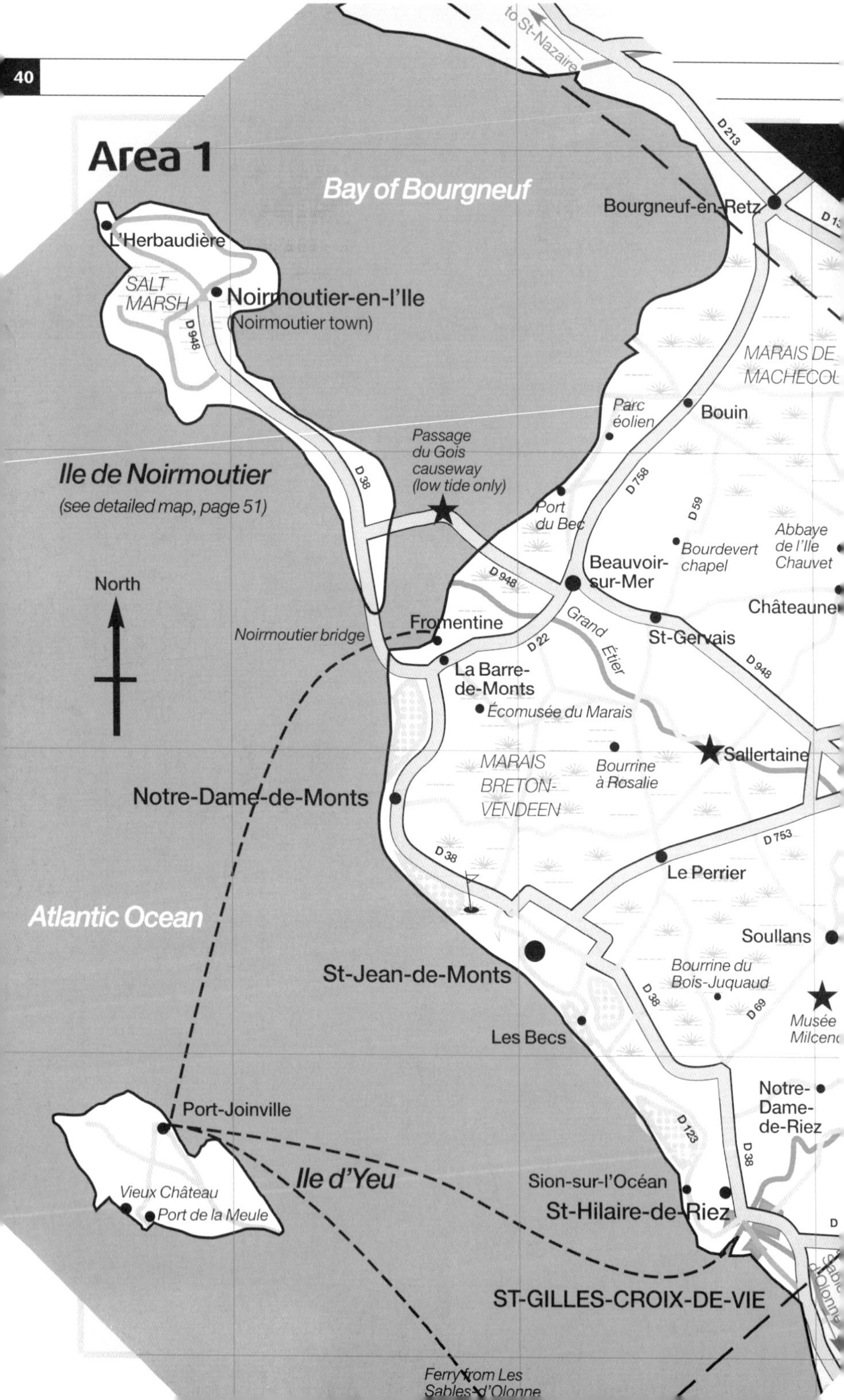

Area 1

Bay of Bourgneuf

Bourgneuf-en-Retz

L'Herbaudière

SALT MARSH

Noirmoutier-en-l'Ile
(Noirmoutier town)

MARAIS DE MACHECOU

Ile de Noirmoutier
(see detailed map, page 51)

North

D 948

D 213

D 1

Parc éolien

Bouin

Passage du Gois causeway
(low tide only)

Port du Bec

Bourdevert chapel

Abbaye de l'Ile Chauvet

Châteauneu

Beauvoir-sur-Mer

D 758

D 59

D 38

Noirmoutier bridge

Fromentine

Grand Étier

St-Gervais

D 948

La Barre-de-Monts

D 22

Écomusée du Marais

Notre-Dame-de-Monts

MARAIS BRETON-VENDEEN

Bourrine à Rosalie

Sallertaine

D 753

Atlantic Ocean

D 38

Le Perrier

Soullans

St-Jean-de-Monts

Bourrine du Bois-Juquaud

D 38

D 69

Musée Milcenc

Port-Joinville

Les Becs

Notre-Dame-de-Riez

Vieux Château

Port de la Meule

Ile d'Yeu

Sion-sur-l'Océan

St-Hilaire-de-Riez

D 123

D 38

D

ST-GILLES-CROIX-DE-VIE

to St-Nazaire

Sabl...'Olonne

Ferry from Les Sables d'Olonne

St-Jean-de-Monts, Challans, St-Gilles and the Islands

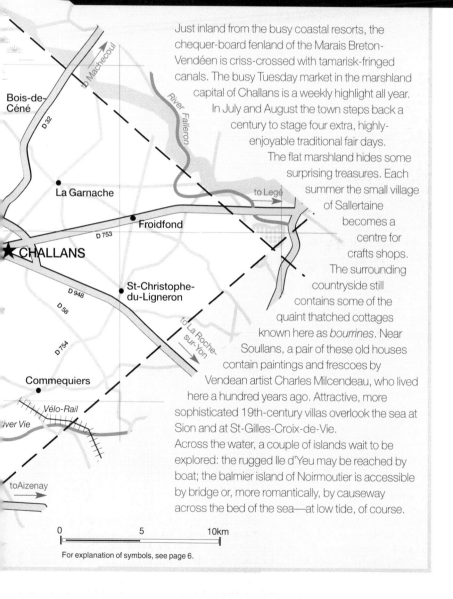

Just inland from the busy coastal resorts, the chequer-board fenland of the Marais Breton-Vendéen is criss-crossed with tamarisk-fringed canals. The busy Tuesday market in the marshland capital of Challans is a weekly highlight all year. In July and August the town steps back a century to stage four extra, highly-enjoyable traditional fair days.

The flat marshland hides some surprising treasures. Each summer the small village of Sallertaine becomes a centre for crafts shops. The surrounding countryside still contains some of the quaint thatched cottages known here as *bourrines*. Near Soullans, a pair of these old houses contain paintings and frescoes by Vendean artist Charles Milcendeau, who lived here a hundred years ago. Attractive, more sophisticated 19th-century villas overlook the sea at Sion and at St-Gilles-Croix-de-Vie.

Across the water, a couple of islands wait to be explored: the rugged Ile d'Yeu may be reached by boat; the balmier island of Noirmoutier is accessible by bridge or, more romantically, by causeway across the bed of the sea—at low tide, of course.

Bois-de-Céné

to Machecoul

River Falleron

La Garnache

D 32

to Legé

Froidfond

D 753

★ CHALLANS

St-Christophe-du-Ligneron

D 948

D 58

to La Roche-sur-Yon

D 754

Commequiers

Vélo-Rail

River Vie

to Aizenay

0   5   10km

For explanation of symbols, see page 6.

LA BARRE-DE-MONTS

ⓘ tel: 02 51 68 51 83 fax: 02 51 93 83 26
www.ville-labarredemonts.fr
ot.fromentine.labarredemonts@wanadoo.fr

Forest walks and cycleways wind through the perfumed pine woods that hold the shifting sands in place to the west of this village 16km north-west of Challans. Here, on the mainland side of the Noirmoutier bridge, look out alongside the marshland canals for the strange wooden *pêcheries*—simple cabins from which dangle contraptions that look like giant spiders, with square nets strung between the tips of their "feet". These are winched down into the water as the tide rises, to catch unwary fish swimming in from the sea. Keep an eye open, too, for the last of the *bourrines*—the small, mud-walled cottages, thatched with reeds from the marshes, which were homes for the poorest farming families.

➤Écomusée du Marais Breton-Vendéen. An ultra-modern entrance building welcomes you to this open-air museum 2km east of La Barre, where methods of fenland agriculture are demonstrated in the context of a late-19th-century farm. To take in the whole of the 12-hectare site requires a good couple of hours—and a fair amount of walking. After an introductory video, with headset translation for English-speakers, you head outside to see furnished reed-thatched *bourrines* (see above, and picture on page 33), and outbuildings full of poultry, spotted Bayeux pigs and old farm machinery. Alongside working salt-pans are interesting descriptions of the region's salt industry. From July to mid-September there are afternoon demonstrations of clog-making, basket-weaving and other country crafts, and in one of the farthest buildings is a hide from which you can watch herons and other marshland birds—if you have your binoculars with you. On summer Sundays you may catch other traditional activities such as folk-dancing, punting in flat-bottomed craft known as *yoles* (a century ago, the only form of transport through the flooded marshland in winter), canal-vaulting, using punting-poles (*saut à la ningle*), or ploughing with oxen and with Breton draught horses. There's not much shade, so take protective clothing in hot weather.
❶ *1 Feb-end Oct (plus Christmas-holiday period), Tues-Sun 2-6pm (1 May-15 Sept, Mon-Sat 10am-7pm, Sun & public holidays 2-7pm). Closed 25 Dec & 1 Jan. Le Daviaud (tel: 02 51 93 84 84). 4.40€, students & children 3.60€.* ♿
➤Pey de la Blet. About 1km south of La Barre you can eyeball passing birds from a wooden platform level with the tops of the pine trees, which gives a magnificent view towards the Ile d'Yeu and across the marshes—as long as surrounding branches haven't encroached too much. Take the road towards Noirmoutier bridge and immediately go left at a roundabout, where Le Pey is signposted along a lane skirting the forest. No further signs to help you, unfortunately, but after about 1km, stop opposite a lane called the Chemin de l'Archambaud, cross the cycle track in the woods, and you'll see a flight of 122 steps leading to the treetops. ●

BEAUVOIR-SUR-MER

ⓘ tel: 02 51 68 71 13 fax: 02 51 49 05 04
www.otsi-beauvoir.com
otsi-beauvoir@wanadoo.fr

Despite its name, this little town 16km north-west of Challans is no longer "on sea" but stranded 3km inland. As you approach from Challans on the D948, the view south across the low-lying

■ **Bourdevert Chapel:** babies' shoes hang by the altar in this tiny church, near Beauvoir.

marshland gives a clear impression of where the waters must once have been. Large signs outside Beauvoir give times of low tide, when you can safely enjoy the amazing experience of driving across the Passage du Gois—the causeway 5km beyond the village that links the island of Noirmoutier (see page 49) with the mainland. Take a moment to visit Beauvoir's 12th- to 14th-century church—indeed, if you drive through the village from Challans the road practically thrusts you in through the north door on a tight double bend. A statue of St Philbert, the church's patron saint, who also founded the abbey at Noirmoutier, can be seen nearby.

> **Chapelle de Bourdevert**. An enchanting little chapel stands at a country crossroads on the D59, 4km east of Beauvoir. Dating from the 12th or 13th century, it is said to have been built by two sailors in gratitude for surviving a shipwreck in the days when the sea still lapped against this spot. Push open the gnarled wooden door (the key may be obtained from a nearby address if locked) and step inside. Light streams through the two simple, arched windows, a model ship is suspended from the painted rafters, and on either side of the ornate altar hangs a collection of babies' shoes—placed there by parents who come and pray to the Virgin to guide their children's first steps. Mass is said at 3pm on the second Sunday of the month; a pilgrimage takes place in early September. ●

> **Maison de l'Ane**. You probably wouldn't believe there could be 25 different types of donkey! At this farm 1km west of Beauvoir you will see many of them on show, from the small, grey Provençal variety to the large, shaggy Baudet du Poitou—not forgetting the Egyptian white and the Berry black—and children can take rides on some of them. ❶ *Easter-30 Sept, daily 2-6pm; (1 July-31 Aug, daily 10am-7.30pm). Route du Gois (tel: 02 51 93 85 70). 3.50€, children 2.50€; family (2+2) 10€.*

BOIS-DE-CÉNÉ

ⓘ tel: 02 51 93 19 75 fax: 02 51 49 76 04
www.otsi-challans.com
info@otsi-challans.com

A few ancient houses dating from Renaissance times add to the attraction of this village 10km north of Challans. The restored 14th-century church contains Romanesque pillars with interesting stone carvings on the top—including some depicting the Seven Deadly Sins (you may wish to cover the children's eyes for the saucier ones).

> **L'Abbaye de l'Ile Chauvet**. The site of this ancient abbey, just to the south-west of the village, was indeed once a small *île*, or island. To reach it, take the Châteauneuf road, and then turn right across marshes drained by 12th-century monks, whose monasteries became prosperous from the resulting salt trade. A driveway leads through woods to a 19th-century mansion, behind which lie the romantic ruins of the church, founded by Benedictines in 1130, much knocked about by the English in 1381, and finally abandoned following further damage by the Republicans after the French Revolution. The guided tour leads through a handsome Romanesque doorway to a roofless chancel. Part of the refectory building still stands, and a museum showing models of the landscape in earlier times has been arranged beneath the magnificent oak beams of the former dormitory on the first floor. ❍ *1 July-30 Sept, daily 11am-6pm. Ile Chauvet, off D28, 2km SW of Bois-de-Céné (tel: 02 51 68 13 19). 4.50€, children under 10 free.*

> **La Route du Sel: Canoë Ornitho**. Early risers will enjoy this magical guided canoe trip, starting at dawn, to look for buzzards, lapwings, and other wildlife. The four-hour journey, along narrow canals spanned by dew-spangled cobwebs, carries you along ancient salt routes through the open marsh landscape. Meet at the well-signposted farm in the heart of the Ile Chauvet marshland (to the left of the abbey driveway—see separate entry). As the sun climbs, it can become scorching, so take hats and suitable clothing. The guide produces a copious breakfast half-way through the trip, but it's advisable to have a snack before leaving home, too. ○ *1-30 July, 6am; 1-15 Aug, 6.30am. Ferme de Belle-Ile, Ile Chauvet, off D28, 2km SW of Bois-de-Céné; booking through tourist offices, or direct (tel: 02 51 93 03 40). 32€ (including breakfast), under-11s 5.50€.*

BOUIN

ⓘ tel: 02 51 68 88 85
www.otsi-beauvoir.com
otsi-beauvoir@wanadoo.fr

This pretty village (once an island), 20km north-west of Challans is full of narrow lanes and ancient houses. Bouin originally made its fortune from salt-making—in the 15th century, 80 per cent of that used in London came from the area. The riches from this valuable commodity endowed the church with three handsome altarpieces.

Today, however, oysters are the most important product. The rich mud of Bourgneuf Bay provides ideal conditions for fattening them, and the oyster-growers based at Port du Bec (see below), Port des Champs and Port des Brochets lay the baby shellfish out under water in sacks of plastic netting. When they reach maturity, after four years, the growers collect them, purify them in water-tanks, and market some 12,000 tonnes each year.

> **Marais Salant: Les Valencières**. In contrast to the 700 salt-producers that worked here in the 19th century, just one today is still making the "*or blanc*" (white gold) on his carefully laid out salt-pans 1km west of Bouin. Unless it's raining (a catastrophe for a salt-maker), you can drop in and see Thierry Odéon at work scraping the precious crystals from the surface of the shallow water, and can buy some salt to take home. ○ *1 July-31 Aug, daily 10.30am-noon & 4.30-7.30pm. Signposted off D21A Port des Champs road; follow signs to Les Evains (tel: 02 51 49 36 01). Free.*

> **Parc Éolien**. The Vendée's first wind farm draws fascinated spectators. Follow "Parc éolien" signs from Bouin out to the coast, where there is no missing the eight 102-metre-high turbines that stand in a breezy spot near the oyster-farming centre. Their output of 19.5 megawatts makes this the most powerful site in France at the time of building, capable of providing around 1 per cent of the Vendée's electricity requirements. ●

> **Port du Bec**. At the southern end of the wind farm road—and also accessible from the main D758 road to Beauvoir—is an unusual oyster-fishing hamlet. The rickety-looking wooden jetties lining the channel that leads out to the sea have, earned it the nickname of "the Chinese port". Lobster-pots litter the quays, and coloured flags flutter from brightly-painted boats. There's tremendous activity about two hours after low tide, as the fishermen return from their expeditions into Bourgneuf Bay, and spectators have to be careful to dodge the ancient tractors that reverse rapidly down to the water's edge to drag in the trailers of oysters. If you want to sample these shellfish at their freshest, you can buy them from Chez Melon, to take home, or drop into the Mord'eau café (see panel), and down a dozen, with a glass of chilled Muscadet. ●

■ **Le Port du Bec: spindly jetties for the oyster boats at Bouin's quaint harbour.**

CHALLANS

ⓘ tel: 02 51 93 19 75 fax: 02 51 49 76 04
www.otsi-challans.com
info@otsi-challans.com

As "*capitale du canard*," or "duck capital," this charming market town 16km from the coast was to France what Aylesbury was to England, and you will find many duck-related dishes on local menus. Formerly reared in enormous numbers in the surrounding marshes, these birds have now been overtaken by the free-range black chicken (*poulet noir*) and guinea-fowl (*pintade*).

Bristling with restaurants and with smart shops, Challans is renowned for its terrific market-day on Tuesday mornings. From the countryside around, shoppers come to stock up on fresh fish, vegetables, cheese (particularly delicious goat's cheeses from a farm at nearby La Garnache) and other produce in the covered food hall. Outside, hundreds of stalls fill the streets and squares with local colour, and offer clothes, farm equipment, gadgets and even live poultry.

The town's imposing, neo-gothic 19th-century church is rather strangely divorced from its bell-tower, which stands across the way in a leafy square on the site of a previous church. Inside are two magnificent rose windows and a *chemin de croix,* or Stations of the Cross, composed of snowy-white, life-sized statues that won for their creator (Maison Beau, of Nantes) a first prize at the great Paris Exhibition of 1900.

You'll find more sculpture behind the *mairie*; a work by the internationally-renowned twin Vendean artists Jan and Joël Martel (1896-1966), created to honour their friend the painter Charles Milcendeau (see page 59). Another Martel sculpture decorates the façade of Le Marais theatre, in Rue Carnot.

> ★ Autrefois Challans . . . la foire. On four days in July and August the clock is turned back to 1910, and more than 1,000 local people dress up in turn-of-the-last-century costume. The men sport blue denim smocks and heavy clogs, or traditional marshland garb of black close-fitting trousers and short, matador-style jacket with jaunty small-brimmed hats. The women wear pretty lace *coiffes* or the face-shading bonnets

■ **Challans: live poultry is still on sale at the Tuesday street market.**

known as *quichenottes* (supposedly a corruption of the English "Kiss not," a name said to date from the time of English occupation during the Hundred Years War) that were a common sight until 30 years ago. Horse-drawn carts clatter through the streets, children re-enact schoolroom scenes, farmers trade ducks and chickens, the fire brigade stages a dramatic "rescue", and old folk spin, weave, strip kernels from corncobs and indulge in noisy, old-fashioned diversions like *l'aluette* (a boisterous local card game) or *palets* (a riotous contest involving metal discs thrown at a board). O *Two Thurs in July & two Thurs in Aug, 10am-7pm. Throughout town (tel: 02 51 68 19 10). Admission free; charges for some events.*

❯**Karting Loisirs Challandais**. There's a family feel to this go-kart centre, where adults, and children from seven years and up, can don helmets and overalls and play at being Formula 1 drivers on the 700-metre-long circuit. Lots of chicanes help to spice up the driving. ● *Daily 10am-noon & 2-6pm (1 July-31 Aug, daily 9.30am-9.30pm). Route de Cholet, take Montaigu exit from Challans bypass, and turn east on D753 following signs to "KLC" (tel: 02 51 93 33 44). From 14€ for 10 mins, children from 11€.*

❯**Planète Racing**. Adoring 20-something girls video their dashing boyfriends zooming on jet-skis around the disused gravel pits on this 30-hectare lake, 7km south-west of Challans. A sandy beach, the odd palm tree, and the sun-loungers provided for clients give a tropical feel; a trim wooden clubhouse sells drinks and snacks. There are also water-borne "bananas" and "do'nuts", plus paint-ball, cross-country karting and a mini-circuit for children's quad bikes (for ages five to 12). Minimum age for most vehicles is 16. ◑ *1 Apr-31 Dec, Fri-Mon & public holidays 10am-7pm (1 June-30 Sept, daily 11am-8pm). Les Fontenelles, Route d'Apremont, about 4km along D58 (tel: 02 51 49 80 78). 10-min jet-ski session, 22€; 30-min quad trial 35€; passports or cheque required as deposit on some vehicles.*

❯**Les Puces Ligneronnaises**. A fantastic open-air flea-market is held twice a year on the edge of a village 7km south-east of Challans. Enjoy many hours of happy treasure-hunting among its 200 stalls selling chunky linen sheets, old picture-postcards, furniture, glass and bric-à-brac. O *Mid July & mid Aug, Sun 10am-5pm. St-Christophe-du-Ligneron, off D948 (tel: 02 51 35 27 27). 1€, in aid of charity.*

■ Autrefois Challans: ladies in quichenottes relive olden times.

CHALLANS EXTRAS

Toutoccas. Huge shed full of furniture & bric-à-brac. Tues-Sat 9.30am-12.30pm & 2.30-7pm; Sun 3-7pm. 3km SE of Challans, on D948 (tel: 02 51 68 29 41).

Shops:

Billet. Small tea-room & wonderful patisserie opposite market-hall. 4 Place Aristide-Briand (tel: 02 51 35 35 45).

Côtes et Lacs. Fishing equipment, from bait to high-tech rods. 32 bis Rue Carnot (tel: 02 51 35 58 53).

Festivals:

Autrefois Challans (see main entry). July & Aug.

Puces Ligneronnaises (see main entry). July & Aug.

Foire des Minées. Trade & agricultural fair. Sept.

CHATEAUNEUF

ⓘ **tel: 02 51 93 19 75 fax: 02 51 49 76 04**
www.otsi-challans.com
info@otsi-challans.com

This small village, 8km north of Challans, still has an ancient *motte féodale*, or feudal mound, standing at the side of the Bois-de-Céné road. Try climbing the steep sides to appreciate what a good lookout point it must have made over the flat countryside, before the trees grew up. A variety of birds nest in the surrounding meadows and marshland including, from April to October, pairs of storks who roost on tall trees and specially-built platforms. You can spy on them from a wooden observatory, signposted off the D28.

❯**Le Petit Moulin**. The sails of this windmill, built in 1703, still provide the power to grind corn, though now essentially for animal feed. Monsieur Vrignaud, seventh-generation miller, explains the process animatedly (ask for an English information sheet at the outset, to help you keep up) as he demonstrates the engaging of the wooden gears and the adjusting of the slatted sails that strain and groan in high winds like the sails of a ship at sea. Keep an eye on children among the clanking machinery and on the spiral stairs, which are potentially perilous even for a nimble adult. Downstairs, Madame Vrignaud produces delicious pancakes in her *crêperie* and sells wheat, buckwheat and millet flour. Outside there are a children's play area, picnic tables and signposted footpaths. ◐ *1 Feb-mid Nov, daily 2-7pm (mid July-31 Aug, daily 10am-noon & 2-7pm). Signposted to W of village centre (tel: 02 51 49 31 07). 3€, children 1.50€.*

COMMEQUIERS

ⓘ **tel: 02 51 54 80 56**
www.cc-atlancia.fr

The attractive village on the edge of the *bocage*, 9km south-east of Challans was, until the end of the Middle Ages, a centre of considerable feudal power—as testified by the remains of its imposing castle. Visitors flock here today to enjoy strenuous outings on the Vélo-Rail (see below), an ingenious re-use of an abandoned section of railway track.

➤**Château.** The eight handsome—though crumbling—round towers of the stone castle lying off the D754, north of the village, give these ancient ruins the appearance of the best kind of sandcastle. Take a wooden footbridge across the water-filled moat to explore the inner secrets of the fortress, demolished in 1628 on orders from Cardinal Richelieu. ●

➤**Vélo-Rail.** With two people to do the pedalling and a couple of others travelling on a deck-chair arrangement in between them, an afternoon on one of these flat-bed wagons, known as *draisines*, that run on a stretch of disused railway line makes a brilliant outing. The 10km route takes in a viaduct over the river Vie and level-crossings across the D82 road (watch for traffic!). Take some food and drink to keep up your strength; when you meet another 80kg wagon on the single track, the two crews have to join forces and lift one off the line to let the other pass. The weight of the wagon also means you need to allow plenty of braking distance if the track is wet. ◐ *Easter-end Sept, Wed, Sat, Sun & public holidays 2-7pm (mid June-mid Sept, daily 2-7pm; 1 July-mid Aug, daily 10am-9pm; 16-31 Aug, daily 10am-8pm). Last departure two hours before closing time. Booking essential. Gare du Vélo-Rail (tel: 02 51 54 79 99). From 16€ per wagon for two hours (20€ in July & Aug).*

➤**Tannerie.** The strong of stomach will be fascinated to take the carefully-labelled, self-guided trail at Monsieur Bocquier's tannery, 1km west of the village, that shows how he soaks, stirs, washes, mashes and cures horrible-looking skins to make fluffy rugs and other products. It's a bit of a smelly process, so queasier folk might prefer to browse in the shop for goatskin rugs and lambskin slippers—even here you'll find strange items made out of horses' hooves, ducks' feet and other unusual materials. ● *Mon-Wed & Fri 8am-noon & 2-7pm; Sat 9am-noon & 2-7pm (1 June-30 Sept Mon-Fri 8am-noon & 2-7pm; Sat 9am-noon & 2-7pm). Closed public holidays. Route de St-Gilles (tel: 02 51 55 93 42). Free.* ♿

➤**Pierres-Folles.** In a copse along the lane opposite the tannery is one of the region's many mysterious neolithic monuments. Turn left at the edge of the wood, park on the verge and then follow a footpath in among the trees. In a clearing is a huge dolmen, a table-like structure of giant stones erected as a tomb and originally covered with earth. ●

■ **Commequiers castle: medieval summer fun among feudal remains.**

COMMEQUIERS EXTRAS

Market: Wed & Sat.
*Restaurant: **Hotel de la Gare**. Good food, & an unusually friendly welcome for English-speaking children, who are given special menus pasted into Ladybird books to keep them amused while waiting for lunch. Menus from 11.50€. Rue de la Morinière, opposite Vélo-Rail (tel: 02 51 54 80 38).*
***Festival: Fête Médiévale.** A day of entertainment in lively medieval style, around the castle. Aug.*

FROMENTINE
ⓘ tel: 02 51 68 51 83 fax: 02 51 93 83 26
www.ville-labarredemonts.fr
ot.fromentine.labarredemonts@wanadoo.fr

Sprucely-kept village 16km west of Challans, on the edge of La Barre-de-Monts. Its charming beach in the shadow of the Noirmoutier bridge continues south to merge into wild, empty dunes and gradually blend with a forest of pines. You won't easily spot the recently-renovated sea-front promenade, but it's worth persevering. Now pedestrianised, it is hidden from the view of passing motorists, but park in a side street to the south of the ferry port and stroll to the beach through one of the sandy alleyways that run between the houses. Lining the sea front are some quirkily-designed villas of the 1920s and 30s—from Art Deco to frankly fake Arabian—though, sadly, others had to be sacrificed during the last war to make way for military lookout posts and gun emplacements.

Some forlorn vestiges of those times emerge from the waters from time to time. On 8 August 1944 four German minesweepers took refuge in the narrows here, but were spotted, attacked and sunk by Allied aircraft. To this day, at extra-low tides, ghostly sections of their rusty hulls can be seen protruding above the waves.

The main port for transporting passengers, vehicles and cargo to the Ile d'Yeu, Fromentine has imposed meters or pay-&-display machines everywhere in order to discourage long-term parking. If you are considering travelling to the island, see below for details of ferry companies and for information on garage facilities.

FROMENTINE EXTRAS
Market: *Sat (mid June-mid Sept).*
Restaurant: Les Navigateurs. *Tuck into tasty croque-monsieur (toasted cheese-&-ham sandwiches), as well as more substantial dishes, on the seafront.*
2 Avenue de l'Estacade (tel: 02 51 49 03 03).

➤**Ile d'Yeu trips.** Fromentine is the departure point for excursions to the Ile d'Yeu, 25km off shore (see page 60); boats or fast *vedettes* convey foot-passengers across from around 22€ for a day return. If you are hoping to park for the day while you visit the island, make sure you arrive in good time. Meters in the village are designed for short-term parking only, so it is essential to sort out a space in one of the long-stay garages (about 8€ per day); the more distant ones offer a shuttle service to the boat.
● *Information on crossings from Compagnie Yeu-Continent (tel: 0825 85 3000); ask the tourist office for details of companies offering garage parking.*
➤**Route de l'Huître.** Fromentine is the southernmost point of the Oyster Route—a link-up between producers from here to La Bernerie-en-Retz who give tours of their establishments and, usually, a chance to sample the prized mollusc, too. Brochures are available from most tourist offices. If you'd like to buy locally-harvested oysters, mussels and other shellfish direct, check out the quaint waterside oyster-shacks. These lie just off to the left from Avenue de l'Estacade; head east from the village centre, then follow the Chemin des Ostréiculteurs for a few hundred metres. ●

LA GARNACHE
ⓘ tel: 02 51 93 19 75 fax: 02 51 49 76 04
www.otsi-challans.com
info@otsi-challans.com

Clustered around the ruins of its medieval castle, this large village 6km north-east of Challans was for four centuries an important feudal stronghold and the base of a regional government. Later, at the outbreak of the Vendée Wars in 1793, the future Vendean general Charette was dragged from his bed at a nearby country house (not open to the public) by local peasants, who insisted his former experience as a naval officer made him ideally suited to lead them in their revolt against the Republican army (see page 31).

■ Fromentine, by the Noirmoutier bridge: departure point for the Ile d'Yeu, and a perfect beach for families.

In the 19th-century church are some colourful Stations of the Cross in mosaic, and a wooden figure of Christ, carved in 1938 by Vendean sculptor Arthur Guéniot.

Exhibitions of contemporary art are held in summer at the Maison de Pays, in Grand'rue, where you can also pick up a leaflet that leads you around the village's most notable features.

>Château Féodal. Excellent guided tours (in English as well as French) of the ruined 13th- to 15th-century stronghold built by the lords of La Garnache. Partially destroyed in 1622 at the behest of Louis XIII, and further damaged under the Revolution, the castle retains just its 12th-century keep and two vertical slices of its original round stone towers. Rooms in the keep contain medieval-style draperies, examples of weapons (which you can sometimes handle), a chilly provisions store, and a model of the château in its former glory. In one of the castle's rooms, the delightful local-history museum—the **Musée Passé et Traditions**—presents a comprehensive and well-explained collection of local costume (including *coiffes*, or lace head-dresses) and lovingly-polished furniture. Outside, the ramparts and the remains of the defences conjure up more of the castle's history; elegant gardens have been planted in the former moat, and brightly-coloured birds chirrup inside an outdoor aviary. O *Mid June-mid Sept, Sat, 10.30am-12.30pm & 2.30-7pm, Sun 2.30-7pm (1 July-31 Aug, Tues-Sun 10.30am-12.30pm & 2.30-7pm). Route de Nantes (tel: 02 51 93 11 08). 4€ (guided tours, 11am, 3pm & 5pm, 5€), children free.*

>Chapelle de la Victoire. The stocky stone chapel at the east end of the village, with its elegant little spire, was built to commemorate a decisive Christian victory over the Turks at far-away Lepanto in 1571. After a period of neglect, the building was restored during the 18th century by St Louis-Marie Grignion de Montfort (see page 148), who preached there on two occasions. O *1-30 June, Sat, Sun; 1 July-31 Aug, Tues-Sun. Opening hours not available at time of writing. Route de St-Christophe (tel: 02 51 93 11 08). Free.*

LA GARNACHE EXTRAS

Specialities: "Le Garnachoix" cheese.

Restaurant: Le Petit St-Thomas. Smart restaurant opposite the castle, strong on eels, fish, duck & chicken; menus from 12€. 25 Rue de-Lattre-de-Tassigny (tel: 02 51 49 05 99).

ILE DE NOIRMOUTIER

ⓘ tel: 02 51 39 80 71 (Barbâtre), 02 51 39 12 42 (Noirmoutier town)
fax: 02 51 39 53 16
www.ile-noirmoutier.com
info@ile-noirmoutier.com

Barely 1km off the coast, this long, thin island 20km north-west of Challans is connected to the mainland by a bridge from Fromentine and, at low tide, by "Le Passage du Gois", a 4.5km causeway that is one of the wonders of France. Thanks to its microclimate, Noirmoutier produces the first yellow pompoms of mimosa in the dark depths of February, delectable early potatoes (served at the smartest tables in France), and a tremendous harvest of seafood—particularly conger eel, sole, squid and oysters. The island's economy once depended to a great extent on salt-production. Today you can still see the rectangular drying-pans (especially north of the road between Noirmoutier-en-l'Ile and L'Épine) where sea-water is allowed to evaporate, leaving crystals to be raked up into glistening white pyramids.

Much of the island's appeal is based on the charming villages of low, white-painted cottages, with their red-tiled roofs and blue-painted shutters, which you pass through on the side roads and sandy byways. The colourful, animated port of L'Herbaudière, on the north coast, is a centre for fishing and yachting. To the east of it lies the chic village of Le Vieil, with trendy little shops and restaurants. Then comes Bois de la Chaise (sometimes written "Chaize"), a wooded area on the north-east coast, its forest of holm oaks criss-crossed by sandy tracks lined with elegant 19th-century villas. In this sheltered corner, the air in February is heavy with the perfume of mimosa blossom; in summer its pleasant, rather Breton-style beach called La Plage des Dames is so popular that it's best to visit it by bike or on foot to avoid traffic and parking problems.

The island's capital, Noirmoutier-en-l'Ile, is an attractive place with smart shops and restaurants along its quayside and around its stalwart 12th-century castle. The street on the south side of St Philbert's church leads you into the Banzeau district, one of the most picturesque parts of town, with narrow lanes and alleyways lined with whitewashed houses that were formerly homes of fishermen, but are now desirable holiday retreats for Parisians. Across the harbour channel you can walk along to the end of the track beyond the boat-building museum for the melancholy sight of a boat "graveyard", full of abandoned craft half-sunk in the mud.

One word of warning: the island's shape and road system makes Noirmoutier-en-l'Ile something of a traffic bottleneck. In July and August the number of vehicles attempting to enter the town—especially when low tide has lured thousands of extra visitors across the causeway—can create impossible hold-ups on the fast dual-carriageway that is the main approach road. On such days, it is better to investigate the sleepy charms of the island's southern shore: the beaches of Barbâtre, the little museum of La Guérinière (see page 52) and, farther north-west, the village of L'Épine and the small harbour of Port de Morin. (If you have a good map, you can turn north after L'Épine and cut across the salt-marshes to the L'Herbaudière road, west of Noirmoutier town.) Strung out along the former main road of the island, these south-coast villages are full of shops selling beach-balls, shrimping nets and other traditional holiday equipment. You may even spot some old windmills at La Guérinière, today transformed into covetable beach houses.

> ★ **Passage du Gois**. A drive either to or from the island along this submersible roadway, edged with seaweed and glistening with sea-water, is an unforgettable experience—particularly on a moonlit night. Until 1971 the 4.5km causeway, passable just twice a day either side of low water, was the only access to Noirmoutier, except for a passenger ferry from

NOIRMOUTIER EXTRAS

Markets: Mon (1 July-31 Aug), L'Herbaudière. Tues (1 Apr-30 Sept), Fri, & Sun (late June-early Sept), Noirmoutier-en-l'Ile. Wed, Barbâtre. Thurs & Sun (1 July-mid Sept), La Guérinière. Sat, L'Épine. **Specialities:** Potatoes, especially the Bonnotte. Salt. The marshland plant salicorne (samphire). **Restaurants:** **Le Blé Noir**. Quayside crêperie, for savoury & sweet pancakes. 14-16 Place St-Louis, Noirmoutier-en-l'Ile (tel: 02 51 39 18 17). **Le Petit Bouchot**. Close to castle, with open-air courtyard for summer evenings. Menus from 12€. 3 Rue St-Louis, Noirmoutier-en-l'Ile (tel: 02 51 39 32 56). **Shops: Giraudet**. Buy crunchy "St Philbert" biscuits from this patisserie on the main street. 28 Grande Rue, Noirmoutier-en-l'Ile (tel: 02 51 39 07 83). **Brocante:** Vide-Grenier (car-boot sale), Thurs (1 July-31 Aug), Place St-Louis, Noirmoutier-en-l'Ile. **Festivals:** **Mimosa weekends**. Buy flowers outside the grand woodland villas. Bois de la Chaise. Jan/Feb. **Festival de Noirmoutier-en-l'Ile**. Open-air theatre in castle courtyard. Aug. **Régates du Bois de la Chaise**. Vintage-yacht racing & parade. Aug.

Pornic. Its dog-leg route is studded with sturdy poles and platforms that provide windswept sanctuary for anyone caught out by the rising waters; if you return for a look at high tide you can see why they might be necessary!

Nature and tides are merciless, and you should treat this phenomenon with the greatest respect. Tide-tables (*horaires des marées*) are available from tourist offices in the area to indicate safe crossing times, which vary each day. Times are also published in local papers and shown on huge roadside panels around Beauvoir-sur-Mer and on the Noirmoutier side of the causeway, supplemented with flashing signals of warning once the tide begins to rise. Cross only within 60 minutes either side of low water (*basse mer*), and never park on the causeway itself, which is wide enough for just one lane of traffic in each direction. You'll probably notice the locals parking on occasional hard areas of sea-bed to take advantage of extra-low tides to scrabble in the mudflats for shellfish. Allow plenty of time to cross at peak periods (summer Sunday afternoons, and throughout July and August); it can be a bit worrying to find yourself stuck in a traffic jam, beginning to fret about the tide. The handsome bridge from La Barre-de-Monts provides alternative—if considerably less exciting—road access. For the return to the mainland, follow signposts to the quaintly-termed "*continent,*" either *par le pont* (by bridge) or *par Le Gois* (by causeway). ● *Causeway passable twice a day, for approximately two hours each time. (Consult current tide-tables.) Free.*

➤ **Église St-Philbert**. Beneath the tall church that lies to the north of the castle, and accessible from near the side of the main altar, is a beautiful 11th-century crypt that holds the empty tomb of St Philbert (sometimes called St Philibert), who founded a monastery on the island in AD674. Because of repeated Viking invasions, the saint's remains were removed by his followers to St-Philbert-de-Grand-Lieu (see page 167) and, later, across France to the abbey of Tournus in Burgundy. In a casket on the altar, just a vertebra and a rib remain to be venerated here. Press the button for a taped explanation of the church's history, with musical accompaniment. ●

➤ **Musée du Château**. The imposing, dry-moated castle in the centre of the island's capital is visible from afar across the flat landscape. During its turbulent, 800-year history the building served as a prison for insurgents of the Paris Commune in 1871, as a centre for internees in World War I, as a victualling centre for the Germans during the World War II occupation, and then held German prisoners after the Liberation. Steep stone steps lead to rooms displaying stuffed birds, navigational equipment, maritime maps, archaeological remains and local history—anyone of gory disposition will appreciate the bullet-ridden chair in which the Vendean general the Duc d'Elbée was shot, in January 1794, by Republican troops in the square outside the castle gates (also the subject of one of the paintings on view). On the top floor is a proudly-displayed but rather gaudy collection of lustre-ware from Jersey, the type of souvenir cherished by 18th- and 19th-century sailors and fishermen. ◑ *Early Feb-early Nov, Wed-Mon 10am-12.30pm & 2.30-6pm (16 June-7 Sept, daily 10am-7pm). Place d'Armes (tel: 02 51 39 10 42). 3.70€, children 2€. Joint ticket with Musée de la Construction Navale (see below) 5.40€ & 3.10€.*

➤ **Musée de la Construction Navale**. The different stages in the building of wooden boats are explained in a reconstructed 19th-century workshop, where the graceful curves of the ships' timbers echo those of the solid roof rafters above. ◑ *Early Apr-early Oct, Tues-Sun 10am-12.30pm & 2.30-6pm (16 June-7 Sept, daily 10am-7pm). Rue de l'Écluse, Noirmoutier-en-l'Île (tel: 02 51 39 24 00). 3.10€, children 1.55€. Joint ticket with castle (see page 51).* &

➤**Sealand**. All the names on the fishmonger's slab come to life in the huge tanks that line the walls of this excellent aquarium: turbots swim with elegant wave-like movements of their bodies, lobsters and crabs stalk haughtily across the gravel floor, small sharks cruise nonchalantly through the water, octopuses pulsate in the depths, the sinister *murène* (moray eel) lurks in rocky crevices, and sealions splash in a semi-open-air pool—you can go down steps to watch their underwater antics from behind 60mm-thick glass. Some jewel-coloured tropical fish are on view, with useful explanations for anyone who is contemplating keeping them at home. If you are thinking of this as a wet-weather outing in summer, be warned: you won't be the only ones! ◑ *Early Feb-mid Nov, daily 10am-12.30pm & 2-7pm (1 July-31 Aug, daily 10am-7pm). Rue de l'Écluse, Noirmoutier-en-l'Île (tel: 02 51 39 08 11). 9€, children 7€.*

➤**Océanile**. Stylishly-designed aqua park on the southern outskirts of Noirmoutier town, its silhouette resembling that of a huge wrecked ship. It offers several different pools, indoors and out, including hot tub, chutes, wave machine and paddling pool. Some of the water features may be a bit dramatic for very small children, but older ones love it. It's best to take a picnic to eat on the lawns, as the queues for the café can be tedious. ○ *Mid June-mid Sept, daily 10am-7pm. Noirmoutier-en-l'Île (tel: 02 51 35 91 35). 17.50€, children 13€; from 3pm, 10€ for all.*

➤**Musée des Traditions de l'Île**. A charming small museum beside the church of La Guérinière, showing the islanders' activities and way of life linked to fishing, salt-production, farming and the manufacture of linen in the early 20th-century. Everything from rowing boats to wedding dresses is displayed in a series of rooms, several of them arranged to show typical interiors of island homes. ◑ *1 Apr-15 Oct, daily 2.30-5.30pm (1 July-31 Aug, daily 10am-7pm). Place de l'Église, La Guérinière (tel: 02 51 39 41 39). 3.50€, children 1.50€.*

➤**L'Île aux Papillons**. Artfully arranged pathways wind through a covered enclosure where hundreds of butterflies—some of them gigantic—flutter freely about your head and settle on the tropical plants growing around. Peering into a glass case, you can watch others struggling from their chrysalises to join the fun, and there's an interesting video to tell you about their life-cycle. ◑ *1 Apr-30 Sept, Mon-Fri 2-7pm; Sat, Sun & public holidays 10am-7.30pm (1 June-31 Aug, daily 10am-7.30pm). 5 Rue de la Fassonnière, Zone d'activités des Mandeliers, La Guérinière, behind Intermarché (tel: 02 51 35 77 88). 6.40€, children 4.50€.* &

➤**Bird reserve**. The jetty leading south-east from Noirmoutier town quay towards the site of Fort Larron offers panoramic views across the mud-flats to the right and the Marais de Müllembourg salt-marsh on the left. In winter you should see ducks, geese and small waders; in spring and summer plenty of avocets, egrets and redshanks, especially if you are there around the time of high tide. Wardens from the Ligue pour la Protection des Oiseaux are often on hand with telescopes to help with identification (dates from tourist office, or by calling the

■ Road to the isle: high wooden platforms are refuges for drivers caught by the tide on Noirmoutier causeway.

■ End of the line: Noirmoutier's boat graveyard.

wardens' office, below). The site is extremely exposed, so wrap up warmly in winter; take drinks and sun protection in high summer. ● *Information on guided walks from the LPO (tel: 02 51 35 81 16). Admission free; guided walks 5€, students 3.30€, children 1.70€.* ♿

➤Marais salants. At several of Noirmoutier's salt-marshes some of the the island's 100 or so salt-makers (known as *sauniers*) welcome visitors to their salt-pans where they demonstrate the process of producing salt crystals through the evaporation of sea-water by wind and sun. The annual cycle of draining, cleaning and reshaping the square clay pans in March; letting in the sea-water in May; raking up the crystals as they form, and barrowing the harvest to a giant salt heap, or *mulon*, between June and September; and then flooding the salt-pans again to protect them from the vicissitudes of winter is back-breakingly hard work. Heavy rain is disastrous for the *sauniers*, as it dilutes the brine and can set the process back several weeks. ○ *Mid June-early Sept (in fine weather). L'Épine area (dates & times from Noirmoutier tourist office).*

➤Route de l'Ile. A 40km route, signposted in blue, highlights the prettiest spots on the 20km-long island. As Noirmoutier is pretty flat, it's fun to follow the route by bicycle—which also avoids any summer traffic jams and parking problems. ● *Map & cycle-hire details from tourist office.*

NOTRE-DAME-DE-MONTS

ⓘ tel: 02 51 58 84 97 fax: 02 51 58 15 56
mairie-notre-dame-de-monts.fr
office.tourisme.notredamedemonts@wanadoo.fr

Seaside village 6km south of the Noirmoutier toll bridge, and just north of the huge resort of St-Jean-de-Monts, with the finest-textured sand in the Vendée. Notre-Dame is firmly orientated towards "windy" themes: dinghy-sailing, windsurfing, speedsailing, sand-yachting and kite-flying. A colourful "garden of the wind" (see below) has been created in and around an old mill.

■ Windy: Jardin du Vent.

NOTRE-DAME EXTRAS

***Market**: Sun.*
***Festival**: **Festival du Vent**. Wind festival. July.*

➤Jardin du Vent. There's no missing the collection of triangular sails twirling in the breeze on top of a restored windmill that peep over the rooftops above the town centre. Inside, a new exhibition each year takes a different wind-related theme; once you emerge into the grounds an ingenious series of devices to enjoy include a mirrored "cloud-catcher", wind-chimes, machines that blow bubbles or puff fragrances, colourful windsocks and an unusual sail-powered roundabout. ◐ *1 Apr-31 May (plus Oct half-term), Tues-Sun 2-6pm (1 June-30 Sept, daily 11am-7pm). 29 bis Rue Gilbert-Cesbron (tel: 02 28 11 26 43). 4€, children 2€.* ♿

➤Salle Panoramique. Choose a clear day to take the lift up the 70-metre-high *château d'eau*, or water-tower, 3km east of the village on the D82, for a bird's-eye view of the marshes, the coast, the Ile d'Yeu and the island of Noirmoutier. Headphones give commentary in French, English, German—and even the local *patois*, or dialect. To make the most of the magnificent viewpoint, take a map and binoculars up with you. ◐ *1 Feb-31 Oct (plus Nov public holidays), Tues-Sun 2-6pm (1 May-30 Sept, Tues-Sun 10am-noon & 2-6pm; 1 July-31 Aug, Mon-Sat 10am-7pm, Sun 3-7pm). La Croix, Route du Perrier (tel: 02 51 58 86 09). 3.30€, children 2.50€.*

➤Pont d'Yeu. Not, alas, a bridge to the Ile d'Yeu, this natural phenomenon is a rocky spit of land 50 metres wide and several kilometres long, heading in the direction of the island. Lying to the south of Notre-Dame's main beach, it is uncovered only at the lowest low tides; if you have the current tide-tables, look for days with the highest figures in the *coefficient* column (see page 15). Legend says that St Martin wanted to evangelise the people of the Ile d'Yeu but could find no boat to take him there. In exchange for the soul of the first Christian to use it, the Devil offered to build a path across, and the saint accepted—on condition it was completed before cockcrow. Satan's crew set to work, plying the local cockerel with alcohol to buy extra time. But the confused bird crowed even earlier than usual, so the route was never finished. ● *Signposted off D38.*

ST-GILLES-CROIX-DE-VIE

ⓘ tel: 02 51 55 03 66 fax: 02 51 55 69 60
www.stgillescroixdevie.com
ot@stgillescroixdevie.com

A pair of attractive seaside towns now merged into one, on opposite sides of the river Vie. Croix-de-Vie is on the west bank, where the railway line from Nantes terminates at the buffers alongside the fishing harbour and the main street. Some elegant 19th-century villas line the seafront by Boisvinet beach. Nearby is the recently-renovated Tour Joséphine, a cylindrical stone tower by the Petite Plage. Once a lighthouse marking the entrance to the port, it was built in 1850 and named after Napoleon's empress.

Croix-de-Vie is renowned for sardines and anchovies, and for a large canning industry (trade name "Les Dieux") for these, and for other products like fish soup and tuna. Connoisseurs should look in local shops, or ask at the tourist office, for cans of sardines *millésimées*—vintage sardines, to be laid down and lovingly turned from time to time over the years so that the fish are evenly imbued with oil. The sea is still in the forefront of the town's largest present-day industry: the headquarters of the Bénéteau company, one of the world's biggest manufacturers of yachts and other boats, is located at St-Gilles-Croix-de-Vie.

You can take a ferry from Croix-de-Vie for the 65-minute crossing to the Ile d'Yeu (see page 60) with the Compagnie Vendéenne, (tel: 02 51 26 82 22). The tourist office also has details of half- and whole-day cruises on a *vieux gréement* (a traditional sail-powered fishing boat), or of sea-fishing trips on more conventional craft.

A much smaller ferry, or *passeur*, takes foot passengers on a two-minute journey across the harbour mouth in summer, giving access to the northern end of the Grande Plage on the St-Gilles side, and avoiding the parking problems around that popular beach. The little boat leaves from the quay, just across the railway line from Croix-de-Vie's *mairie*; try parking in the quiet streets a few blocks north.

Across the river, at St Gilles-sur-Vie, stands a picturesque old church (in the tower of which one of Napoleon's generals was killed in 1815, during the second Vendean uprising). A selection of fairground rides is in more or less permanent residence on the quayside. Farther on is the lovely Grande Plage—choose your time carefully on this beach, though, as it can become impossibly crowded when an incoming tide compresses sunbathers onto an ever-narrower ribbon of sand. Some charming French domestic

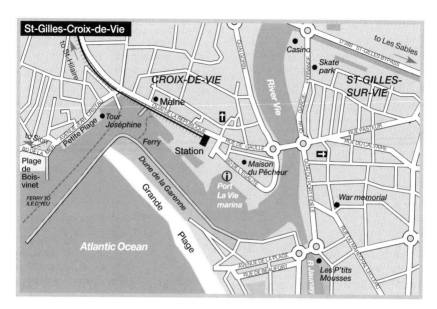

architecture lining the roads leading to the beach provides a reminder of St-Gilles' heyday as a seaside resort in the 1860s. Monuments to look out for on this side of the river Vie include the bust of local navigator Pierre Garcie-Ferrande (at the east end of the main bridge) and a war memorial by the Martel brothers (see page 45) in the form of a grieving Vendean woman, a short distance along Rue du Maréchal-Leclerc, just off the quay.

➤**Maison du Pêcheur**. A tiny, whitewashed, fisherman's house in one of Croix-de-Vie's oldest streets, just across from the tourist office, is furnished with items typical of a Vendean interior in the 1920s. As the whole place measures only about 35 square metres, it doesn't take long to visit its two rooms and backyard; don't miss the intricately laundered *coiffes* (starched head-dresses), and the sepia photographs of sail-powered sardine-fishing boats. ◐ *1 Apr-30 Sept, Wed-Sat & Mon 2.30-6.30pm. 22 Rue du Maroc, Croix-de-Vie (tel: 02 51 54 08 09). 2€, children 1€.*

➤**Les P'tits Mousses**. Children over nine, and parents, can have a great time manoeuvring miniature ferries, tugs, tankers and fishing boats on the quiet Jaunay river, a stone's throw from St-Gilles' Grande Plage. To drive unaccompanied, children must be aged at least 13. Lifejackets provided. ◐ *Easter-mid Sept, Sat, Sun, public holidays & school holidays 10.30am-1pm & 2.30-7pm (1-30 June, daily 10.30am-1pm & 2.30-7pm; 1 July-31 Aug, daily 10.30am-8pm). Port Miniature, Avenue de la Cour St-Laud, St-Gilles (tel: 06 67 62 56 51). From 4€ for 15 mins.*

ST-HILAIRE-DE-RIEZ

ⓘ tel: 02 51 54 31 97 fax: 02 51 55 27 13
www.sainthilairederiez.fr
otsthilairederiez@wanadoo.fr

Well endowed with dunes, pine trees and a huge sandy beach, this little town 5km north of St-Gilles-Croix-de-Vie was one of the Vendée's earliest coastal resorts. Today, St-Hilaire embraces the lively holiday area of Merlin-Plage, the marshland village of Notre-Dame-de-Riez and the more dramatically-sited clifftop resort of Sion-sur-l'Océan, and sees its population swell in summer from 1,500 to 150,000. Among the modern blocks, there are still a few seaside villas dating from the 1880s, and St-Hilaire's 17th-century church contains several religious paintings by well-known local artist Henry Simon (1910-87).

> **Corniche Vendéenne**. As an antidote to the endless sandy beaches, the shoreline between Sion and Croix-de-Vie, 2km west of St-Hilaire centre, provides the northernmost cliffs of the Vendée, and some break-away rock-stacks known as the "Cinq Pineaux" ("Five Pine Cones"). The small beaches among the cliffs are crowded in summer but provide a series of sheltered coves to protect out-of-season visitors—and, above the aptly-named "Trou du Diable" ("Devil's Hole"), some dramatic effects of wind and water during autumn gales. A chic promenade near the pretty Café de la Plage overlooks the main beach. ●

> **Atlantic Toboggan**. Whether you favour the "Kamikaze" or one of the other many different water chutes (*toboggan*, in French, means slide), this family aqua-park, 7km north-west of St-Hilaire, makes a great day out. It has a total of five 15-metre-long water slides, plus pools, playgrounds and picnic-spots, and a huge wave-pool. (Children come running when the siren announces the waves will start breaking!) ◐ *Mid May-early Sept, daily 10.30am-7.30pm. Les Becs, near Merlin-Plage, on the D123 (tel: 02 51 58 05 37). 16€, children 13€, under-threes free; from 4pm, 11€ for all.*

> **Bourrine du Bois-Juquaud**. This attractive limewashed, cob-built cottage and its outbuildings, 4km north of St-Hilaire, are thatched with reeds in local style and are the subjects of countless picture-postcards. A clock ticks softly in the traditionally-furnished living-room, looking onto the neat vegetable garden. The primitive building materials of mud and straw give an insight into the simple, self-sufficient life of the farmers who raised the house with their own hands in 1818. Good visitor centre, with changing exhibitions, and occasional demonstrations of dancing, butter-making or threshing. ◐ *1 Feb-31 Oct (plus Nov holiday period), Sun & public holidays 2-6pm (1 May-30 Sept, Tues-Sat 10am-noon & 2-6pm, Sun & public holidays 3-7pm; 1 July-31 Aug, Mon-Sat 10am-7pm; Sun & public holidays 3-7pm). Le Pissot (tel: 02 51 49 27 37). 2.20€, under-11s free.*

> **Louis de la Rochejaquelein Memorial**. A simple stone cross in a cluster of trees marks the place where the Vendean general Louis de la Rochejaquelein fell, rallying his troops, on 4 June 1815. Brother of the Vendean leader Henri de la Rochejaquelein (see page 37), he had landed from England during Napoleon's brief return to power, and embarked on a short-lived attempt to revive the royalist cause in the Vendée by driving the emperor's forces out of the area. A thousand soldiers from each side faced one another on this sandy terrain, at that time the only route between St-Gilles and Soullans. ● *Les Mattes, 6km NW of St-Hilaire, signposted off the D59.*

ST-HILAIRE EXTRAS

Markets: Mon morning & Wed & Sat afternoons (1 July-31 Aug), Merlin-Plage, 7km NW of St-Hilaire. Tues & Fri, Sion, 2km W of St-Hilaire. Thurs & Sun, St-Hilaire-de-Riez. Sun (mid June-mid Sept), Notre-Dame-de-Riez, 5km NE of St-Hilaire.

Restaurant: **Café de la Plage**. Charming place above the beach at Sion, serving mussels & other simple fare. 1 Rue de l'Océan, Sion, 2km W of St-Hilaire (tel: 02 51 54 51 76).

Brocante: **Chez Pierrot**. Large junk emporium. Fri-Wed 2.30-6.30pm. On D83 at Notre-Dame-de-Riez, 4km NE of St-Hilaire (tel: 02 51 54 45 50).

Festivals: **Vintage car rally**. Easter. **Grand firework display**. Mid Aug. Sion beach.

ST-JEAN-DE-MONTS

ⓘ tel: 02 51 59 60 61 fax: 02 51 59 87 87
www.saint-jean-de-monts.com
accueil@saint-jean-de-monts.com

Large, colourful objects—banana, fish, ball, house etc—erected on tall posts, help families to keep their bearings on the huge sandy beach of this popular seaside resort, 17km west of Challans. It's not surprising that St-Jean calls itself a "Station Kid", since there is plenty going on for children. Teenagers scoot along the seafront on rollerblades or on four-seater *quadricycles*, while younger children can enjoy roundabouts, beach swings, slides and inflatables, or pedal old-fashioned metal pony-carts on the beach. With countless bars, fast-food restaurants, casino and discos, there is no lack of night-time entertainment either.

Anyone looking to expend more energy will find golf, sand-yachting and tree-climbing (see below) near the northern end of the beach, plus tennis, riding and archery. There is a heated salt-water pool at the resort's "thalassotherapy" (sea-water treatment) spa. Details of all these from the tourist office in the Palais des Congrès, itself a venue for regular high-quality art exhibitions.

The 8km of sand and the modern esplanade are, of course, the resort's main attractions. However, the original fishing village of St-Jean, now half a mile inland, contains a prettily-restored church with a 17th-century bell-tower, its spire roofed with wooden tiles. Diagonally across from the church is a wonderful fish shop, though watch that no tiny fingers come close to the lobsters' claws!

> **Arbre et Aventure**. Whirrings, whizzings and whoops of joy fill the air in the fragrant pine forest. Energetic folk of all ages don harnesses and helmets, and are given detailed safety instruction before climbing up into the trees and embarking on one of five circuits—colour-coded to show difficulty—varying between 1 and 12 metres above the ground. Not for very small children or for the faint-hearted. ◑ *1 Apr-30 Sept, Sat, Sun 9.30am-7pm, Wed 12.30-7pm (1 July-31 Aug, daily 9am-11pm). Booking recommended. Parée Jésus, near golf club (tel: 06 22 61 45 98). 16€, 9-14-year-olds 10.50€, five-to-eight-year-olds 8€.*

> **Centre de Thalassothérapie**. Even if you don't have the time or the money to sign up at the resort's sea-water therapy centre for a week's full-time de-stressing, you can at least treat yourself to a few sybaritic hours. "Espace Détente Marine" gives half a day's unlimited use of pool, sauna, gym, and rest room, plus group gymnastic and t'ai chi classes. Rather more pampering, "La Remise en Forme" ("Back in Shape") allows four *soins* (treatments) in the morning, and the rest of the day to use the facilities, above. Take swimming costume; towel and bathrobe provided. Swimming cap and plastic shoes compulsory (may be purchased at spa). ◑ *1 Feb-mid Nov, Mon-Fri 9am-12.30pm & 2-5.30pm. Les Thermes Marins, 12 Avenue des Pays-de-Monts (tel: 02 51 59 18 18; booking essential). Half-day use of facilities, 30€; Remise en Forme 83€ (1 Apr-30 Sept, 88€). www.thermes-st-jean.com/*

> **Ferme des Pommettes**. A great welcome for all the family at this marshland farm just north of the town, on the D82, where you are given supplies of barley to feed to a series of friendly animals—from rabbits to donkeys. Interesting 15-minute video about life on the farm (also in English), though the explicit scenes of birth, artificial insemination etc may need a bit of explanation! There's also a mini-golf and a nine-hole "swin-golf" course. Visitors are offered a slice of brioche before leaving. ◑ *1 Apr-15 June, Sat, Sun, public holidays & school holidays 2-7pm; 16 June-30 Sept, & Oct half-term, daily 2-7pm (1 July-31 Aug, daily 10am-7pm). Le Vieux Cerne (tel: 02 51 59 02 26). 3.20€, children 2.70€ (extra charges for pony & tractor rides, mini-golf & swin-golf).*

> **Promenade en Yole**. Guided 45-minute trip through the open marsh-land in a *yole*, a traditional flat-bottomed boat, poled along the narrow

■ **High adventure: swing through the treetops at St-Jean-de-Monts.**

ST-JEAN EXTRAS

Markets: Wed & Sat (1 July-31 Aug, daily), near church in the old village. Daily (1 July-31 Aug), Rue du Marché, near beach.

Restaurants:
Brasserie et Restaurant du Golf. In the clubhouse, an informal bar serves great croque-monsieur (toasted cheese-&-ham sandwiches); more gastronomic dishes in the restaurant. Avenue des Pays-de-la-Loire, NW of beach (tel: 02 51 58 07 77).
Le Petit St Jean. Delicious food, served in a jungle-themed décor; menus from 25€. 128 Route de Notre-Dame, on D38 2km NW of St-Jean (tel: 02 51 59 78 50).

Festivals:
Kid's Folies. Easter-holiday activities for children. Apr.
Passion Cerf-Volant. Ascensiontide kite festival. Late May.
Golf: Golf de St-Jean-de-Monts. Nine holes among pine trees, nine alongside the sea (see also page 16). Avenue des Pays-de-la-Loire (tel: 02 51 58 82 73).

canals 6km north-east of St-Jean. In July and August you also have the option of doing one leg of the journey by horse-and-cart, making a two-hour outing in all. ○ *15 June-15 Sept. Wed-Mon, departures from 3pm to 6pm (1 July-31 Aug, Wed-Mon, departures from 2pm to 6pm; no horse-drawn section on Sat). Booking advisable. Meet at information point, D753 Route de Challans, Le Perrier (tel: 06 98 85 25 50). 4.10€, children 3.30€ (with wagon ride, 8.20€ & 7.40€).*

SALLERTAINE

ⓘ tel: 02 51 93 19 75 fax: 02 51 49 76 04
www.otsi-challans.com
info@otsi-challans.com

A delightful village on what was once an island, 8km west of Challans, Sallertaine attracts artists and craftworkers throughout the summer months. On a rocky outcrop that rises above the flat landscape of the Marais Breton, the village was formerly a busy centre to which families would travel from isolated marshland farms by flat-bottomed boat on Sundays to attend Mass. In 1899, celebrated writer René Bazin (1853-1932) used Sallertaine and its surroundings as the setting for *La Terre qui Meurt* ("The Dying Land") in which he painted a poignant image of the pressures on rural life brought about by the drift from the land at a time of encroaching industrialisation. You can plunge into the past by following a signposted walk into the countryside in the footsteps of "Jean Nesmy", the fictional farm-worker hero of Bazin's novel; you can further recapture the spirit of those times by taking an enjoyable short trip around the "island" by canoe.

> ★ **L'Ile aux Artisans**. Each summer many village houses are transformed into temporary shops and studios for potters, woodturners and other craftspeople selling everything from wooden toys to weather-vanes. ○ *1 July-mid Sept. Daily 10am-7pm. Village centre (tel: 02 51 35 47 38).*
> **Vieille Église**. A wonderful 12th-century church, saved in the nick of time from total destruction in 1915 by the intervention of French novelist René Bazin (see above). Beneath the flaking white-wash you can just make out vestiges of some ancient frescoes, and where once the congregation sat is a series of tableaux showing aspects of marshland life. As the costumed figures are "retired" shop-window dummies, it does tend to suggest (falsely) that the local peasantry was composed entirely of doe-eyed young men and skinny, over-made-up damsels, but the setting more than compensates for this shortcoming. ○ *Mid June-mid Sept, daily 2.30-7pm (1 July-31 Aug, daily 10.30am-12.30pm & 2.30-7pm). Village centre (tel: 02 51 35 51 81). Free.*
> **Musée du Pain/Le Pain Câlin**. Behind the counter of a restored, 1950s-style bakery—with its racks of baguettes, brioches and cakes—a door leads to a delightful little museum about bread, and about the generations of the Barreteau family who used to live here. In an excellent use of new technology, visitors are issued with neat headsets (ask for English-language ones) with a commentary that automatically starts and stops as you move from room to room. After a small, atmospherically-furnished parlour, where a film recounts the history of the family, you come to other rooms with interesting videos about bread-making and (not surprisingly) about the "Mie Câline" sandwich-bar franchise—brainchild of a present-day Barreteau—that sells snacks, bread and cakes on 100 high streets throughout the Vendée, and beyond. Finally you emerge into a large yard to find poultry, pigs and friendly goats that would have been kept in olden days to provide food for the family. ● *Tues-Fri 7.30am-1pm & 4-7pm; Sat, Sun 7.30am-12.30pm (1 June-30 Sept, Tues-Fri 7.30am-1pm & 3-7pm; Sat, Sun 7.30am-12.30pm. 1 July-31 Aug, daily 9.30am-7pm). 8 Rue du Pélican (tel: 02 51 35 40 58). 4€, children 3€.* ♿
> **La Route du Sel**. One-and-a-half-hour guided canoe trips around the former island of Sallertaine make an excellent introduction to the Marais Breton and its wildlife. There are also two six-hour outings, the first including a convivial barbecue lunch and the second a candlelit barbecue under the stars. It can be scorching on a hot summer day, so take hats and suitable clothing.

🌓 *1 Apr-30 Sept, daily; trips hourly from 9.30am-5.30pm. Meet at Route du Sel office, 41 Rue de Verdun (tel: 02 51 93 03 40). Canoe rental from 7€; guided tours (but do your own paddling) from 13€ per person, accompanied children free. Lunch trip 36€ (includes meal), children 11€; evening trip 46€ (includes meal) & 15.50€; booking essential for both.*

➤**Chêne Vert café**. For an unusual experience, take a look at the taxidermy displays in the bar and an adjoining showroom of this village café. Bizarre items include a stuffed boar's head, a cat, a mouse and the bust of a cockerel, handiwork of the eccentric lady owner. There's an attractive garden, too (though don't venture in without ordering a drink!). ●

➤**Moulin de Rairé**. The miller takes visitors up rickety wooden staircases to visit three floors of his working windmill—built in 1560, 3km north-west of Sallertaine, and claimed to have been in continuous use since. The view across the marshes from the top-floor window, regularly interrupted by the wood-slatted sails creaking past, is breath-taking—though anybody with small children in tow will need to watch out for the flailing machinery and narrow, open stairs. English leaflets are available to clarify Monsieur Burgaud's enthusiastic explanations and demonstrations. Downstairs, organic bread flour is on sale, and in a barn nearby is an interesting display of photographs and milling equipment. 🌓 *1 Feb-31 May, school-holiday periods & public holidays, daily 2-6pm; 1 June-30 Sept, daily 2-6pm (1 July-31 Aug, daily 10am-noon & 2-6.30pm). Off D103, St-Urbain road (tel: 02 51 35 51 82). 3.25€, children 1.50€.*

■ Splashing out: canoe in the marshland around Sallertaine.

SALLERTAINE EXTRAS
Festivals: Foire à la Brocante. Antiques fair. Early Aug.
Fête à la Bourrine à Rosalie (see main entry). *Traditional dancing, crafts & country skills. 5km W of Sallertaine. 15 Aug.*

➤**Bourrine à Rosalie**. A reed-thatched, green-shuttered cottage (picture on page 33) nestles in the marshes 5km west of Sallertaine. The two basic, whitewashed rooms, inhabited until 1971 by the doughty old lady whose photograph hangs on the wall, give an (albeit slightly sanitised) image of the hard life in one of these isolated marshland farms where no roads passed, where electricity was not installed until 1961, and where beds needed long legs to keep their occupants above the winter flood-waters. Neat labels explain in charmingly distorted English the origins and purposes of items on display. Outside are a small orchard, a few ducks and a donkey. 🌓 *Easter-mid May & 1-30 Sept, daily 2.30-6.30pm; mid May-mid June, Sat, Sun & public holidays 2.30-6.30pm; 1 July-31 Aug, daily 10.30am-12.30pm & 2.30-7pm. On C116, between Sallertaine & St-Jean-de-Monts (tel: 02 51 49 43 60/02 51 68 73 61). 1.60€, children under 10 free.*

SOULLANS
ⓘ tel: 02 51 35 28 68

This large village on the frontier of the marshes and the hillier lower bocage, 6km south of Challans, was the birthplace of one of the Vendée's best-known painters, Charles Milcendeau (1872-1919), who cut his artistic teeth by sketching the customers at his father's café on the market square. Today, one of Milcendeau's works, *La Flagellation*, hangs in the local church; plenty more are on display in his former home (see below).

➤ ★ **Musée Milcendeau-Jean Yole**. Charming museum, created from two *bourrines*, or traditional whitewashed cottages, in the heart of the countryside 3km south of Soullans. It is devoted to two of the village's most celebrated inhabitants: the painter Charles Milcendeau, whose home this was, and his contemporary—a doctor and, later, writer and politician—Léopold Robert (1878-1956) who under the pseudonym "Jean Yole" published many books in praise of the Vendée and who is commemorated here by a small collection of photographs and objects.

In the first building, transformed into a bright, air-conditioned, state-of-the-art gallery, hang dozens of portraits of Milcendeau's family and neighbours—exactly the sort of ruddy-cheeked country folk you see at local markets today—as well as atmospheric domestic scenes and some dramatic, wintry views of the flooded fields that surrounded his marshland home. (If you have driven across parched August pastures to reach the museum, you may feel he went a bit over the top in some of these, but February's rains can—and do—produce the same effect today.) Seen through cleverly-shaped windows, the landscapes outside are framed almost like those within.

A couple of lengthy videos, in French, are shown in a corner of the gallery. Think twice, however, about sitting through both if your time is limited. Though the second gives a valuable insight into the life of Milcendeau and the travels in Spain that influenced much of his work, it is preceded by a 20-minute film about Jean Yole, a worthy, but much less visual subject. You would do better to walk around and admire the real paintings while the first film runs, and only to view the second.

When you enter the painter's bedroom-cum-studio in the second house, you are guaranteed to gasp. In place of plain whitewash, Milcendeau covered the walls with stylised birds, cats and flowers in vivid blues and yellows, arranged stuffed pigeons at the windows and reshaped the doorways in Moorish style—all in an attempt to imbue his damp cottage with the sunshine and colour of his beloved Spain.

Outside, under a series of large blue metal awnings, are "listening posts" at which you can hear readings of literary texts about the marshes, by Yole and other authors. (In case you are wondering, these "umbrellas" are a nod towards the marshland tradition whereby—in this flat landscape where there were no trees or hedges to conceal them—a courting couple would disport themselves discreetly behind a large umbrella to be screened from prying eyes.) ◑ *1 Feb-31 Oct (plus the Nov & Christmas holiday periods), Tues-Sun & public holidays 2-6pm (1 May-30 Sept, Tues-Sat 10am-noon & 2-6pm, Sun 3-7pm; 1 July-31 Aug, Mon-Sat 10am-7pm, Sun & public holidays 3-7pm). Le Bois-Durand (tel: 02 51 35 03 84). 3.30€, children 2.50€.* &

ILE D'YEU

ⓘ **tel: 02 51 58 32 58 fax: 02 51 58 40 48**
www.ile-yeu.fr
tourisme@ile-yeu.fr

Time seems to have stood still on this picturesque island of 23 sq km that lies just over an hour's boat-ride off the coast (45 minutes by hydrojet) to the west of St-Gilles-Croix-de-Vie. Few cars travel the gorse-lined lanes, and the island's houses—often topped with pretty weather-vanes—seem bleached by the sunshine that beats down on them.

You can travel year-round from Fromentine (see page 48) to the island's capital, Port-Joinville, by boat, fast craft or helicopter. There are also summer services from Noirmoutier's Pointe de la Fosse, or from the mainland ports of St-Gilles-Croix-de-Vie and Les Sables-d'Olonne—though, at a minimum of around 26.50€ per adult for a day return (19€ for a five- to 17-year-old), it can be an expensive proposition for a family. You need to book ahead in the peak season. On arrival, it is a good idea to hire bicycles (at about 8€ a day) to explore the island—just about feasible in a day. (It is not worth taking your own, as the ferry companies charge more than that to transport each one.) If you intend cycling round the island, consider buying sandwiches and drinks in Port-Joinville, or on the mainland, before you set off; there is a severe lack of places for snacks on the way.

The north-east side of the Ile d'Yeu (pronounced "eeld-yer") is full of sheltered, sandy coves for swimming and picnicking. More dramatic features will be found on the rocky south coast: the 40-metre-high Grand Phare, or lighthouse, built in the 1950s between Port-Joinville and the aerodrome; the caves on the Sables Rouis beach; the ghostly ruins of a feudal fortress (the Vieux Château), south-west of Port-Joinville; the pretty fishing harbour of Port de la Meule, overlooked by the tiny, whitewashed chapel of Notre-Dame-de-Bonne-Nouvelle; a Toytown-sized harbour on the western edge of the sandy Plage des Vieilles; and, in the village of St-Sauveur at the centre of the island, a solid

Romanesque church. Among several neolithic monuments scattered around the island is a gigantic, rat-shaped stone—the *pierre tremblante*—balanced precariously above a cliff to the east of Port de la Meule, which will rock if pressed firmly at a particular spot.

In 1945, the 90-year-old Marshal Pétain (1856-1951), who headed the pro-German Vichy government during World War II, was incarcerated in the gloomy Pierre-Levée fort after his death sentence for treason was commuted to life imprisonment. He died six years later, and lies buried in the island's cemetery.

Travel year-round to Port-Joinville: foot-passengers & vehicles from Fromentine with Compagnie Yeu-Continent (tel: 0825 85 3000). Summer-only foot-passenger services by VIIV from La Fosse (tel: 02 51 39 00 00), or from St-Gilles-Croix-de-Vie (tel: 02 51 54 15 15). Also from St-Gilles-Croix-de-Vie, Compagnie Vendéenne (tel: 02 51 26 82 22). From Port-Olona, Les Sables-d'Olonne, Compagnie NGV "Le Sabia" (tel: 02 51 23 54 88). All from about 30€ return. Flights from Fromentine heliport, on D22 Beauvoir road; summer service from St-Jean-de-Monts Hippodrome (racecourse), Oya Hélicoptères (tel: 02 51 59 22 22); from 64€ one-way, children 39€.

■ **Ile d'Yeu: pedal south by bike to explore the island's Vieux-Château.**

❯**Musée de la Pêche**. Fascinating glimpse of the fishing industry on which the island's economy has depended for so long. An excellent 20-minute video—very visual, even if you don't understand much of the commentary—explains the rigours of the fishermen's lives. There are displays of boatbuilder's tools and navigational equipment, maps of wrecks and models of different craft. ○ *15 June-15 Sept, Tues-Sat 10am-12.30pm (1 July-31 Aug, Mon-Sat 10am-1pm & 3-6.30pm). Abri du Marin, 7 Quai de la Chapelle, Port-Joinville (tel: 02 51 59 31 00). 3.50€, children 2€.*

❯**Monument de la Norvège**. A granite monument on the waterfront at Port-Joinville commemorates a terrible tragedy. In January 1917 the Ile d'Yeu lifeboat went to the aid of an open boat carrying seven survivors from a Norwegian ship torpedoed a few days earlier. Having picked up the starving sailors, the lifeboat crew found that a contrary tide made return to harbour impossible. They anchored a mile off shore, to wait for it to turn, but the anchor rope broke and the helpless craft was blown north-west by icy winter winds. After three days in glacial conditions without food or water, the boat reached the coast of Brittany, but five Norwegians and six of the 12 islanders had died of cold and hunger. ● *Quai de la Norvège.*

❯**Fort de Pierre-Levée/La Citadelle**. Head south or south-west from Port-Joinville and follow signposts up through a forest of holm oaks to a dismal fortress in which the elderly Marshal Pétain (see above) was held after World War II. A wooden bridge leads over the dry moat into the huge courtyard. Pétain is buried in the island's cemetery a little farther east; surrounded by green bushes, his grave backs onto the roadside wall and faces in the opposite direction to all the others. ●

❯**Musée Historial**. Guided tours explaining the history of the Ile d'Yeu in the house where Marshal Pétain's wife lived in the late 1940s during her husband's imprisonment. ○ *1 July-31 Aug, daily 10.15am-12.30pm & 3.15-6.15pm. Hotel des Voyageurs, Rue de la République, Port-Joinville (tel: 02 51 58 31 55). 3.05€, children 1.85€.*

❯**Vieux Château**. The remains of the 14th-century fortress, 1km north-west of Port de la Meule, seem to grow from the rocks themselves. Built during the Hundred Years War, it changed hands several times between the French and the English. ● *Exterior only;* ○ *15 June-15 Sept, guided tours Tues-Sun, every half-hour 11am-5.30pm (1 July-31Aug, daily 11am-7.30pm). 3€, children 1.50€. South coast (tel: 02 51 58 32 58).*

ILE D'YEU EXTRAS

Markets: Daily, Port-Joinville. Daily (1 July-31 Aug), St-Sauveur.
Specialities: Tuna. "Patagos", or palourdes (clams), with cream sauce. Tarte aux pruneaux (prune tart). Min-Min (prune-&-butter sweets).
Restaurant: Le Père Raballand. Gastronomy on the first floor; simpler, brasserie fare downstairs, overlooking the port, near the Monument de la Norvège. 6 Place de la Norvège, Port-Joinville (tel: 02 51 26 02 77).

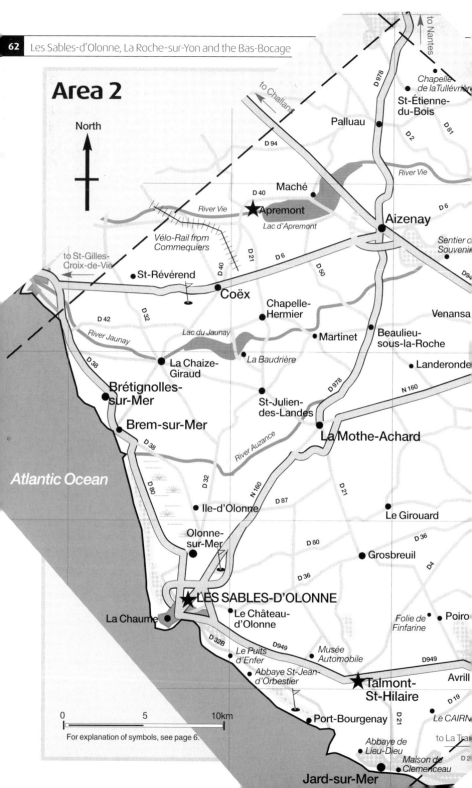

Area 2

North

to Nantes

D 978

Chapelle de la Tullévrièr

St-Étienne-du-Bois

D 2

D 81

Palluau

to Challans

D 94

River Vie

Maché

D 40

D 6

Apremont

Lac d'Apremont

Aizenay

Sentier d Souvenir

Vélo-Rail from Commequiers

D 21

D 40

D 6

D 50

D 94

to St-Gilles-Croix-de-Vie

St-Révérend

Coëx

Chapelle-Hermier

Venansa

D 42

D 32

River Jaunay

Lac du Jaunay

Martinet

Beaulieu-sous-la-Roche

Landeronde

D 38

La Baudrière

La Chaize-Giraud

N 160

Brétignolles-sur-Mer

St-Julien-des-Landes

D 978

Brem-sur-Mer

D 38

River Auzance

La Mothe-Achard

Atlantic Ocean

D 80

D 32

N 160

D 87

D 21

Ile-d'Olonne

Le Girouard

D 36

Olonne-sur-Mer

D 80

Grosbreuil

D 4

D 36

LES SABLES-D'OLONNE

La Chaume

Le Château-d'Olonne

Folie de Finfarine

Poiro

D 32B

D949

Le Puits d'Enfer

Musée Automobile

D949

Avrill

Abbaye St-Jean-d'Orbestier

Talmont-St-Hilaire

D 19

0   5   10km

Port-Bourgenay

D 21

Le CAIRN

to La Tra

For explanation of symbols, see page 6.

Abbaye de Lieu-Dieu

Maison de Clemenceau

D 2

Jard-sur-Mer

Les Sables-d'Olonne, La Roche-sur-Yon and the Bas-Bocage

to Nantes

to Montaigu

Belleville-sur-Vie

Poiré-
-Vie

D 937

Dompierre-sur-Yon

River Yon

to Les Herbiers

D 100

D 37

Lac de Moulin-Papon

N 160

A 87 (opens 2005)

paye des
tenelles

La Chaize-le-Vicomte

D 948

A 83

LA ROCHE-SUR-YON

s
ouzeaux

D 747

D 746

River Yon

St-Florent-des-Bois

to Fontenay

bigny

Nesmy

D 36

ul-le
ent

Chaillé-sous-les-Ormeaux

D 50

D 12

Piquet

to Luçon

L'Aubonnière

Lac de Graon

Moutiers-les-Mauxfaits

to La Tranche

to Luçon

e Bernard

21

Richard the Lionheart was probably the first Briton to appreciate holidaying in this popular area—though he came for the hunting rather than for the beaches. Today, visitors can follow in his footsteps, day or night, amid the ruins of his fortress at Talmont. Endless golden sands stretch along this part of the Vendée's coastline, with the smart resort of Les Sables-d'Olonne providing good year-round shopping, eating, culture and entertainment even for those venturing to the Vendée out of season. Among inland villages, picturesque Apremont with its lake, ruined Renaissance castle and steep, narrow streets is a favourite with families.

AIZENAY

ⓘ tel: 02 51 94 62 72
www.mairie-aizenay.fr
aizenay.tourisme@wanadoo.fr

Situated on the edge of a 228-hectare forest 16km north-west of La Roche-sur-Yon, the pleasant little town is easily pinpointed on any map of France as it usually sits on the centre fold. The woods conceal some interesting finds, including the poignant Sentier du Souvenir, remembering an American bomber crew shot down in World War II (see below). The forest, also accessible from the D6 Le Poiré road, is criss-crossed with signposted walks and is home to large wildlife such as roe deer and wild boar.

>Piste Cyclable. Aizenay is at the centre of the smoothly tarmacked cycle route (also popular with rollerbladers) that links Coëx (see page 70) with the county town of La Roche. It meanders through 30km of peaceful countryside, along the path of an old railway line. You can use your own bikes or rent some at Aizenay tourist office by the hour, the day or the week. ● *Cycleway crosses D948 in front of tourist office.*

>Sentier du Souvenir. On the eastern fringe of the forest, a moving memorial commemorates five members of a US bomber crew who died when their Flying Fortress crashed into a field (gradually encroached on since by the woodland) in March 1944. Among the trees, several modern aluminium shards have been artfully placed bearing on them the tale (in French) of the survivors, five in all, of whom two escaped to Spain. You can still see the crater where part of the fuselage hit the ground. ● *4km SE of Aizenay. From the D948 La Roche road, turn off on D101A, towards La Genétouze; car park on left in 100m, sometimes with flags flying.*

Market: First & third Mon.
Shop: *Pâtisserie Angélus*. *Irresistible cakes, sweets & hand-made chocolates; delectable home-made ice-creams in summer. 9 Rue Maréchal Foch, by church (tel: 02 51 94 61 21).*
Crafts: *Poterie Ismail et Marie-Claire*. *Large pottery, indicated by an old tree festooned with pots of all sizes. Mon-Sat 9am-noon & 3-6pm. Route de La Roche, SE of town centre (tel: 02 51 48 32 08).*
Factory: *Tuileries Gauvrit*. *Traditional terracotta bricks & tiles, made using wood-fired kilns, & much sought after for restoration of historic houses. Mon-Fri 9am-noon & 2-6pm. La Gombretière, 3km SE of Aizenay, off D948 (tel: 02 51 94 66 89).*

APREMONT

ⓘ tel: 02 51 55 70 54 fax: 02 51 60 16 65
otapremont@wanadoo.fr

★ Delightfully unspoilt village, clinging picturesquely to the rocky sides of the Vie valley. Lying 26km north-west of La Roche-sur-Yon, Apremont is dominated by a tall water-tower and by the romantic remains of a Renaissance castle. Around Rue des Bretons, south of the river, a few imposing mansions line the narrow streets; on the north side, smaller houses stagger up a steep slope alongside the church. A dam, or *barrage,* signposted east of the bridge, has created a 170-hectare lake—the largest in the Vendée—with a sandy beach and shady riverbanks, which attract lovers of fishing, swimming and water-sports from miles around.

>Château d'Apremont. Two towers and a chapel remain of the fine castle (pictured, left, in its original state, and on page 34 as it is today) built in 1534 by Admiral Philippe Chabot de Brion on the site of an earlier stronghold. A childhood friend of the French king François I, the admiral had accompanied

Specialities: *Traditionally-cured Jambon de Vendée (ham or gammon).*
Restaurant: *Restaurant du Centre*. *Popular place, with outdoor terrace for sunny days. Menus from 15€. 14 Rue Clemenceau (tel: 02 51 55 70 22).*
Festival: *Fête des Battages*. *A day of demonstrations of old-time rural crafts. July.*
Le Château en Fête. *Renaissance-style entertainment. July.*

■ **Setting sail: the lake at Apremont.**

François to his summit meeting with England's King Henry VIII at the Field of the Cloth of Gold 14 years earlier. On 17 April 1622 the young King Louis XIII is said to have slept here after defeating a Protestant army at Riez. The castle later fell into disrepair and, in 1733, it was partially demolished.

You can climb its east tower via a series of empty rooms, looking out over the village rooftops, until you reach the magnificent network of wooden beams that supports the pointed roof. The recorded commentary indoors, and the descriptive leaflet, are available in English. Back at ground level, follow the signs to the 16th-century *voûte cavalière*, a steep indoor ramp cut into the rock. When visitors arrived by boat below, they would be conveyed up this dark slope on horseback,

and emerge dazzled by daylight into Chabot de Brion's glorious courtyard. The other interesting feature, half-buried beneath a corner of the garden, is the *glacière*—a Renaissance-style refrigerator hewn into the rock, where winter ice would have been stored to preserve food in hotter months, or even to create chilled desserts. It still provides welcome cool air in the height of summer.

The more recent buildings surrounding the inner courtyard contain Apremont's *mairie*, local fire station, and occasional art exhibitions. On summer evenings, you may catch an open-air theatrical or other entertainment performed there. ◑ *Mid April-late Sept, daily 2-6pm (1 June-31 Aug, daily 10.30am-6.30pm). Place du Château (tel: 02 51 55 27 18). 3€, children 2.50€, under 12s free (1 July-31 Aug, 4€, children 3€; includes ascent of water-tower, see below).*

➤**Salle Panoramique**. Let yourself be whisked by lift up the 80m-high *château d'eau*, or water-tower, for a stupendous view westward to the sea and islands, and eastward towards the plain and the distant *haut-bocage*. Choose a clear day, and take binoculars and a map for an interesting exercise in orientation. ○ *1 July-31 Aug, daily 10.30am-6.30pm. Route de Maché (tel: 02 51 55 27 18). Admission charge combined with château, see above.*

➤**La Venise d'Apremont**. Rent rowing boats, canoes or pedalos at the "Venice of Apremont", a stretch of the River Vie, downstream of the dam. You can paddle along the placid waters past the restored *lavoir*, or washing-place, and below the castle's majestic towers. If you take a canoe, which can be dragged around the occasional obstacle, you can ultimately reach the hamlet of Dolbeau, 4km to the west. ◑ *1 May-30 June, Sat & Sun 10am-7pm; 1 July-31 Aug, daily 10am-7pm. Apremont riverside (tel: 02 51 55 70 22). 18€ an hour per boat.*

AVRILLÉ
ⓘ **tel: 02 51 22 30 70 fax: 02 51 22 34 00**
www.mairie-avrille.fr

Its large number of prehistoric remains have earned the area around Avrillé, 23km east of Les Sables-d'Olonne, the nickname of "the Carnac of the Vendée" (after the famous megalith-rich site in Brittany). More than 20 dolmens and 100 menhirs are scattered around the area. Behind Avrillé's *mairie* is one of the largest standing-stones in France (see picture, page 66); even Asterix's muscular menhir-deliveryman, Obelix, would have found moving the 7-metre-high "Menhir du Camp de César" a challenge. The tourist office beside Avrillé's 19th-century market-hall has maps showing sites of ancient stones around here and nearby Le Bernard, and organises guided visits to some of them. The CAIRN centre (see page 66) produces a leaflet on the location of additional stones.

➤**Château de la Guignardière/"L'Aventure Historique"**. Such a well-preserved Renaissance stately home is a rare sight in the Vendée. La Guignardière, about 1km west of the village, was built in 1555 by Jean Girard, who held an important post in the court of the French king Henri II.

Having been occupied during the Wars of the Vendée by Republicans, the château escaped destruction in the post-Revolutionary conflicts. Guided tours (in English, as well as French) take you from vaulted cellars to beamed attics, by way of dining-room, kitchens and a granite staircase pierced with holes through which defenders could shoot at attackers below. Outside in the grounds, which contain no fewer than 14 menhirs of varying sizes, is the award-winning "Aventure Historique", an entertaining trail (available in English) for seven- to 12-year-olds; allow two hours for its 20 clues and activities. ◑ *Early Apr-mid June, Wed-Mon 11am-6pm; mid June-31 Aug, daily 10am-7pm; 1-30 Sept, daily 11am-6pm. Route des Sables-d'Olonne (tel: 02 51 22 33 06). 9€, children 6€.* &

➤**Fontaine St-Gré**. Miraculous properties are ascribed to the holy spring trickling from a granite stone, signposted along a footpath off the D105 Longeville road, 2km south-west of Avrillé. A tranquil pond holds water that was collected on St Peter and St Paul's Day (29 June) and treasured by countryfolk for its effectiveness against asthma, heart disease, paralysis and rheumatism. ●

➤**Le CAIRN**. If you'd like to have a go at lighting fires with two sticks, making jewellery from shells, polishing stone axes, making pottery, or weaving in the style of our early ancestors, visit this archaeological neolithic research centre 3.5km south-west of Avrillé. On July and August afternoons, visitors can try one or two crafts, or help with erecting a menhir (standing-stone), constructing a stone wall, or daubing mud on the side of some neolithic-style building. With two exhibition rooms to take in first—fortunately one is sometimes enlivened by an archaeologist chipping flints inside a giant glass case—and the screening of a rather worthy video, the tour does get off to a slightly slow start. However, it comes to life outside, with hands-on experiences that are both fun and enlightening. ◑ *Easter-30 Sept, Sun-Fri 3-6pm (1 July-31 Aug, Mon-Fri 10am-1pm & 3-7pm; Sat, Sun 3-7pm; neolithic techniques demonstrated daily 3.30-6.30pm). St-Hilaire-la-Forêt (tel: 02 51 33 38 38). 4.20€, children 1.70€ (1 July-31 Aug, 5.80€, students 4.20€, children 2€).* &

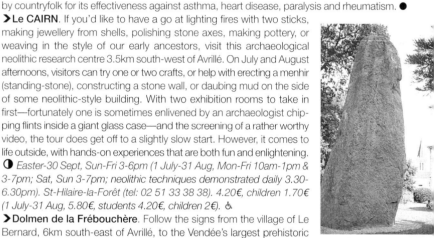

➤**Dolmen de la Frébouchère**. Follow the signs from the village of Le Bernard, 6km south-east of Avrillé, to the Vendée's largest prehistoric burial-chamber (see picture, page 33). In spite of the incongruous pink gravel spread around it to prettify the area, the mighty structure—its top slab weighing 100 tonnes—remains an impressive sight. ● &

■ **Rock of ages: the giant menhir at Avrillé.**

➤**Géosciences**. Endearingly home-made museum of earth sciences, 5km east of Avrillé, created by a family passionate about ancient stones, stars and fossils. In an old barn they show casts of footprints of small, three-toed dinosaurs that roamed the nearby beaches 204 million years ago, and use combinations of Christmas-tree lights to demonstrate the outlines of the constellations. Weekly astronomy nights are held in summer. ◑ *1-30 Apr, daily 2-6pm; 1 May-mid June, Sun & Wed 2-6pm; mid June-7 Sept, daily 2-7pm. La Chauvière, signposted off D91, Le Bernard to Moutiers-les-Mauxfaits road, just N of the main D949 (tel: 02 51 22 34 36). 5€, children 2.50€.* &

AVRILLÉ EXTRAS

Market: Wed (1 July-31 Aug), & second Thurs of the month.

Crafts: Marché Artisanal. Large crafts fair. July.

➤**La Folie de Finfarine.** Signposted in the centre of Poiroux, 6km north-west of Avrillé, is the visitor centre of a forest park designed to give a feeling of woods and their flora and fauna. With true Gallic flair, the presentation is great: wild flowers are artfully framed through a window; a romantic video shows the changing seasons; blocks of wood have handles so you can test their relative weight; and litmus paper is ready to be dipped into various tree essences so you can sniff the difference. (Slightly confusingly, the French word *essence* in connection with trees means "species".) Outside, you can wander round and look at groups of trees; the paths are somewhat overgrown and the map is a bit sketchy, but it's pleasantly shady in hot weather, and there's a great children's playground—made of wood, of course. ◑ *Early Apr-late Sept (plus Oct half-term), Sun-Fri 2-6pm (1 July-31 Aug, daily 10.30am-7pm). Poiroux (tel: 02 51 96 22 50). 4.60€, children 2.60€.*

BEAULIEU-SOUS-LA-ROCHE

ⓘ tel: 02 51 98 80 38 fax: 02 51 98 21 47.

This pretty village, clustered around a tree-shaded square 19km west of La Roche-sur-Yon, has become a well-known focus for cultural and arts-orientated events. Beaulieu's streets are full of artists and craftspeople: bookbinder Armelle Delaunay works on the square; a glass-blower and a designer of decorative objects are in Rue des Forges; and potter Marie-Christine Grangiens is at La Cantardière, 3km to the north.

High-quality exhibitions are mounted in the Maison de l'Art, while the hidden courtyard off the village's main square (see below) offers even more delights, including a view of Beaulieu's steep-sided public gardens.

➤ **Maison de l'Art**. Interesting changing exhibitions of arts and handicrafts and, from December to February each year, several delightful, animated Christmas nativity scenes. ● *During exhibitions: Daily 3-6.30pm. Place de l'Église (tel: 02 51 98 23 80). Admission charge varies.*

➤ **Cour des Arts**. The archway on the south side of the square leads to a shady courtyard where you will find Antiqvaria—an Aladdin's cave for French-reading book-collectors—as well as the studio of artist Régis Delène-Bartholdi who creates attractive paintings and collages inspired by his travels among the nomadic peoples of Africa. ● *Free.*

➤ **Église de Landeronde**. The small, squat 11th-century church of Landeronde, a village on the D50 4km south-east of Beaulieu, is known for its decorated altarpieces and painted wooden sculptures. Look out for plague-sufferer St Roch, accompanied by the faithful dog that brought him food during the saint's self-imposed isolation. ●

BEAULIEU EXTRAS

Restaurant: Café des Arts. The cosy bar-restaurant opposite the church holds occasional exhibitions of the work of local artists. Menus from 15€. 2 Rue de la Poste (tel: 02 51 98 24 80).

Brocante: Brocante La Grolle. Furniture & collectors' items in two rooms of a house on the old La Roche-Les Sables road, now bypassed by the dual carriageway N160. Daily 3-7pm (1 June-30 Sept, Mon-Sat 3-7pm). La Grolle, near Landeronde; on N2160, 7km SE of Beaulieu (tel: 02 51 40 36 92).

Festivals:

Foëre à Bialu. Old-time street market. July.

Foire à la Brocante. Antiques fair. Aug.

Marché de Noël. Christmas market. Dec.

BREM-SUR-MER

ⓘ tel: 02 51 90 92 33 fax 02 51 20 14 67
www.bremsurmer.com
ot.brem.sur.mer@wanadoo.fr

Though now a kilometre from the sea, this pretty village 15km north of Les Sables-d'Olonne was formerly, as its name implies, a seaside port. Today it's thronged with holidaymakers, though you can still find a bit of tranquillity to the south, in the Forest of Olonne or on the wonderfully wild sand dunes and beach of Le Havre de la Gachère.

Strange as it seems to think of salt-breezes wafting over vineyards, Brem is a centre of wine-making. A dozen growers produce reds, whites and rosés—served, it is said, at the table of Cardinal Richelieu, and today marketed under the Fiefs Vendéens label.

➤ **Musée du Vin**. A small wine museum on the south-east edge of the village tells the history of the local vineyards through displays of old tools and equipment, and offers tastings and sales of some of the local wines. You can also read the curious tale of a discovery allegedly made at nearby Brétignolles in 1908. On finding a large barrel washed up on the beach, the villagers bored a hole in it and tasted the contents—a delicious amber-coloured liquid. Keen to take it home, they began to load the barrel onto a cart when it fell and broke open—revealing a pickled orang-utan that had been en route for a museum! ◑ *Easter-mid Sept. Moulin de Bellevue, Route des Sables-d'Olonne. Opening hours & charges not available at time of writing.*

❯**Parc des Dunes**. This excellent amusement park on the D38, north-west of Brem, is perfect for active children, who can spend all day in boats and ball ponds, on roundabouts and bobsleighs, bouncing on inflatables or trying out pedal go-karts and mini-golf. Best for over-sixes; many activities are restricted to over-10s and over-14s. Most notices are in English as well as French, but play is not supervised so keep an eye on your children. Take picnics (lots of places to sit), plus drinks, sunhats, swimwear and towels. ◑ *Easter-mid Sept, daily 10.30am-7.30pm. Rue de l'Écours (tel: 02 51 90 54 29). 6.50€, children under three free.*

❯**Église St-Nicolas-de-Brem**. A few hundred metres north-west of Brem you come across a real delight, the remains of a Romanesque church, built in 1020. Of its original three naves, just the central one survived destruction by Protestants during the Wars of Religion. The carving above the west door is thought to show St Nicholas, surrounded by sculpted acrobats and other figures; on the south wall two fire-breathing serpents intertwine above a small window. Enter through the low north doorway to admire the simple, whitewashed interior, where some 12th-century frescoes were revealed in the early 1980s beneath layers of paint: on the left, a crucifixion and on the right, women at Christ's tomb . ●

❯**Dolmens and menhirs**. Neolithic man was busy raising stones and building tombs here 5,000 years ago. North-west of Brem, off the D38, is a small dolmen on the lane leading to La Normandelière beach. Other prehistoric stones are the Menhir de la Crulière (signposted north of the D54, 2km east of Brem), and the Menhir de la Conche Verte (on the GR364 footpath, in the forest of Olonne, 3km south of Brem). ●

■ **In a spin: fun at the Parc des Dunes, Brem.**

BRÉTIGNOLLES-SUR-MER

ⓘ tel: 02 51 90 12 78 fax: 02 51 22 40 72
www.bretignolles-sur-mer.com
ot.bretignolles.sur.mer@wanadoo.fr

A cheerful seaside atmosphere pervades this village 19km north-west of Les Sables, with shops selling buckets, spades and other holiday paraphernalia. La Parée beach has something for everyone: sandy enough for digging and sunbathing, it is also covered with interesting-shaped pebbles and, at low tide, good rockpools. Other fun at Brétignolles includes an enjoyable mini-golf on Avenue de la Plage, good waves for surfers at La Sauzaie (to the north), and an attractive beach at La Normandelière (to the south), with bars, rockpools and a shallow sea-water pool where small swimmers and sailors can safely try new skills.

❯**Vendée Miniature**. Exquisitely detailed model houses, churches, windmills and farm buildings, built in wood, tiles and local stone by a former cabinet-maker. Not ideal for small children, as it's strictly hands-off, but you marvel at the skill of its creator, who took 20,000 hours to make them all. ◑ *1 Apr-30 Sept, Mon-Sat 10am-noon & 2-6.30pm; Sun 2-6.30pm (1 June-31 Aug, daily 10am-7pm). Rue du Prégneau, Les Morinières, NW of Brétignolles (tel: 02 51 22 47 50). 6€, children 4€.*

❯**Labyrinthe**. An amazing maze, in a field of—what else?—maize, on the D38 just south of Brétignolles. Layouts, taking the form of a treasure hunt, with clues in English and French, change each year. Wandering among the dead-ends and the "walls" of vegetation, hearing voices of other, unseen, visitors makes for a strangely disorientating experience. ○ *Mid July-31 Aug, daily 1-7pm; 1 Sept-31 Oct, Sun 1-7pm. Near La Normandelière road (tel: 06 68 41 67 99). 5€, children 4€.*

■ Mist and magic: the River Yon swirls past boulders and weirs near Chaillé.

➤ **Église de La Chaize-Giraud.** Although the interior of this Romanesque church 5km north-east of Brétignolles has been heavily restored, it retains much of its original atmosphere. Outside, the west façade is all that remains of the 12th-century construction; you can make out, on the right, the Adoration of the Kings and, on the left, Gabriel making his momentous announcement to the Virgin Mary. Some carved stone faces adorn the roof-line and the imposing doorway. ●

CHAILLÉ-SOUS-LES-ORMEAUX
ⓘ tel: 02 51 36 00 85 fax: 02 51 36 90 27
www.ot-roche-sur-yon.fr
info@ot-roche-sur-yon.fr

One of the best-kept secrets of the Vendée is the valley of the River Yon. From Chaillé "Under-the-Elms" (14km south-east of La Roche-sur-Yon) south to Le Champ-St-Père, narrow lanes run either side of the river—though offering the motorist hardly a glimpse of this picturesque stretch of water. However, signs to the "Vallée de l'Yon" encourage you to turn off towards several pretty waterside spots from the D101 on the west side of the water. On the east side, off the D50, follow signs to Piquet to find a traditional *guinguette* (see below, and page 70). If you walk down the steep slope from this open-air bar, you discover on the riverbank the roofless remains of a 19th-century spinning mill, its jagged top-floor window-openings giving it the appearance of a ruined castle.

In Chaillé there are plans to set up a Maison de la Vallée de l'Yon, a museum to explain the ecology of the river and the industries that grew up alongside it. However, until this becomes a reality, you can learn much about the subject in the small museum, below.

➤ **Écomusée de l'Aubonnière.** Allow a good hour for the curator's guided tour of this little museum, located next to an old stone building that is now a hostel for hikers, 5km south-east of Chaillé. He describes the history and geology of this beautiful spot where, in the 19th century, the rapid current created by the steep descent of the Yon between here and Luçon was harnessed to drive many mill-wheels, providing energy for tanning, fulling, paper-making and other industries. An English leaflet is available.

CHAILLÉ EXTRAS

Restaurant: La Guinguette de Piquet. Snacks & grills outdoors, with dancing in summer (see page 70). Coteau de Piquet (tel: 02 51 46 73 52).

From the museum, walk down the sloping, stony track to a magical spot where the fast-flowing Yon tumbles over weirs and swirls around alder trees, islands and granite boulders (see picture, page 69). Beneath ivy and brambles you can make out the ruins of the many little watermills that once made the area so busy. Some parts of the bank are pretty steep, particularly if you walk to the right, so hold securely on to any small children. ● *River walks accessible at all times. Museum open Sat, Sun 2.30-5.30pm (1 July-31 Aug, daily 2.30-5.30pm). L'Aubonnière; from D101, follow "gîte d'étape" signs to hostel (tel: 02 51 34 90 66). 1.50€, children 0.75€.*

➤**Piquet**. On the opposite side of the Yon is an attractive spot where, on fine weekends, you can sip drinks, eat simple meals and even step out to live accordion music outdoors in the style of the old *guinguettes* (open-air, waterside bars or dance-halls). From Chaillé, take the D50 on the east side of the valley, towards Rosnay; after the village of Le Tablier, turn right and continue about 2km to the Piquet car park. ◗ *April-Oct (in good weather), Sat, Sun from 11am (1 June-30 Sept, daily from 11am; dancing Sat from 8.30pm; Sun from 4pm). Piquet (tel: 02 51 46 73 52).* ♿

COËX

ⓘ tel: 02 51 54 28 80
www.cc-atlancia.fr

This flower-filled village 25km west of La Roche-sur-Yon—the locals pronouce its name "kwex", rather than "coh-ex"—is renowned for its scented garden. The village lies at the far end of the Vélo-Rail line from Commequiers (see page 47), and on the cycleway that links La Roche-sur-Yon to the coast along the route of another old railway line.

Coëx is also known for its large carnival held in the middle of Lent (usually in March, depending on the date of Easter), which draws thousands to watch the giant decorated floats parade through the streets.

➤**Jardin des Olfacties**. In the village centre is a breathtakingly colourful garden laid out with all kinds of plants endowed with intense fragrance. The scents of geraniums and roses mingle with more unusual floral aromas of aniseed, chocolate and even tar. There are herb and woodland gardens, waterside walks, exotic plants, a kaleidoscopic bank of wild flowers, a children's play area around a little Japanese-style house, and plenty of benches for just sitting and contemplation. Friendly signs encourage you to sniff certain flowers or to stroke the leaves. Children can try a few hands-on activities, including trying to create bird calls. ◗ *Mid Apr-mid Sept, daily 2-7pm (mid June-31 Aug, daily 10.30am-7pm). Entrance behind church (tel: 02 51 55 53 41). 6.10€, students 4.60€, children under 12 free. Guided tours 4pm, 1.50€.* ♿

COËX EXTRAS

Market: Sat.

Restaurant: **Crêperie du Pré**. Pretty café on Jaunay lake. 4km S of Coëx, off D42. (tel: 02 51 34 68 20).

Festival: **Fête de la Confiture**. Festival of jam & preserves. Sept.

Golf: **Golf des Fontenelles**. An 18-hole course, 3km W of Coëx, on D6 (tel: 02 51 54 13 94).

■ Heaven-scent: Coëx's garden of fragrance.

■ Retiring gracefully: cottage at Jard, where Georges Clemenceau received friends and foreign dignitaries.

JARD-SUR-MER

ⓘ tel: 02 51 33 40 47 fax: 02 51 33 96 42
www.ville-jardsurmer.fr
tourisme@ville-jardsurmer.fr

A charming seaside town 20km south-east of Les Sables-d'Olonne, with a small harbour providing moorings for up to 500 boats, plus three sandy beaches, and many
attractive villas half hidden among pine woods. The port is overlooked by the Moulin de
Conchette which, with the neighbouring Moulin de Bellevue, is the last of nine windmills
that ground corn in the area a century ago. Among some delightful walks is the Circuit
du Payré, starting just beyond the turning to the Abbey of Lieu-Dieu (see page 72), which
leads along clifftops and past wind-sculpted holm oaks to the mouth of the Payré river.

➤**Église Ste-Radégonde**. Jard's Romanesque church is dedicated to a one-time queen of
France (see page 78). Fortified in the Middle Ages and sacked by Protestants in 1568, it has many
interesting features, including a Renaissance-style chapel. It is often locked, so your best opportunity to see the interior is around the time of a service—on Saturday evening or Sunday morning.
● Church open all year. ○ Guided tours in summer (tel: 02 51 33 40 47).

➤**Musée de la Machine à Coudre**. Unexpectedly fascinating collection
of 225 sewing machines of all sizes and ages—the first dating from
1852—set out in an immaculate building not far from the town's Super U
store. Although the American Isaac Singer is generally credited with this

JARD EXTRAS

Market: Mon, Jard town
centre. Sun, St-Vincent-
sur-Jard, 2km SE of Jard.

■ **Inspirational: Clemenceau's view.**

revolutionary invention in 1851, it seems that a Frenchman, Barthélémy Thimonnier, had already come up with a similar idea in 1830. Thimonnier, however, was forced to abandon his brainchild after the tailors of Paris, angered by the anticipated loss of work, threatened to lynch him. ◑ *1 May-30 Sept, Sat, Sun 3-7pm (1 July-31 Aug, daily 3-7pm). 3 Rue du Rayon (tel: 02 51 33 57 93). 5€, children 2.50€.* ὁ

➤**Maison de Clemenceau.** As soon as you see this enchanting low-built cottage on the sands, 2km south-east of Jard (see pictures, right, and page 71), you can understand why Georges Clemenceau (see pages 32, 119 and 146) chose this idyllic spot for his retirement in 1919. After his momentous work on the Treaty of Versailles, which brought an end to World War I, the fiery politician withdrew here to write his memoirs at his desk overlooking the sea. The interior is full of books, furniture and objects, as if the "Tiger" (as he was affectionately known) had just left it to go out for a stroll round his beloved garden with his friend the Impressionist painter Claude Monet—reputed to have given him some ideas for its design—or with visiting dignitaries like the young Hirohito, later to become emperor of Japan. A 20-minute video precedes the guided tour; English notes available. ● *Tues-Sun 10am-12.30pm & 2-5.30pm (mid May-mid Sept, daily 9.30am-12.30pm & 2.15-6.30pm; 1 July-31 Aug, daily 9.30am-6.30pm). Closed 1 Jan, 1 May, 1 & 11 Nov & 25 Dec. St-Vincent-sur-Jard (tel: 02 51 33 40 32). 4.60€, students 3.10€, children under 18 free.* ὁ

➤**Abbaye de Lieu-Dieu.** A once-imposing abbey built more than 800 years ago by Richard Coeur-de-Lion—King of England and Duke of Aquitaine—stands 2km to the west of Jard, and towers over the unspoilt agricultural buildings around it. After a long period of prosperity, the abbey suffered greatly in the Hundred Years War and was further ruined by Protestants during the Wars of Religion. The interior is not currently open for visits, but you can sneak a look from the farmyard at its unusual architecture, embellished by a strange pair of slate-roofed octagonal turrets. ●

➤**Indian Forest.** Follow signs for Plage de la Mine, another kilometre west beyond the Abbey of Lieu-Dieu (see above) to find this adventure park for adults and children in 2 hectares of Jard's coastal pine forest. Helmets, harnesses, ropes and shackles are provided; you are recommended to come in tough clothing, and wear trainers or other solid shoes. Several grades of treetop trails include a special supervised course for small children. Instruction given in English if required. It's popular, so you may have to book ahead in July and August; count on spending a good two hours there. On the same site there is also paint-ball, a 12-metre climbing wall, and bungeeing from a trampoline. ◑ *Late Mar-end June, Wed, Sat, 2-6.30pm; Sun & public holidays 10am-7.30pm. 1 July-31 Aug, daily 9am-9pm. 1 Sept-15 Oct, Wed & Sat 2-6pm; Sun 10am-5pm. Route du Payré, near Plage de la Mine (tel: 02 51 20 38 02). 17€; children: two to five years 10€; five to eight years 9€; nine to 11 years 11€; 12-15 years 15€.*

MACHÉ

ⓘ tel: 02 51 55 72 05 fax : 02 51 55 64 06
www.mairie-de-mache.com
mairie-mache@wanadoo.fr

The casual passer-by would hardly suspect this small lakeside village off the D948, 24km north-west of La Roche-sur-Yon, to be one of the world's leading quail-rearing centres, yet three local enterprises sell 10 million table-ready birds (each about the size of a plump thrush) every year to shops and restaurants as far away as Japan. If you want to try one, pop along to the annual quail festival when 1,000 are barbecued for supper beside the lake.

Maché's 170-hectare lake, stretching west for 6km to the dam at Apremont, is a paradise for fishermen—especially for carp enthusiasts, who will find a special section for night-fishing near the bridge on the D50 (Rue du Lac). Other fishing places are near the open ground at the bottom of Rue du Moulin-à-Eau. Walkers can follow a signposted route from here along part of the lake's north shore: easy terrain to the left; quite precipitous in places to the right—though you are rewarded for scrambling up the steep, rocky slopes with some magnificent views over the water.

> **Eurotruche**. A forward-looking poultry farmer has moved upscale into ostrich-breeding so if you're keen on these birds (*autruches* in French), this visit is for you. After watching a 10-minute video on raising ostriches, you can walk around the enclosures to observe them and their near relatives, emus and rheas. There is a collection of ducks, guineafowl, donkeys, goats and other farmyard animals, plus a shop selling decorated eggs. In summer the farm opens its "ferme-auberge"—a restaurant, where you can sample ostrich steaks and other delicacies. ◐ *1 May-mid Sept, Sat, Sun & public holidays 2-6pm (1 July-31 Aug, daily 10am-6pm). La Logerie, on D948, 2.5km NW of Maché (tel: 02 51 55 63 74). 5€, children 3€. Restaurant open 1 July-31 Aug, lunchtime only; booking advisable. Restaurant clients have free admission to the ostrich enclosures.*

MACHÉ EXTRAS

Specialities: Quail. Ostrich.

Restaurants:

Le Fougerais. Try quail, deliciously marinated, & other dishes, in a renovated barn. Off D948, 2km NW of Maché (tel: 02 51 5●75 44).

Eurotruche Ferme-auberge. See main entry.

Festivals:

Fête de la Caille. Quail feast & entertainment. July.

Fête du Lac. Games & fireworks on lake. 15 Aug.

MARTINET
ⓘ tel: 02 51 05 90 49 fax: 02 51 05 95 51
www.cc-pays-des-achards.fr
tourisme.pays.des.achards@wanadoo.fr

A pleasant little village near the Jaunay river, Martinet offers fishing possibilities in its landscaped park, Les Ouches du Jaunay, and signposted footpaths highlighting such rustic features as some unusual *chênes-lièges*, or oak trees with cork bark.

■ **Walking tall in Maché.**

St-Julien-des-Landes, 5km to the south-west, has preserved its old-world village atmosphere, and attracts many British visitors to its top-of-the-range campsites. Among other attractions in the area are the popular waterside activities on the Lac du Jaunay (see page 74), and a pretty chapel in the centre of La Chapelle-Hermier, 4km west of Martinet, in which you can see some newly-discovered medieval wall decorations.

> **Chapelle Notre-Dame de Garreau**. The unusual 16th-century chapel near the banks of the Jaunay river on the D42, on the western edge of Martinet, is the site of a pilgrimage on the first Sunday of September each year. A panel near the water tells the legend of a knight returning from the Crusades, who prayed to the Virgin for help as he was almost swept away trying to ford the fast-flowing Jaunay river. A large boulder on the Martinet side is said to have risen from the water enabling him to reach the bank, and is supposed still to bear the hoofprint of the knight's horse. ●

> **Ferme des Thibaudières**. An interesting little farm outside the village, restored by its owners to display animals typical of those that were traditionally raised in the area until recent intensive farming methods banished most of them indoors. You can stroke sheep, have pony rides, watch strutting geese and wallowing pigs, and feed stale bread to rabbits and guinea pigs. Keep your

distance from the tethered goats though—they can butt! ❶ *Early Apr-early Oct, Wed & Sun 3-5.30pm (1 July-31 Aug, Wed-Mon 2.30-5.30pm). Les Thibaudières, signposted E off D55, 3km SW of Martinet (tel: 02 51 46 63 73). 4€, children 2.50€; pony-rides 5.50€.* &

➤**Stèle de la Brionnière.** A sombre granite monument beside a country lane marks the isolated spot where the Allies parachuted a consignment of arms to Resistance workers on 11 August 1943. ● *3km N of Martinet, signposted from D55, & also from D6 Aizenay-to-Coëx road.*

➤**Lac du Jaunay.** This 114-hectare, fish-filled lake lies 3km west of Martinet as the crow flies, though a bit farther by car. It is strangely invisible from the surrounding network of roads, but if you drive south-west to St-Julien-des-Landes and then take the Chapelle-Hermier road from there, you'll find a sign to the hamlet of La Baudrière off to the left. One of the most attractive places on the lake's tree-lined shores, it has the atmosphere of a seaside fishing village, and in summer you can rent canoes, pedalos and mountain-bikes. A footpath has been created around the whole lake; to walk the easier half, you can set off anticlockwise from La Baudrière and return via the nearby road bridge that crosses the lake. Near the north-west end of the lake, at Le Pré, is a pretty waterside café (see page 70), surrounded by signposted walks and cycle trails. ●

LA MOTHE-ACHARD

ⓘ **tel: 02 51 05 90 49 fax: 02 51 05 95 51**
www.cc-pays-des-achards.fr
tourisme.pays.des.achards@wanadoo.fr

Large village midway between La Roche-sur-Yon and Les Sables-d'Olonne with a picturesque 1920s iron-and-glass market-hall. Among local curiosities are Château-Gaillard, an eccentrically-battlemented former presbytery in the village of Le Girouard, 6km south-east of La Mothe, and a couple of stone wolves that—appropriately—stand guard outside the *mairie* of Ste-Flaive-des-Loups (St Flavia of the Wolves), 5km to the east.

■ **Bizarre vegetables at La Mothe-Achard.**

➤**Le Potager Extraordinaire.** Every curcubitaceous plant (marrow, pumpkin, squash, gourd etc) you could imagine—more than 300 different types, including the curiously-contorted Devil's Claws and Turban Squash, and many rare varieties—is grown here, 2km north of La Mothe. A meandering path leads past a series of themed plots: decorative, organic, perfumed and prickly; medicinal, poisonous and tropical, and signs (mostly in French) prompt you to touch or smell. Regular guided tours are led by enthusiastic staff, who often suggest how to cook their favourite vegetables; afterwards you can buy whatever's in season, and take it home to try for yourself. ○ *Mid June-mid Oct, daily 10.30am-12.30pm & 2.30-6pm (1 July-31 Aug, daily 10.30am-7pm). Les Mares, on N2160, old La Roche road (tel: 02 51 46 67 83). 4.50€, children 2€.* &

➤**Katsika.** Like shaggy poodles, the frisky, curly-coated angora goats skip around this farm 5km south of La Mothe. Vividly-coloured wool, sweaters and delectably fluffy rugs, plus home-made goat's cheese and other produce, are for sale in the barn; photographs show the process of transforming fleece into knittable wool. Children will love stroking the cuddly kids from the milking herd. ❶ *Early Apr-early May, Sun-Fri 3-7pm; early May-30 June (shop only), Sun 3-7pm; 1 July-31 Aug, Sun-Fri 3-7pm; 1 Sept-15 Nov (shop only), Sun 3-7pm. Le Moulin du Puy-Gaudin, off D21, Talmont road (tel: 02 51 46 61 79). 3€, children 2€; guided tours in July & Aug, Sun & Tues-Fri 3.45pm; 4.50€ & 3€ (including admission).* &

➤**Mémoires du Pey.** A fascinating collection of agricultural implements fills two large barns on a farm 8km south of La Mothe. The owner has

LA MOTHE EXTRAS

Market: Second, third & fourth Fri of the month (food hall only); first Thurs (larger market).

Festival: *Fête de la Citrouille. Pumpkin festival, with competition to find the heaviest. Oct.*

amassed a huge number of tools—from bread-making materials and dairy equipment to a fork used for fending off wolves, and some examples of murderous-looking weapons manufactured during the 18th-century civil war by the Vendeans, who ingeniously adapted their sharp scythes and billhooks into lethal bayonets. O *1 July-30 Sept, daily 10am-noon & 2-6pm. Le Puy-Babin, signposted off D87, 1km E of St-Mathurin (tel: 02 51 22 74 11). Free, but donations welcome.*

MOUTIERS-LES-MAUXFAITS

ⓘ tel: 02 51 98 94 13 fax: 02 51 31 42 67
www.moutiers-les-mauxfaits.fr
contact@moutiers-les-mauxfaits.fr

The pride of this ancient village 21km south of La Roche-sur-Yon, on the road to La Tranche-sur-Mer, is its unusual 18th-century market-hall, whose roman-tiled roof rests on an intricate structure of solid oak beams and 41 stalwart stone columns. The historic atmosphere of the village centre is accentuated by the collection of old houses clustered around the market, alongside the well-preserved Romanesque church of St-Jacques. This 12th-century building was familiar centuries ago to travellers on the road to Santiago de Compostela; in memory of those times, Moutiers has taken a pilgrims' scallop shell as part of its present-day emblem.

■ Moutiers market-hall.

MOUTIERS EXTRAS

Market: Tues (1 July-31 Aug) & Fri, & last Mon of month.
Garden centre: Boutin et Fils. See main entry.
Festival: Puces. Large annual flea-market. Aug.

➤ **Pépinières Boutin et Fils**. Take a present home for your garden from these large nurseries 6km west of Moutiers. Outdoors, alongside the glasshouses full of gnarled olive trees and tender shrubs, are exhibition gardens and plenty of good-value plants in superb condition. ● *Mon-Sat 9am-12.30pm & 2-6pm. Belle-Fontaine, on D45 W of St-Avaugourd-des-Landes (tel: 02 51 98 94 44).*

NESMY

ⓘ tel: 02 51 36 00 85 fax: 02 51 36 90 27
www.ot-roche-sur-yon.fr
info@ot-roche-sur-yon.fr

Since the 13th century, local clay deposits have sustained a pottery industry (see below) at this village 6km south of La Roche-sur-Yon. The council has even seen fit to include a red pottery jug on Nesmy's colourful coat of arms.

The nearby village of Aubigny has put itself on the tourist map for its unlikely feat of having an incredible number of outsized objects listed in the French *Guinness Book of Records* (see page 76).

➤ **Vieille Poterie**. Monsieur Charpentreau's family has been working this pottery since 1890. Inside the rickety buildings, in the centre of Nesmy, you can look into the clay-spattered workshops that are a hive of industry on weekdays. A pleasantly chaotic shop sells the hand-turned and hand-painted products for a wide range of tastes, that range from pretty, flower-decorated plates, candlesticks, jugs and dishes to traditional 60-litre salt-glazed storage jars suitable for a lifetime's supply of gherkins. Descriptive leaflet available in English. ● *Shop: Mon-Sat 10am-noon & 2-7pm, Sun 2-7pm. 57 Rue Georges-Clemenceau (tel: 02 51 07 62 57).*

NESMY EXTRAS

Factory shop: Old pottery. See main entry.
Festival: Fête des Vendanges. Festival of new wine. Oct.
Fête des Vieux Métiers. Day-long festival of weaving, rope-making & 80 other old skills & crafts. Aubigny, 4km W of Nesmy. Aug.
Golf: Golf de la Domangère. An 18-hole course (the seventh hole is the longest in France) laid out around a 15th-century mansion (see page 16 for Formule Golf pass). On D85, 3km N of Nesmy (tel: 02 51 07 65 90).

➤**Moulin de Rambourg**. Restored watermill in a verdant spot beside a ford across the river Yon, signposted off the D85 some 2km north-east of Nesmy. It ceased commercial activity in 1981, but panels have been installed to explain the workings of the machinery that was renowned for producing an extremely fine flour. Guided tours in summer. Outside there are picnic places and waterside footpaths plus, in summer, canoe hire on the river. ○ *1 July-31 Aug, Tues-Sun 1-7pm. Near Nesmy (tel: 02 51 07 63 83). 2€, children 1.50€, under 12s free.*

➤**Musée des Records**. A huge key, 7 metres long, draws attention to this curious collection of giant objects—that includes vastly oversized skittles and coffee-grinder, a grandfather clock made of 280,000 matches, a 3.1-metre high spinning-wheel, a clothes peg measuring 3.8 metres in length and a 10.5-metre-diameter replica of Maurice Chevalier's straw boater. The criterion is that everything must be functional, however enormous the scale. ◑ *Easter-31 May, daily 2-6pm; 1-30 June, daily 2-6.30pm; 1 July-31 Aug daily 10.30am-6.30pm (guided tours 11.30am, 2.30pm & 4.30pm; craft demonstrations Tues & Thurs afternoons); 1-30 Sept, daily 2-6pm; 1 Oct-mid Nov, Sun & public holidays 2-6pm. Parc de Loisirs de la Tournerie, Rue Jules-Verne, on N side of village, near junction with D747 (tel: 02 28 15 50 63). 4.50€, children 2.50€.*

➤**Les Clouzeaux**. Beside the church in this small village 10km north-west of Nesmy stands one of the most elegant of the war memorials created during their long career by the Martel brothers (see page 45). Commissioned in 1947, this beautiful sculpture represents a pensive Vendean girl.

If you have time for a walk, there's more stonework to be admired along the irresistibly-named "Chemin de l'Amour" ("Path of Love"), a footpath that starts some 200 metres north-east of Les Clouzeaux' central crossroads. A pretty little stone fountain awaits those who brave the mud along this sunken lane, which is signposted off Rue du Moulin de la Polka.

OLONNE-SUR-MER

ⓘ tel: 02 51 90 75 45 fax: 02 51 90 77 30
www.olonnesurmer.fr
office-de-tourisme.olonne@wanadoo.fr
ⓘ tel: 02 51 33 11 72 Ile-d'Olonne
ⓘ tel: 02 51 21 09 67 Le Château-d'Olonne

In the area globally known as the Pays-des-Olonnes, you could be forgiven for finding the names of the individual villages misleading. Ile-d'Olonne, at the north-west tip of the group, is no longer an island; Olonne-sur-Mer, lying due south, is now stranded 2km from the sea; and at Le Château-d'Olonne, to the south-east, there is little sign of a château. Les Sables-d'Olonne, on the other hand, spreading out to the south and west of these three, has no shortage of *sable*, or sand.

Of the first group mentioned, Olonne-sur-Mer has the largest tourist office, so this entry will embrace all three. (For Les Sables-d'Olonne, see page 81.)

➤**Musée des Traditions Populaires**. Museum of local costume, customs and way of life laid out in five rooms of a former school building in the centre of Olonne. It includes a good collection of agricultural and woodworking tools and some expertly-starched local *coiffes*, or headdresses, plus amusing relics from the early days of the area's seaside holiday industry. ● *Tues 2.30-5.30pm (1-30 Apr, & 1 June-30 Sept, Mon-Fri 2.30-5.30pm; 1 July-31 Aug, Mon-Fri 3-6.30pm, Tues & Thurs 10am- noon & 3-6.30pm). Closed public holidays. 30 Rue du Maréchal Foch, 500m W of church (tel: 02 51 96 95 53). 3.10€, children 1.50€.*

OLONNE EXTRAS

Market: Sun (1 July-31 Aug), Olonne. Daily, (1 July-31 Aug), Le Château-d'Olonne.

Festivals:

Fête des Vieux Métiers. More than 100 old crafts demonstrated in village centre. Ile-d'Olonne. July.

"Cette nuit...Pierre-Levée". Annual son-et-lumière production. Château de Pierre-Levée, Olonne (see page 77). Aug.

Golf: Golf des Olonnes. Plenty of water features on an 18-hole course, 2km E of Olonne. Near large roundabout on N2160 (tel: 02 51 33 16 16).

➤**Château de Pierre-Levée**. Although this pretty stone house modelled on the Trianon château at Versailles is only rarely open to the public, you can get a good view of it from the road that leads to the golf club, 2km east of Olonne and just east of the N2160. In August some 200 local residents take part in an excellent *son-et-lumière* presentation (see page 76) in the grounds, telling the history of the house and of the surrounding area. ○ *1 July-31 Aug, guided tours Wed 10am. Near Olonne-sur-Mer (tel: 02 51 90 75 45). 3€, children free. Son-et-lumière show, five days in Aug (booking tel: 02 51 90 75 45); tickets approximately 14€, children 7€.*

➤**Observatoire d'oiseaux**. Wood-built bird-watching post 2km north of Olonne, overlooking the old salt-marshes that are home to France's second-largest colony of avocets. Telescopes are provided and help is given in identifying the curlews, stilts, spoonbills and other wading birds that take up temporary residence in this wetland: huge migrating flocks pass by in March/April and August/September. ◑ *Observatory: Easter-mid Sept, daily during school-holiday periods 10am-5pm (1 July-31 Aug, daily 9.30am-7pm). Champclou, near Ile-d'Olonne, signposted off D38 (tel: 02 51 33 12 97). 2.40€, children 1.20€.*

➤**Musée de la Petite Gare**. Housed in a former station building in the centre of Ile-d'Olonne is an interesting collection of artefacts and photographs relating to the local trades of salt-making and wine-producing. Strangely, the two are perfectly complementary, since the first requires most of its work to be done in spring and summer while the second has a busy autumn and winter schedule. You can also climb the tower of the village church, with its witch's-hat-shaped spire, for a bird's-eye view—though try and avoid a time when the clock might strike! ○ *1 July-31 Aug, daily 10am-noon & 4-6pm. Chemin de la Ceinture, Ile-d'Olonne (tel: 02 51 33 11 72). 2€ (includes admission to church tower), children 1€.*

➤**Puits d'Enfer**. About 2km south-east of Les Sables, and 3km south of Le Château-d'Olonne, the coastline turns to water-eroded cliffs and gullies, where spray is driven up like geysers on stormy days, earning the site its name of "Hell's Well". (Be careful not to stray near the edge in fierce weather conditions.) This was the site of a gruesome discovery in February 1949, referred to as "la malle sanglante" ("the blood-soaked trunk"), when a laundry basket containing the body of an elderly Parisian, murdered by his housekeeper, was found at the bottom of the cliff. ●

➤**Abbaye St-Jean-d'Orbestier**. The solid remnants of a 12th-century abbey, said to have been built by Richard the Lionheart, stand just back from the sea 3km south of Le Château-d'Olonne. Half-hidden by some institutional buildings, the partially-restored church now provides a venue for exhibitions and concerts, with an open-air clifftop area outside for summer films and plays. ○ *1 July-31 Aug, Tues-Sun 3-7pm (tel: 02 51 21 09 67). Admission charges vary.*

LE POIRÉ-SUR-VIE

ⓘ tel: 02 51 31 89 15 fax: 02 51 31 89 14
www.ville-lepoiresurvie.fr
tourisme.poire@free.fr

The picturesque village perched on a rocky outcrop 13km north-west of La Roche-sur-Yon is clustered around a central market place that is overlooked by a well-preserved Renaissance house dating from 1613. Among Le Poiré's artistic treasures are a wonderfully baroque altarpiece in the church and, across the square, a wall decorated with an enormous painting of a wedding, created by distinguished local contemporary "naïve" artist Raphaël Toussaint.

Le Poiré is the hub of a large network of footpaths (maps may be obtained from the tourist office in the Moulin à Elise watermill). If, in autumn, you see strange piles of vegetation stacked to dry around single poles in the fields you will be looking at the harvest of the ubiquitous *mogettes*—the white haricot beans that appear on so many menus, often accompanying local gammon. In July and August, new season's beans are on sale still in their pods. Known as *demi-secs*, these can be cooked without any preliminary soaking.

If you take the D4 towards Les Lucs, you pass two interesting country houses (neither of them open to visitors). At the Château de Pont-de-Vie, 1km north of Le Poiré, General Charette spent a few nights as a prisoner after his capture (see page 147) by Republicans on 23 March 1796. Some 2km farther north, the Château de la Métairie has its own tragic links with the Vendée Wars: three daughters of the Vaz de Mello family, who owned the house in the 18th century, met their deaths at the guillotine in 1793.

> **Moulin à Élise**. The large wheel of this restored 19th-century water-mill creaks and splashes around while the miller gives a 15-minute explanation of the process, with the aid of a complex diagram showing the to-ings and fro-ings the wheat undergoes before emerging as bags of flour. You can climb the stairs for a look at the hopper feeding the mill-stones with grain, and buy little bags of both ordinary and *blé noir* (buckwheat) flour in the shop below. Nearby are picnic tables, a series of signposted footpaths, and a *crêperie*. ● *1 Apr-31 Oct, Sun 3-6pm (1 July-31 Aug, Mon-Sat 10am-noon & 3-6pm). On lakeside (tel: 02 51 31 61 38). 2€, children free.*

> **Aux P'tites Puces**. Not, strictly speaking, on the tourist circuit, but a visit to these two huge warehouses, selling every conceivable type of fabric by the kilogram, is an unmissable experience for anyone who can sew. If you have ever needed material to make mackintoshes, or those odd bits to repair dungaree or bra straps, this self-service bazaar is the answer. It also offers bedspreads, *bleus de travail* (blue workman's overalls), cast-iron firebacks and even wire-netting. Stock changes fast, as much of it is end-of-range stuff. ● *Wed-Sat 9.30am-12.30pm & 2.30-6.45pm. Route d'Aizenay (tel: 02 51 06 49 50).*

> **Pierre de la Merlière**. The neolithic boulder also known as the "Pierre des Farfadets", or "Goblins' Stone", is located about 4km west of Le Poiré on a footpath known as the "Sentier des Farfadets" ("Goblins' Path"). The top of this 12-tonne block of granite bears more than 300 myste-rious signs, indentations engraved on it by prehistoric or—some say—by fairy hands. Others maintain that they are the fingermarks of Gargantua, Rabelais' legendary giant (see page 115), who allegedly used this "pebble" for playing games of marbles. ●

> **Chapelle Ste-Radégonde**. In the depths of the countryside, 3km south of Le Poiré and sign-posted off the road north of the village of La Genétouze, stands a small chapel, rebuilt in 1863 on the site of an earlier one, dedicated to a 6th-century saint who was once a queen of France. According to legend, Radégonde was fleeing from her cruel husband, King Clotaire, when she came across a peasant sowing oats and besought him not to tell anybody that she had passed that way. He agreed, whereupon the seeds he had sown germinated instantly and sprung up high enough to hide the fugitive. Her pursuing husband, witnessing this miracle, recognised the hand of God, and abandoned his chase. The door of the chapel is generally locked, but the setting is picturesquely wooded; you can walk down a sunken lane to a stream that runs below, and join a circuit of local footpaths. (A map of these is available from the *mairie* of La Genétouze.) ●

> **Circuit Philippe Alliot**. Named after its owner—a French racing driver who came third at the Le Mans 24-Hour race in 1983, and enjoyed a brief Formula 1 career—this karting circuit 7km north-east of Le Poiré has 1,000 metres of twisting track and claims to be for everyone between the ages of seven and 77. Vehicles for children (booking essential) as well as for adults—and even one specially adapted for handicapped drivers, with steering-wheel-mounted controls. Signposted from D937 La Roche-to-Nantes road, and located next to a conspicuously tall water-tower. ● *Daily 10am-7pm (no children after 3pm). Zone Industrielle (ZI) Le Petit Bourbon, Belleville-sur-Vie (tel: 02 51 41 05 05). From 13€ for 10 mins, children from 10€ for eight mins.* &

LE POIRÉ EXTRAS

Market: Thurs (larger on first & third Thurs) & Sat.
Specialities: Mogettes (haricot beans).
Restaurant: *Crêperie du Moulin à Élise*. Crêpes, galettes (savoury pancakes) & salads for lunch from around 7€; open Sun evening in July & Aug for mussels & chips. On lakeside, by watermill (tel: 02 51 06 42 86).
Factory shop: *Aux P'tites Puces*. See main entry.
Festivals: *Nuit de la Mogette*. White-bean festival, with evening beanfeast. 14 Aug. *Fête du Blé Noir*. Buckwheat festival. Sept.

LA ROCHE-SUR-YON

ⓘ tel: 02 51 36 00 85 fax: 02 51 36 90 27
www.ot-roche-sur-yon.fr
info@ot-roche-sur-yon.fr

■ Art Deco splendour: the 1930s
post office in La Roche-sur-Yon.

After the Wars of the Vendée, Napoleon Bonaparte wished to create a new capital for the unruly *département* (having decided that the existing one of Fontenay-le-Comte was too far away from the centre), and in 1804 picked on the small village of La Roche-sur-Yon. Demolishing much of the old part (though a corner of it can still be seen around Place de la Vieille Horloge), he created a "new town" of Classical-style buildings and die-straight streets around the central parade-ground, from which radiated avenues designed to give 20,000 soldiers instant access to any trouble-spots. Modestly, he called it "Napoléon". With the fluctuating status of France over the next 66 years the town's name was changed no fewer than seven times, reverting finally to that of the original village in 1870. (However, "Napoléon-Vendée"—the name the town bore under Napoléon III at the time the railway arrived in the 1860s—is still etched indelibly into the stone above one of the station platforms.) A signposted Circuit Napoléon leads you on a 2.5km perambulation around some of the most obvious sights.

The lack of interesting nooks and crannies that the grid layout imposed helped earn La Roche the unenviable description of "about the dullest town in France" from the 19th-century travel writer John Murray. However, efforts have since been made to liven up its image. Excellent art exhibitions are held in the Conseil Général's Hôtel du Département, or county hall. A witty fountain of oil drums now makes a splash in front of the theatre; the few old buildings around Place de la Vieille Horloge have been restored; and on summer weekends you can sip evening drinks in the Jardin de la Mairie to the strains of jazz.

Famous past residents include artist Paul Baudry (1824-86), who decorated the foyer of the Paris Opéra and was born in the street that now bears his name; and if you ever eat Vache-qui-Rit cheese, you have probably stared at the work of another La Roche citizen, Benjamin Rabier (1864-1939) who designed the original Laughing Cow logo. Rabier, however, is better known in France as the creator of Gédéon, a sort of Gallic Donald Duck, whose cartoon exploits gripped the nation in the 1920s and 30s.

There are two principal shopping areas in town: Rue Georges-Clemenceau, where the tourist office stands opposite La Roche's elegant Art Deco post office; and the market area to the north of the large Classical-style church of St Louis on Place Napoléon, with smart shops on Rue des Halles and other pedestrianised streets.

A few words of warning to drivers: remember the very low (30kph) speed limit in the centre, and avoid the town's many bus lanes (particularly tricky around Place Napoléon). Also, if you should plunge into the network of small side streets, beware of the occasional *priorité à droite*—this means that traffic approaching you at a junction from your right-hand side may have right of way. So, unless you can see a definite stop sign for cars approaching you—give way!

❯ **Haras National**. This national stud—one of the largest in France—was founded by Napoleon in 1843 to breed horses for his army. Today its roomy boxes are home to around 45 stallions of various breeds—from draught animals to elegant riding horses, and from Connemara ponies to thoroughbred trotters. The guide on the hour-long tour of this impeccably-kept city farm explains how the animals are exercised, shod, and generally cared for—and lets you stroke a few, too. The stud is a well-known training centre for saddlers and blacksmiths. ○ *1 June-30 Sept, Mon-Sat (except public holidays), guided tours 3pm (1 July-31 Aug, Mon-Sat 10.30am-noon & 1.45-5pm; guided tours 10.45am & throughout afternoon. Sun & public holidays 2.45-5pm; guided tours 3pm). Boulevard des États-Unis (tel: 02 51 46 14 47). 4.50€, students & children 2€.* 占

➤**Musée de La Roche-sur-Yon**. Awaiting a move to a larger location, the town's museum puts on a series of changing cultural exhibitions in its present home off Rue Clemenceau, just behind the town's tourist office. ● *Tues-Sat 1-6pm. Rue Jean-Jaurès (tel: 02 51 47 48 35). Free.*

➤**Maison Renaissance**. On the corner of the oldest square in town is an elegant Italianate house dating from 1566, which contains summer exhibitions about the growth of La Roche from a humble village to the focal point of the Vendée, and also about one of the region's famous sons, visionary aircraft designer René Couzinet (1904-56). ○ *1 July-31 Aug, Mon-Sat 2.30-6pm. Closed public holidays. Place de la Vieille Horloge (tel: 02 51 47 90 86). Free.*

➤**Les Flâneries**. Large shopping mall 7km north of La Roche which, as well as providing retail therapy, offers a haven for holidaymakers in wet weather (for shelter) and on hot days (for its air-conditioning). Shops, mostly open through lunchtime, include a pet shop, DIY, electrical, clothes and furniture stores; there are also several fast-food outlets (including McDonald's).

For food shopping, you can head a few hundred metres north to a Carrefour hypermarket. It is part of another large complex that also contains a Norauto store, for car accessories, and a Jardiland for everything to do with gardens and which also has an extensive pet department. ● *Mon-Sat 9am-7pm. Route de Nantes.* 占

➤**Lac de Moulin-Papon**. You'll need a good map in order to find your way to the shore of this 5km-long lake just north of La Roche. Although no swimming is permitted, you can sail or fish, and there is a very lengthy footpath that makes almost a complete circuit, with information panels on the way giving details of local flora. ●

➤**Abbaye des Fontenelles**. The proud remains of a Romanesque abbey, built in 1210 and partially destroyed by the English during the Hundred Years War, loom half-hidden among outbuildings and trees at a farm 3km west of La Roche. Inside is the tomb of Béatrice de Machecoul, an ogress reputed to have eaten the hearts of small children. After repenting, she did penance by walking 25km barefoot from Talmont to here, on a route strewn with brambles. Today it is private property, and the interior is accessible only to pigeons. However, the owners do permit visitors to walk discreetly around the outside to glimpse the tracery of the church's vaulting through the tall, glassless windows, to admire the carved stone faces grimacing beneath the eaves, and to peek into the roofless chapter house on the south side. ● *Signposted N of N2160. Follow the lane for a couple of kilometres, park outside farm entrance & walk up the drive.*

➤**Musée Ornithologique Charles Payraudeau**. About 2,000 stuffed birds—from sparrows to spoonbills—were left to the town of La Chaize-le-Vicomte by a 19th-century naturalist. Restored, perky and impeccably displayed against a black background, they are neatly labelled and given

Market: Tues-Sat, in Les Halles, or food hall. Second Mon of the month (large open-air market), Place Napoléon.
Restaurants:
Le Clemenceau. *Brasserie downstairs for quick lunches (dish of the day from 7€), & upstairs for more leisurely meals; main courses from 11€. 40 Rue Georges-Clemenceau (tel: 02 51 37 10 20).*
Le St-Charles. *Small, elegant restaurant to the north of Place Napoléon; set menus from 17€. 38 Rue de Gaulle (tel: 02 51 47 71 37).*
Crafts: **Halles Artisanat**. *High-quality textiles, baskets, lamps, furniture & pottery made by local craftspeople. Tues-Sat 9.30am-12.15pm & 2.30-7pm. Carreau des Halles, near market-hall (tel: 02 51 62 51 33).*
Brocante: **La Trocante**. *Huge junk emporium. Mon, & Wed-Sat 10am-noon & 2-7pm. Route de Nantes, 1km N of La Roche (tel: 02 51 08 83 61).*
Factory shop: **Intercycles**. *Bikes for men, women & children, plus helmets & other accessories. Mon 3-7pm, Tues-Sat 9am-noon & 2-7pm. Zone Acti-Sud, 9 Rue Ampère (tel: 02 51 44 51 50).*

coloured codes showing which can legally be shot! The museum is located on the first floor of La Chaize's *mairie*, on the western fringe of the village. Before you leave La Chaize, it's worth exploring the back streets a bit. The town contains the Vendée's largest Romanesque church—an austere, fortified building with unadorned granite walls within and some detailed sculpted tops to the columns—and, below the east end of the church, some solid medieval walls edging the grounds of a 19th-century château. ● *Museum: Mon-Fri 9am-noon & 2-5pm. Mairie, La Chaize-le-Vicomte, 9km E of La Roche (tel: 02 51 05 70 21). 2€, children free.*

LES SABLES-D'OLONNE
ⓘ tel: 02 51 96 85 85 fax: 02 51 96 85 71
www.ot-lessablesdolonne.fr
info@ot-lessablesdolonne.fr

By far the most ritzy seaside resort in the Vendée, Les Sables offers a vast and gently-shelving beach of ultra-manicured sand. On the other side of the same spit of land is a busy fishing port lined with good restaurants. Between the two is an area of narrow, surprisingly hilly streets full of old houses and interesting shops. Don't miss the witty shell murals adorning the walls of the area called l'Ile Pénotte (see page 82).

The dazzling glass building on the seafront houses the tourist office, and also a theatre, disco, restaurant and one of the town's two casinos. From about 8.30pm on summer evenings the main beachfront promenade—usually referred to as "Le Remblai"—is full of lively street performers entertaining passers-by in front of the pavement cafés.

Shoppers will enjoy the pedestrianised streets to the east and north of the church, while small children will probably prefer the little roundabouts in Place de la Liberté, the gardens near the *hôtel de ville* (town hall), just to the east of the Muséum des Coquillages.

If you fancy a trip out to sea—for a simple jaunt round the bay, an opportunity to fish for mackerel to take home for supper, or to spend a few hours on board a working trawler—various possibilities are available through the tourist office. For those who like things a little speedier, between Easter and September a 30-knot craft can take you in an

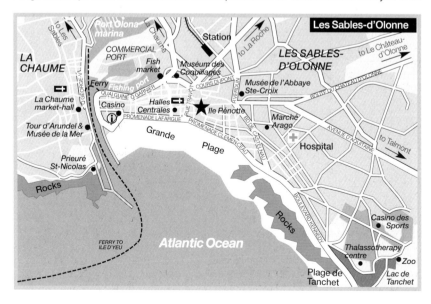

hour to the Ile d'Yeu where you can spend an enjoyable day cycling around this attractive island (see page 61).

Parking can be a problem. Meters function relentlessly in season, even on Sundays and public holidays. Alternatives are to find a car park, to make for one of the residential streets behind the eastern end of the beach, or to drive around to La Chaume (see page 83), where there is less pressure on space, and then take the inexpensive little passenger ferry across the harbour mouth.

➤**Halles Centrales**. If you enter the lovely glass-and brick-built market-hall from Rue du Palais, on the seaward side of the building, you arrive at first-floor level where small farmers sell their produce on Wednesdays and Saturdays. From here, an escalator carries you down to the ground floor where you find a terrific selection of colourful food stalls offering glistening shellfish, heaps of golden *mirabelle* plums, gleaming mountains of butter, and fragrant bunches of fresh herbs such as basil and coriander. ● *Tues-Sun 8am-1pm (15 June-15 Sept, daily 8am-1pm).* ♿

➤**Rue de l'Enfer**. This street, off the south side of Rue des Halles and several blocks west of the central market-hall, is reputed to be the narrowest in France. You'll need to breathe in to squeeze along it—at the bottom, the walls on either side hardly allow for the width of an average person's shoulders. ●

➤ ★ **Ile Pénotte**. Among the quirkiest features of Les Sables is an ever-extending series of shell murals created by one of the residents of a little street just behind the seafront promenade. Near the beachside clocktower, and just to the north of it, you will see a street called Rue Travot heading inland from the Remblai. Start walking along it, and take the first right into Rue d'Assas. Facing you is a splendid representation of Neptune (see picture, page 34, and another design below). Along both sides of this and adjacent streets is a variety of further decorations made from mussel, scallop, cockle and limpet shells. Look up, look down and look round corners—some are in the most unexpected places. ● *Rue d'Assas.* ♿

➤**Muséum du Coquillage**. More than 50,000 shells of all kinds, from familiar winkles and sea-urchins to the colourful, speckled and exotic produce of the South Seas. Beautifully presented in glass cases, most of them have chatty descriptions in English as well as French. ● *Mon-Sat 9.30am-noon & 2-7pm, Sun 2-7pm (1 Apr-31 May & 1 Sept-31 Oct, daily 9.30am-noon & 2-7pm; 1 July-31 Aug, daily 9.30am-8pm). 8 Rue du Maréchal Leclerc, at eastern end of fishing harbour (tel: 02 51 23 50 00). 6€, children 4€.* ♿

➤*Baron Rouge II*/**Parachute Ascensionnel**. If you've a head for heights and don't mind being suspended 80-130 metres above a boat bobbing on the Atlantic, you can try the sport of parascending. Instructor Robert Garrido will send you up on a tethered parachute, and let you walk on the water—if you wish—before he winches you back on board. ○ *Late June to early Sept, daily 10am-7pm (advance booking recommended). Les Circaètes, Port Olona (tel: 06 09 80 28 70); departures from the dinghy base at western end of Les Sables main beach. Individual flight 36€; tandem flight 57€; boat trip with no flight 14€.*

➤**Musée de l'Abbaye de Ste-Croix**. Delightful museum and gallery of modern art in one wing of a 17th-century building that was formerly a

LES SABLES EXTRAS

Markets: Tues-Sun (late June-mid Sept, daily), Halles Centrales (see main entry). Daily (plus open-air stalls on Tues, Fri, Sun & public holidays), Marché Arago. Wed & Sat, Cours Dupont. Mon-Sat (fish) 8.30am-12.30pm & 4-7pm, Fish-market building, Quai Franqueville.
Specialities: *Tuna. Langoustines. Sole.*
Restaurants:
Le Bistrot du Port. *Divine mussels served in a choice of five ways at around 11€, plus grills & seafood, on the fishing harbour. 7 Quai Garnier (tel: 02 51 21 55 45).*
La Fleur des Mers. *Chic dining overlooking the fishing harbour. Weekday lunches from 15€, other menus from 21€. 5 Quai Guiné (tel: 02 51 95 18 10).*
Brocante: ***Marché aux Puces.*** *Flea market. 1 July-31 Aug, Fri 8am-7pm. Place de la Liberté, SW of station.*
Festivals:
Festival Georges Simenon. *Celebration of the Belgian writer, who spent time in Les Sables during World War II. June.*
Régates de la Ch'nou. *Old-style fishing boats & maritime traditions. Aug.*

Benedictine convent. Temporary exhibitions are held throughout the year; the permanent collection, which is often shifted around to different parts of the building, includes a couple of charming pictures of Les Sables in the 1920s by Albert Marquet (1875-1947), a large selection of colourful collages and paintings by Gaston Chaissac (1910-64), an exponent of *"art brut"*, and a collection of mixed-media Surrealist works by Romanian artist Victor Brauner (1903-66). Some of the latter are a bit explicit, so you might want to preview them before finding yourself compelled to give children an impromptu sex-education lesson!

Under a network of beams in the attic is a marvellous collection of local costumes, model ships and items relating to the fishing industry, including some wonderful naïve paintings of boats by fisherman-turned-artist Paul-Émile Pajot (1873-1929) and his son Gilbert. With their accurate depictions of fishing boats and their rigging, of dolphins cavorting in front of the bows, and of rows of freshly-caught fish hanging along the decks, the Pajots were in great demand from shipowners, who commissioned them to portray their sardine- and tuna-fishing vessels. Many of the pictures represent dramatic events such as battles, or storms on the high seas. ● *Tues-Sun 2.30-5.30pm (15 June-30 Sept, Tues-Sun 10am-noon & 2.30-6.30pm). Closed public holidays. Rue de Verdun (tel: 02 51 32 01 16). 4.60€ (first Sun of month, free), children 2.30€.*

➤ Zoo des Sables. Beyond the southernmost end of the seafront, or promenade, some 2km from the town centre, is a small but delightfully laid-out zoo, with a collection of reptiles, exotic birds, big cats, wallabies and other animals in a tree-filled park alongside the River Tanchet. Free-roaming monkeys swing down from the trees to investigate the rubbish bins among the rose bushes and fragrant frangipani trees, and otters dive into a glass-sided pool so you can watch their underwater antics. Feeding-times are posted at the gate. It's very family-friendly, with ramps for pushchairs, lots of picnic spots, and notices telling you that the ducks love popcorn. (You can buy bags of corn at the gate.) ● *Daily 2-6pm (15 Feb-1 Nov, daily 10.30am-noon & 2-6pm; 1 Apr-15 Sept, daily 9.30am-7pm). Route du Tanchet (tel: 02 51 95 14 10). 11€, children 6€.* &

LA CHAUME (LES SABLES)

On the other side of the channel that links the port of Les Sables with the sea lies the picturesque former fishing village of La Chaume. You can drive around to it, passing round the north side of Port Olona marina on the large boulevard, or take a three-minute ferry ride across the harbour mouth from the Quai Guiné pontoon, on the Les Sables side. Near the little market building, at the side of the imposing Château St-Clair, is one of La Chaume's most distinctive pieces of architecture—the square-sided Tour d'Arundel that still serves as a lighthouse. If you

■ La Chaume: maritime tradition.

make your way to La Chaume's other major landmark, the church—a few blocks inland from the busy quay—you'll find in the square outside that a once-dreary blank wall has been transformed by the hand of an artist into a jokey and imaginative view of the village.

➤ Port Olona. More than 1,000 yachts are moored in this busy marina, full of shops, restaurants and bars—occasionally with live music in the evenings—near the north end of La Chaume's quay. The port hits the headlines every four years as the start and finish of the single-handed, non-stop, round-the-world sailing race known as the Vendée-Globe Challenge. Brainchild of the famous yachtsman Philippe Jeantot, the event has given rise to some heroic exploits by competitors, including many British. Among those who made the UK news were Pete Goss, in 1996/97, and Ellen MacArthur, in 2000/01. The winner usually accomplishes the gruelling circumnavigation in about 110 days. In a Vendée-Globe year, the start of the race is usually in early November; for a month or so beforehand the competitors are gathered at La Chaume for final trials and preparations,

■ **All at sea: the Tour d'Arundel overlooks the busy harbour channel between Les Sables and La Chaume.**

and the public can visit the race pontoons to inspect the tall-masted, smartly fitted-out single-hulled yachts, and may even have a chance to encourage their favourite skipper. (To miss the crowds on these occasions, it's advisable to turn up around lunch-time—and to avoid weekends.)
● *Capitainerie (harbourmaster's office), Port du Vendée-Globe (tel: 02 51 32 51 16).*
➤**Les Salines: En bateau**. This remarkable river-boat journey gives a real insight into the salt industry that used to flourish in the marshes north of Les Sables, as well as into the fish-farming that has taken over. Don't be put off by the rows of plastic chairs on the flat craft that carries you on the guided, two-hour excursion into the marshes. En route, you disembark and watch the guide pick up a long-handled, rake-like *simouche* to skim the salty crystals from the surface of the salt-pans, or demonstrate the sluices and channels that let the salt water in to dry out under the baking sun. (There's no shade on board, so take sunhats, and garments with sleeves in hot weather.) From June to September, one *oeillet*—the series of square pans in which the sea-water evaporates to form salt—produces between 15 and 35kg of salt, depending on how much rain falls to hinder the process. Fifty years ago, the area contained 30,000 *oeillets*, but today only about 100 remain in production. The salt-pans are flooded for the winter to protect them from the cold, and then drained and tidied up in March ready for a new season. Ask for the explanatory leaflet in English before you set out. ◑ *Mid Apr-30 Sept, days & times vary according to tides (booking essential). Port Olona car park, Boulevard de l'Ile-Vertime; car park entrance is next to the Bowling building (tel: 02 51 21 01 19). 14€, children 6€.*
➤**Les Salines: Site Historique**. An open-air trail winds along bumpy paths, and up and down steps, among old salt-workings 3km north-west of Les Sables. Ask for an English leaflet first to help understand the taped commentaries at various points. These explain the history of the salt industry—so vital for preserving foodstuffs in days before canning and refrigeration. A reconstructed Roman clay oven shows how heat was used to evaporate salt from sea-water 2,000 years ago, and a present-day salt-maker demonstrates how he harvests the "white gold" from

LA CHAUME EXTRAS

Market: Tues, Thur, Sun
(1 July-31 Aug, Tues-Sun).
Restaurants:
Le Port. *Traditional fishy dishes; menus from 13.90€; first-floor tables have view over harbour channel. 24 Quai George-V (tel: 02 51 32 07 52).*
Loulou Panoramique. *Unprepossessing exterior, but from inside this smart restaurant you enjoy amazing views over waves crashing onto the rocks below, & delicious menus from 20€.*
19 Route Bleue, 2km W of La Chaume by clifftop road (tel: 02 51 21 32 32).

his *oeillets* (see previous entry). The crippling salt tax (*la gabelle*), introduced in 1340, is described, and a building designed with ropes and flapping canvas to evoke a sailing ship houses an exhibition on Les Sables' once-great cod-fishing industry. (Until the time of Louis XIV, the boats went on three-month voyages to fish off Newfoundland, or *Terre-Neuve*, taking salt to preserve their catches till they could be sold on return to France.) Allow a couple of hours to see it all. You can rent canoes at the same spot; from 11€ an hour for up to three people, to use on the narrow marshland canals nearby. ❶ *1 Apr-30 Sept, daily 10am-12.30pm & 2-6pm (1 June-31 Aug, daily 9am-7pm). 120 Route de l'Aubraie (the D87A, north of the Bowling building); in L'Aubraie village follow the sign to the canoe base (tel: 02 51 90 87 74). 7.50€, children 4€.*

➤**Musée de la Mer et de la Pêche**. Scale-models, naval objects, plans and documents are on show—though slightly lacking in explanation—in the 12th-century Château St-Clair, alongside the imposing Tour d'Arundel. The small museum devotes its downstairs area to nautical matters and the floor above to La Chaume's important fishing industry. You can also read a little about the local sailor-turned-pirate, the bloodthirsty "Nau l'Olonnois", who mercilessly tortured his victims in the Caribbean and was himself eaten by cannibals in 1671. ❶ *1 Apr-30 Sept, daily 10.30am-12.30pm & 3-7pm. Château St-Clair (tel: 02 51 95 53 11). 2.50€, children 1.30€.*

➤**Prieuré St-Nicolas**. Beautifully restored Romanesque church, and one-time fort, in a wonderful position on the point, overlooking the ocean and the entrance to Les Sables harbour channel. Exhibitions and concerts are held in the summer, giving a chance to view the plain stone interior. ● *Open during exhibitions; times & admission charges vary.*

ST-ÉTIENNE-DU-BOIS
ⓘ tel: 02 51 34 52 11 fax: 02 51 34 54 10

This inland village 19km north-west of La Roche-sur-Yon still has a few Renaissance houses clustered around its church—though one side of the square has been somewhat blighted by an ultra-modern *mairie*. Walk down the hill behind the church to the *lavoir*, or washing-place, and you'll find a noticeboard with maps of local footpaths: if you've an hour to spare, the Sentier du Coteau—through woodland and across an ancient bridge made of megalithic stones—makes a delightful walk.

➤**Chapelle de la Tullévrière**. A cockerel and a cross decorate the roof of this small chapel in a hamlet 5km north-east of St-Étienne, on the D94. It was rebuilt in 1835 on the site of an earlier building where one of the rebel priests (see page 32) celebrated Mass during the Wars of the Vendée. Within the simple interior, two stained-glass windows show clandestine religious services of the time. On the wall is a memorial to 22 local martyrs—men, women and children—who were slaughtered on 1 March 1794, as they attempted to hide from a Republican death squad. ●

ST-RÉVÉREND
ⓘ tel: 02 51 54 61 11 fax: 02 51 55 94 40
www.cc-atlancia.fr

If you approach this small village, 8km east of St-Gilles-Croix-de-Vie, from the direction of Coëx you'll notice two significant landmarks as you drive along the D6. One is the giant water-tower, painted with beach and golfing scenes by an artist who must have had a good head for heights; the other is St-Révérend's 19th-century windmill (see below), its picturesque white, slatted sails rotating gently above the treetops.

➤**Moulin des Gourmands**. The restored windmill is an imposing sight from the road, and tells the story of milling—from the field of corn you pass on the way in, to the bread oven and *crêperie* you can stop at before you leave. During the guided tour visitors are taken from top to bottom of the building, while the miller explains how he controls the sail area by pulling levers from inside, and points out some carefully-preserved sketches of the mill and of a miller's donkey, drawn on the wall by a long-vanished predecessor. ◑ *Late Mar-mid June, Sat, Sun & public holidays 2-6pm; mid June-late Sept, Sat, Sun & Wed 2-6pm (1 July-31 Aug, daily 10am-7pm). St-Révérend (tel: 02 51 60 16 72). 4.60€, children 2.30€.*

❯**Roseraie de Vendée.** Early June is the best time to catch the flowers in bloom at this garden, 2km to the west of the village, which exhibits 8,000 roses (950 varieties) within its 3 hectares. They are grouped by name (countries, first names, famous people and so on), and also by type—such as perfumed, old-fashioned, and varieties for special situations—and the owners make a virtue of the fact that they don't spray for pests or diseases, so that you can see which varieties might be most susceptible. Take a sunhat in hot weather, as the grounds have little shade. Rose-flavoured jams, liqueurs and syrup available in the shop. ◑ *Mid May-mid Oct, daily 10am-7pm (guided tours May & June, Sat; July & Aug, Wed). Rond-Point des 4 Chemins, signposted off D6, near the D32 crossroads (tel: 02 51 55 24 03). 2€, under-13s free.*

TALMONT-ST-HILAIRE

ⓘ tel: 02 51 90 65 10 fax: 02 51 20 71 80
www.ot-talmont-bourgenay.com
ot.talmont.bourgenay@wanadoo.fr

A former port of great charm nestles below the impressive remains of a medieval castle that once belonged to the powerful Princes of Talmont and, between 1152 and 1204, to the English crown. A little less ancient, up the hill behind the castle, are some beautiful old ivy-covered mansions. And very much more of today is the modern Vendée Air Park, 4km along the D4 towards La Roche-sur-Yon—a private, American-style development where owners of light aircraft can buy a house with a plane-sized garage, and a taxiway running past the front door.

Talmont and Port-Bourgenay tourist offices can advise on visits to the nearby oyster beds and salt-marshes, organised between July and September around the village of La Guittière. There are also guided tours of the woodland and dunes around the lovely little beach of Le Veillon, 5km to the south-west, where dinosaur footprints have been found in the rock, and are still sometimes uncovered at the lowest tides.

❯ ★ **Château de Talmont.** Richard Coeur-de-Lion (the English king Richard the Lionheart, son of Henry Plantagenet of England and of his French wife, Eleanor of Aquitaine) spent a good deal of time hunting in the neighbouring forests and was responsible for building Talmont castle. The imposing ruins you see today are for the most part 12th-century; the castle was much fought over during the Wars of Religion, and reduced to its present state in 1628. From the top of the keep there are marvellous views over the town, countryside, marshes and sea. Throughout July and August there is a daily programme of medieval events—including some in English—with costumed performers encouraging visitors to try archery or calligraphy, to watch "knights" kneeling to be dubbed, or to learn the steps of medieval dances. Extra combats and cannon-firing take place on most Wednesdays in summer and children's games on most Thursdays. ◑ *Late Mar-15 June, daily 10.30am-12.30pm & 2-6.30pm; 16 June-21 Sept, daily 11am-7pm; 22 Sept-2 Nov, daily 2-6pm. Place du Port (tel: 02 51 90 27 43). 3.65€, children 1.90€ (plus 2€ for "King's Ransom" historical trail); 1 July-31 Aug, 6.50€, children 3.10€ (includes entertainment); under-sevens free.*

❯ ★ **Les Nuits de Richard Coeur-de-Lion.** After nightfall, you can follow an atmospheric, hugely enjoyable self-guided trail around the castle (see above) and its grounds, with fantastic lighting effects and scenic projections illustrating the castle's history. Take a torch to help light your way on the sometimes uneven ground, and to read the English/French captions at various points along the way. You are advised to wear stout shoes and warm, windproof clothes, and to avoid the initial crush of visitors by not arriving till at least 30 minutes after the opening time. *Place du Port (tel: 02 51 90 27 43).* ◐ *May (dates vary each year; ring for information); 1-30 June, Wed & Sat from 10.30pm; 1 July-31 Aug, daily 10pm; 1-20 Sept, Wed & Sat 9pm. Closed 14 July. 7.25€, children 3.20€; under-sevens free.*

■ **Fine vintage: cars at Talmont's Musée Automobile.**

❯**Musée Automobile de Vendée.** More than 150 immaculately-presented vehicles (mostly French, of course, but well labelled in English) dating from 1885 to the 1960s are lined up in this large motor museum 6km west of Talmont. Alongside such famous names as De Dion-Bouton, Bugatti and Hispano-Suiza are selections of horse-drawn carriages, bicycles and motor-bikes, and some beautiful old posters advertising glorious cars of the past. The collection comes up to date with Maserati and Ferrari, and a Jeep Grand Cherokee with the side cut away to show the transmission system. ◐ *1 Apr-early Oct, daily 9.30am-noon & 2-6.30pm (1 June-31 Aug, daily 9.30am-7pm). On D949, Route de Talmont (tel: 02 51 22 05 81). 7.80€, children 4.20€.* ♿

❯**Port de la Guittière.** The waterside area of this salt-making and fishing village lies 4.5km south of Talmont, where the sheltered waters of the Payré river provide perfect conditions for fattening oysters. Although the port is not specially picturesque, you can be certain that down here at the water's edge you will be buying the very freshest shellfish direct from the various producers. ●

❯**Port-Bourgenay.** Traffic-free holiday development and sports complex 5km south-west of Talmont, with plenty of activities ranging from tennis to croquet, swimming to golf (see listings, right). Down on the waterside, beyond a comically-turreted private castle, is a marina with cafés, restaurants and yacht-orientated shops. ●

❯**Aquarium.** A new project, due to open in 2005, 7km south-west of Talmont, promises visitors 24 large aquariums containing Atlantic fish, coral fish, and the ever-popular sharks. ● *Near the Viviers de la Mine, La Mine, near Port-Bourgenay. Opening details, hours & charges not available at time of writing.*

❯**Figurines d'Art, Éditions Vanot.** Patrick Vanot makes incredibly detailed lead figures for specialised collectors in his studio on the Querry-Pigeon road, 3km west of Talmont. You can watch him at work, pouring molten metal into moulds and spinning them to fling the liquid lead into the farthest recesses. Soldiers on sale—painted or plain—range in period from the Middle Ages, through the Revolution and the Wars of the Vendée to World War I. ○ *1 July-31 Aug, daily 2-7pm. 207 Rue de la Dagoterie, turn off the D4A opposite the Cave Ferré (tel: 02 51 22 28 28). Free.*

❯**Souffleur de Verre.** Jean-Michel Gauthier holds his audience spellbound as he extracts glowing lumps of heat-softened glass from his furnace, and twists, turns and blows them into fantastic shapes full of swirling colour. The shelves in his converted barn are full of vases, lamps and figurines for sale. ● *Tues-Sun 2.30-6.30pm (1 July-31 Aug, daily 9.30am- 12.30pm & 2.30-7.30pm). Rue de Chevrefoy, off D4A, 500 metres N of Port-Bourgenay (tel: 02 51 22 27 13). Free.*

TALMONT EXTRAS

Market: Sat (1 July-31 Aug), & third Thurs of the month.

***Specialities:** Oysters.*

***Restaurant: Le Pierrot Bar.** Literally on the beach; local oysters, plus mussels, chips & a dessert for 13.70€. Plage du Veillon, 5km SW of Talmont (tel: 02 51 22 22 04).*

***Brocante: Dépôt-Vente.** Furniture & collectibles in town centre. Tues, Wed 3-6.30pm; Thurs-Mon 10am-noon & 3-6.30pm. 42 Rue du Centre (tel: 02 51 20 71 10).*

***Crafts: Lead figures & glass-blowing.** See main entries.*

Festivals:

***Fête Médiévale.** Historical fun. June in odd-numbered years.*

***Fête de la Soue.** Salt festival. La Guittière, 2km S of Talmont. Aug.*

***Golf: Golf de Port-Bourgenay.** 18-hole seaside course (see page 16 for Formule Golf Pass). Port-Bourgenay, 6km SW of Talmont (tel: 02 51 23 35 45).*

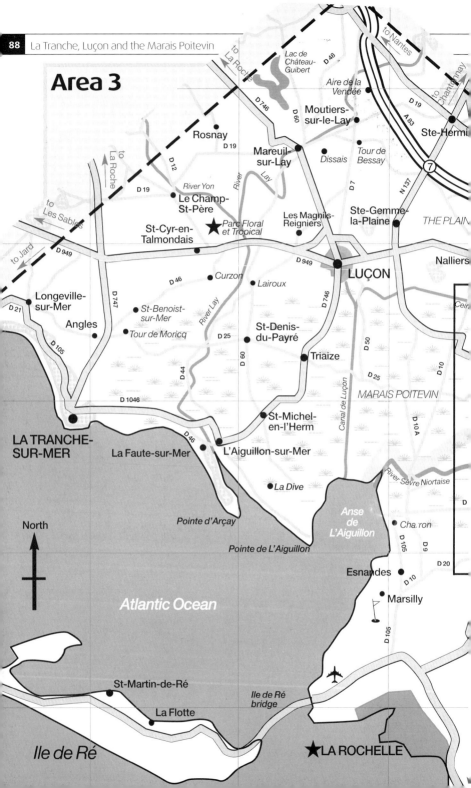

Area 3

to Nantes

to Chantonnay

Lac de Château-Guibert

D 48

Aire de la Vendée

D 60

D 19

A 83

Moutiers-sur-le-Lay

Ste-Hermi

to La Roche

Rosnay

D 19

D 746

Mareuil-sur-Lay

Dissais

Tour de Bessay

Ste-Hermi

7

to La Roche

D 12

River Yon

River Lay

D 7

N 137

Le Champ-St-Père

D 19

St-Cyr-en-Talmondais

Parc Floral et Tropical

Les Magnils-Reigniers

Ste-Gemme-la-Plaine

THE PLAIN

to Les Sables

D 949

D 949

LUÇON

Nalliers

to Jard

Curzon

Lairoux

D 46

D 747

Longeville-sur-Mer

St-Benoist-sur-Mer

River Lay

St-Denis-du-Payré

D 746

D 50

D 25

D 10

D 21

Angles

Tour de Moricq

D 25

Triaize

MARAIS POITEVIN

Cein

D 105

D 60

D 44

Canal de Luçon

D 10A

D 1046

St-Michel-en-l'Herm

D 46

LA TRANCHE-SUR-MER

La Faute-sur-Mer

L'Aiguillon-sur-Mer

River Sèvre Niortaise

D

La Dive

Pointe d'Arçay

Anse de L'Aiguillon

Cha.ron

D 105

D 9

D 20

Pointe de L'Aiguillon

Esnandes

D 10

North

Marsilly

D 105

Atlantic Ocean

St-Martin-de-Ré

Ile de Ré bridge

La Flotte

Ile de Ré

★ LA ROCHELLE

Known for its sunshine, its windsurfing and its flowers, La Tranche has always been a popular holiday destination. If you're looking for relief from the flatness of the surrounding countryside, however, just head north-east to the wine village of Mareuil, the lotus gardens of St-Cyr or the dignified streets of Luçon—for centuries the seat of the bishops of the Vendée. No one should miss a trip east to the magical "Venise Verte", or "Green Venice" marshland. This carefully preserved corner of the Marais Poitevin (Poitou Marshes) is full of picturesque villages where you can travel by boat or bike among a maze of tranquil, tree-shaded waterways. South-east lies historic La Rochelle. This historic port is worth a day-trip for its museums, its shops and its magnificent aquarium. If you'd like ideas for motoring routes the booklet *Balades et Saveurs* ("Trips and Tastes"), free from tourist offices around Luçon, suggests itineraries, and picks some good restaurants to eat at on the way.

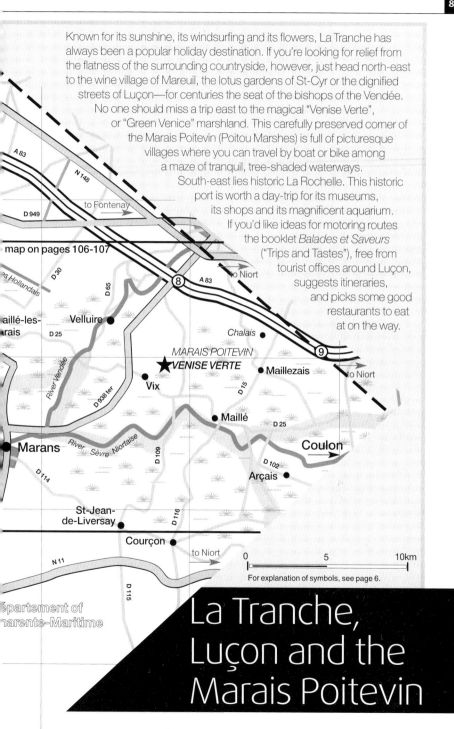

map on pages 106–107

A 83

N 148

to Fontenay

D 949

es Hollandais

D 30

D 65

to Niort

8

A 83

aillé-les-rais

Velluire

D 25

Chalais

MARAIS POITEVIN

VENISE VERTE

Maillezais

to Niort

9

River Vendée

Vix

D 15

D 938 ter

Maillé

D 25

Marans

River Sèvre Niortaise

D 109

Coulon

D 114

D 102

Arçais

St-Jean-de-Liversay

D 116

Courçon

to Niort

N 11

D 115

0   5   10km

For explanation of symbols, see page 6.

Département of Charente-Maritime

La Tranche, Luçon and the Marais Poitevin

L'AIGUILLON-SUR-MER

ⓘ tel: 02 51 56 43 87 fax: 02 51 56 43 91
www.laiguillonsurmer.com
ot.aiguillon.sur.mer@wanadoo.fr

From the quayside of this former trading port at the mouth of the river Lay, 21km south-west of Luçon, ships once loaded cargoes of cereals cultivated on the reclaimed land of the *marais desséché*, the "dry" marsh, or open fenland, to the north-east. L'Aiguillon Bay is one of the largest shellfish-producing areas of France, and oyster- and mussel-farming are still the livelihoods of many who live in the whitewashed cottages and keep their boats alongside the spindly wooden jetties. Legend has it that, in 1255, a shipwrecked Irishman named Patrick Walton was the first to try planting a stake in the water and encouraging mussels to grow on it. Today, at low tide, hundreds of thousands of these *bouchots* are revealed standing in the mud, each holding a rich crop of shellfish.

An artificial lake on the waterfront has its own sandy beach for swimming; if you prefer something bigger, just across the bridge is a vast stretch of fine sand at neighbouring La Faute.

L' AIGUILLON EXTRAS

Market: Tues & Fri.
Specialities: Mussels.
Oysters. Eels.
Restaurant: **Chez
Gégène**. Seafood is much
to the fore at this large
establishment near the
bridge; menus from 12€.
Le Port (tel: 02 51 56 40 43).
Brocante: *Dépôt-Vente*.
Wed, Thurs, Sat 10am-
noon & 3-7pm; Fri 3-7pm
(1-30 Apr & 1 July-31
Aug, Tues-Sat 9.30am-
noon & 2.30-7pm. Zone
Artisanale, Boulevard des
Courlis (tel: 02 51 97 17 17).
Factory shop: *Aux P'tites
Puces*. See main entry.

➤**Aux P'tites Puces**. If you're in search of fabric for upholstery, summer frocks, mackintoshes or lace curtains try the three outlet shops on this site. They sell every conceivable type of material, much of it end-of-range—priced by the kilogram. Snip off the length that you want and it will be weighed, and the price calculated, at the checkout. ● *Wed-Sat 9.30am-12.30pm & 2.30-6.45pm (1-30 Apr & 1 July-31 Aug, Tues-Sat 9.30am-12.30pm & 2.30-6.45pm). Zone Artisanale (signposted from D746, St-Michel road), Boulevard des Courlis (tel: 02 51 56 46 97).*

➤**Pointe de l'Aiguillon**. A long spit of land juts out into L'Aiguillon Bay, bordered by a concrete dyke that protects the hard-won fields from the sea. From the road alongside it you have views of the wind-carved cliffs of La Dive—a former island rising to a dizzy 15 metres above the flat fields—and, to the south, of the gracefully curving bridge linking the city of La Rochelle with the Ile de Ré. A high, crumbling wall beside the road blocks the outlook on the seaward side, but you can clamber up primitive steps that stick out of it to see the mussel-posts stretching away to the horizon at low tide. To the east lie the mud-flats of the Anse de L'Aiguillon, a bay that is now a wildfowl reserve visited by avocets and other waders.

■ Snipe: wetland birds.

Between September and November nearly half a million migrating birds pass this way—in greatest numbers just after sunrise. Volunteers from the Ligue pour la Protection des Oiseaux (a French equivalent of the RSPB) organise guided visits. ● *Bird-watching information from LPO (tel: 02 51 46 21 91), or from L'Aiguillon tourist office.*

ANGLES

ⓘ tel: 02 51 97 56 39 fax: 02 51 97 56 40
www.angles.fr
tourisme@angles.fr

The primitive bear sculpture that peers down from above the west door of the ancient church is the main curiosity of this attractive village, 20km west of Luçon. According to local folklore, the beast was a dangerous animal that abducted and ate the village's youngest and most beautiful maidens. A holy man managed to tame the "malabête," as the animal is known, turn it to stone, and place it in this elevated position where it could do no further harm.

> **Église d'Angles**. The interior of the village's handsome church arouses a great deal of interest for the way its design bridges the Romanesque and the later Plantagenet styles. Rounded arches characteristic of the 12th century rub shoulders with the finer, more graceful architecture that followed. Three statues look down on visitors. A simply-carved figure high above the nave is thought to represent Henri Plantagenêt (who, as King Henry II, ruled England from 1154 to 1189); the two more sophisticated works are said to be of his wife, Eleanor of Aquitaine, and of their son Richard Coeur-de-Lion (Richard I of England). ●

> **Église de St-Benoist**. Another church with a strange animal on the roof is that of St-Benoist-sur-Mer, a village 3km north-east of Angles. If you stand back far enough (don't worry about falling into the sea; it's retreated 12km over the centuries) you can just make out the figure of a rabbit, apparently placed there as a joke by the original monastic builders, and it's—yes—smoking a pipe! Inside the cool, stone-flagged, 11th-century nave, the church's mossy walls are outshone by a surprisingly ornate and colourful Renaissance altarpiece. ●

> **Tour de Moricq**. Marooned in the marshland 2km east of Angles, at the eastern end of the village of Moricq, rises a majestic isolated square tower built in the 15th century, on what was then the coast, to defend the mouth of the river Lay. The port of Moricq silted up four centuries later, and the tower fell into disrepair. Today partially renovated, it can be viewed from the outside; during occasional guided visits of the interior, you can look up inside at the imposing fireplaces still clinging to the walls at the different levels. ● *Exterior only;* ○ *1 July-31 Aug, guided tours; days & times from Angles tourist office (tel: 02 51 97 56 39). Free.*

ANGLES EXTRAS

Market: Sun & Wed (both 1 July-31 Aug). Third Thurs of month.

Shop: *L'Aluette*. A large selection of locally-made crafts, from hand-blown glass to wooden toys. Late June-early Sept, daily 10.30am-12.30pm & 3-7.30pm. Rue des Forges.

Festivals:
L'Été des 4 Jeudis. Folk music & dancing. Four Thursdays in July & Aug.
La Guinguette. Music & singing in the streets. Aug.

CHAILLÉ-LES-MARAIS

ⓘ tel: 02 51 56 71 17 fax: 02 51 56 71 36
ot.islesmaraispoitevin@wanadoo.fr

CHAILLÉ EXTRAS

Market: Thurs.
Speciality: Melons.
Brocante: *Dépôt-Vente Sud-Vendée*. Tues-Sun 2-7pm. On N137 at entrance to Chaillé (tel: 02 51 56 79 07).

The ancient capital of the "dry" marsh, or drained fenland area of the Marais Poitevin, 14km south-east of Luçon, was once an island; cliffs rising alongside the D25 make you realise you are, indeed, driving along the former sea bed. If you drive through here in July and August, you'll get closer to the soul of the region (and probably move faster) by taking the smaller roads through the little marshland villages.

The monks from five nearby abbeys who began drainage work in the 12th century, when the estuary that covered this region began to silt up, are commemorated in the Canal des Cinq Abbés (dug in 1217). Lying just south of Chaillé, it runs roughly north-east/south-west and divides the fertile, open meadows of the "dry" marsh *(marais desséché)* from the more picturesque, tree-lined "wet" marshland *(marais mouillé)* known as the "Venise Verte", or "Green Venice", to the east (see page 105). Another canal, the Ceinture des Hollandais (1645), separates the marshes from the plain lying to the north. It takes its name from the Dutch engineers brought in centuries later by Henri IV and Louis XIII to rescue the intricate system from the effects of a succession of wars.

All this water makes the area a fishermen's paradise, and Chaillé tourist office—tucked against the bottom of a small cliff on the busy N137—provides especially good information on the subject, with maps, and tips on where to look for black-bass, zander, carp and pike, as well as details about permits, shellfish-digging and different fishing techniques.

>**Maison du Petit Poitou**. A charming little museum, lying just to the north-west of Chaillé. Local farming traditions are explained, including the making of cowpat fuel that was highly prized for cooking and heating, and the sport of "cow hunting" (going out shooting, using an obliging cow as cover so as to be able to approach wild ducks unseen). Snowy-white skeletons of different marshland animals and birds are beautifully displayed, along with dissected pellets revealing the diets of owls, herons and other birds. Outside, are some typical livestock of the region: goats, cows, mules and a rather grumpy *baudet du Poitou* (a shaggy-coated local breed of donkey). ◑ *1 Apr-30 Sept, daily 2-6pm (1 July-31 Aug, Mon-Sat 10am-7pm, Sun 2-7pm). On N137 (tel: 02 51 56 77 30). 3.70€, children 2€; family (2+2) 11.40€.*

>**Réserve Biologique Départementale de Nalliers/Mouzeuil-St-Martin**. A marshland nature reserve 6km north of Chaillé is home to otters, kingfishers and herons, and also to many rare plants typical of this watery habitat. You can visit it at any time (trainers or walking-boots are the recommended footwear), but from spring to autumn the warden leads guided walks from the small Maison de la Réserve (visitor centre), pointing out signs of bird and animal life and drawing your attention to the most interesting vegetation of the season. ● *Access at all times.* ◑ *Guided tours: mid Apr-31 Aug: Wed, Sat, Sun, 9am, 11am, 4pm & 6pm; 1 Sept-31 Oct: Wed, Sat, Sun, 9am, 11am, 2pm & 4pm. Les Huttes, on D10 near Nalliers (tel: 02 51 30 96 22). Free.*

ESNANDES (Charente-Maritime)
ⓘ tel: 05 46 01 32 13

ESNANDES EXTRAS
Speciality: Mussels, especially mouclade (a dish of mussels, served in a cream & curry sauce).

Since the 13th century, fishermen from this village 12km north of La Rochelle, and from neighbouring Charron, have used sturdy, flat-bottomed boats called *acons* to collect a daily harvest of mussels from the thousands of stakes planted in L'Aiguillon Bay. The finer points of the business are explained in Esnandes' fascinating mussel-farming museum. The village's strongly-fortified Romanesque church is visible for miles, and offers superb vistas over marshes and countryside. For another great view, this time over the sea, drive west along the D106E to Pointe St-Clément, past crumbling cliffs and the damp salt-meadows known as *mizottes.* Be aware of the tide times, though, as the rising waters can flood the road.

>**Maison de la Mytiliculture**. Once you have watched this museum's video about the labour-intensive mussel-farming industry (*mytiliculture* in French), you will be amazed that these succulent shellfish can still be so inexpensive. The air-conditioned, renovated building, across the square from the church, contains interesting displays on the geography and biology of the area and explanations of the tides that bring daily nourishment to the shellfish fattening on the mud-flats. More than a million *bouchots*, or mussel-posts, are planted out in the shallows; each mussel takes 16 months to reach maturity. ◑ *Late Feb-early Nov, Wed-Mon 2-6pm (1 June-15 Sept, daily 10.30am-12.30pm & 2-7pm). Place de l'Église (tel: 05 46 01 34 64). 3.50€, children 2.50€.* ♿

>**Église St-Martin**. At first glance, the battlemented 12th-century church across from Esnandes' mussel museum looks more like a fortress. Built on the edge of what was the coast, before the long-vanished Picton Gulf was drained, it has a rooftop sentry-way that still commands extensive views over l'Aiguillon Bay and the marshes. ◑ *Mid May-early Nov, Wed-Mon 2-7pm (15 June-15 Sept, daily 10am-12.30pm & 2-7pm). Place de l'Église (tel: 05 46 01 34 64). 1.50€.*

>**Musée des Graffiti Anciens**. At the top of a church tower in the nearby village of Marsilly is a curious collection of plaster copies of drawings and inscriptions from the walls of buildings in the region. The oldest shows a 12th-century knight with his shield; the most recent is a poignant note from a German soldier in hospital during World War II. You can climb higher for a view across the marshland. (Don't forget the binoculars; you won't want to go down the 113 steps to get them.) ◑ *1 Apr-11 Nov, Sat, Sun 10.30am-12.30pm & 2-5.30pm (1 Apr-30 Sept, Wed-Sun 2.30-6.30pm). Marsilly, 3km SW of Esnandes (tel: 05 46 01 49 06). 2.80€, students 2.30€, children under 12 free.*

LA FAUTE-SUR-MER

ⓘ tel: 02 51 56 45 19 fax: 02 51 97 18 08
www.lafautesurmer.com
ot.lafautesurmer@wanadoo.fr

LA FAUTE EXTRAS

Market: Thurs & Sun
(both 15 June-15 Sept).
Specialities: Oysters.
Mussels.
Festival: Les 24 Heures
du Roller. Rollerblading
weekend. Early June.

Set on a sandy peninsula between the sea and the river Lay, 23km south-west of Luçon, La Faute has successfully resisted the high-rise developments that mar so many of today's seaside resorts. Its 10km of beaches and much-vaunted microclimate attract a host of summer visitors; in July and August the town's population increases from its normal 1,000 souls to more than 40,000. However, there is room for all on the golden sands—though to reach any of them does require quite a hike over the dunes.

Among the beaches, the Grande Plage is overlooked by La Faute's casino, which has a restaurant and nightclub open to all—not just to gamblers; the Plage des Bellugas has an area given over to sand-yachting; and the Plage des Chardons is backed with pine woods that offer welcome shade in summer. Parking can be difficult in peak season in the areas by the casino; it's slightly easier farther south, near the forest.

➤**Parcours de Santé**. Athletic holidaymakers will find a circuit laid out near the Plage des Chardons, with a selection of wooden obstacles to jump over or swing from. Anyone is welcome to use these as a fitness aid. You are, however, advised to choose a level that is appropriate to your physical capabilities, and to spend a minimum of 15 minutes warming up before you get started. ●

➤**Bird-watching**. The Belle-Henriette lagoon, behind the beach at the northern end of town, attracts large numbers of gulls, terns, plovers, grebes, herons and occasional spoonbills in summer, as well as migrating chiff-chaffs, redstarts and wagtails. South of La Faute, at the extremity of the Pointe d'Arçay, lies a strictly-protected nature reserve, a staging-post for thousands of wading birds at migration times. Though it is closed to the public, you can observe the edges of it from the sea-wall beyond L'Aiguillon, on the opposite side of the Lay estuary. ●

■ **Dig in: the Vendée
has 140km of beaches.**

LONGEVILLE-SUR-MER

ⓘ tel: 02 51 33 34 64 fax: 02 51 33 26 46
www.longevillesurmer.com
info@longevillesurmer.com

LONGEVILLE EXTRAS

Market: Mon (1 July-31
Aug). Fri.
Restaurant: Les Flots
Bleus. Popular eating-
place, almost overlooking
Le Rocher beach, with
exotically tropical décor.
Lunchtime menus
from 8€. Plage du Rocher
(tel: 02 51 96 10 78).
Festivals: Festival de
Jazz. Music in
the open air. Mid Aug.

A thick fringe of pine forest shelters the vast sandy beaches that lie 2km south-west of Longeville. Some 25km west of Luçon, and set slightly inland, the village has winding streets and white-washed cottages clustered around a handsome 12th-century church. Aptly-named Plage du Rocher ("rock beach") is good for rockpools at low tide, as well as for fossils down near the water's edge; Les Conches beach, farther south, draws the surfers. A popular jazz festival fills the air with music during August, with concerts on beaches, and also on boats among the marshes.

➤**Walking and cycling trails**. Among the many woodland footpaths is an entertaining *parcours de santé*, or fitness trail (see La Faute-sur-Mer, above), which is known as a CRAPA (short for

Circuit Rustique d'Activité Physique Aménagé). It's on the D105, just south of the turning for Le Rocher beach, with some 20 sturdy obstacles to walk along, jump off or climb over. There's also a 13km mountain-bike (*VTT*, in French) circuit to the east of Longeville village. Maps available from the tourist office, near the church. ●

➤ Pierre qui vire. Unless a farmer has surrounded it with a towering maize crop, you can see a large standing-stone (also known as the Menhir du Russelet) in the fields, 1km west of Longeville. According to local legend, the giant stone spins around each night as the clock strikes twelve. ●

LUÇON

ⓘ tel: 02 51 56 36 52 fax: 02 51 56 03 56
www.ville-lucon.fr
officetourisme.paysluconnais@wanadoo.fr

This pleasant town at the junction of the plain with the Vendée's southern marshes is rather misrepresented by the garish light-industrial sprawl around its fringes. Artfully-trained trees, with green or copper-coloured foliage, are trimmed into leafy arches above the roads leading to the centre. The heart of the town is dominated as much by a crazily-decorated concrete water-tower near the Champ-de-Foire (built in 1912 to supply a regiment of dragoons garrisoned in the town) as by the elegant 85-metre spire of its cathedral. (If you pass through at night in summer, look out for the exquisite illumination of the cathedral spire; it becomes progressively more intense between 10pm and 12.30am.)

Luçon's most famous inhabitant was the future Cardinal Richelieu, who arrived in 1606 as the region's bishop and declared the place to be "the filthiest and most unpleasant in France". The town suffered a great deal at the hands of the Huguenots during the Wars of Religion but, as a Republican stronghold, emerged relatively unscathed from the later Wars of the Vendée.

Immaculately well-groomed today, Luçon's streets are lined with substantial two-storey houses of solid, white stone and

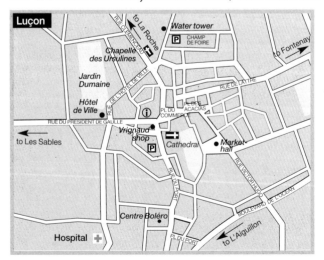

Market: Wed & Sat.
Specialities: Kamok & other liqueurs (see main entry).
Restaurants:
La Mirabelle. *Smart setting & gastronomic food on the Les Sables road. 89 bis Rue du Président de Gaulle (tel: 02 51 56 93 02).*
Le Bordeaux. *Great for steak-&-chips & other straightforward dishes; menus from 9.90€. Place des Acacias (tel: 02 51 29 09 66).*
Brocante:
Antiquités. *Browse among bric-à-brac in the courtyard of an elegant townhouse. Fri 4-6pm; Sat 10am-noon & 3-6.30pm. Rue du Président de Gaulle, opposite post office.*
Dépôt-Vente de Vendée. *Furniture & objects for sale. Thurs-Mon 2-7pm. Ste-Gemme-la-Plaine, 5km E of Luçon on D949, near junction with N137 (tel: 02 51 27 00 55).*
Festivals:
Nocturnes Océanes. *Concerts of romantic music. July.*
Fête de Nuit. *Music by lamplight, in the lovely surroundings of the Jardin Dumaine. July.*

■ Richelieu: preached in Luçon's cathedral.

organised into a complicated one-way system. If you want to stop and look around, it's best to leave the car in the huge car park opposite the cathedral and explore the quaint side streets on foot.

The main shopping areas are Rue Clemenceau, heading north from the cathedral, and Rue de Gaulle, leading west. There is a covered market-hall behind the cathedral, and a tourist office (which dispenses excellent English brochures on the town) near the Hôtel de Ville.

➤**Cathedral**. Richelieu, who was bishop here from 1606 to 1622, said Mass beneath the graceful spire and soaring white columns of the cathedral, and is reputed to have preached from the painted wooden pulpit now kept in the north aisle. In a mixture of architectural styles, the interior features Romanesque carved faces of humans and animals alongside 17th-century stone garlands. Concerts are sometimes given on the monumental organ, made by the celebrated 19th-century organ-builder Aristide Cavaillé-Coll and presented to the city by the Emperor Napoléon III. The cathedral is linked on its south side to the bishops' palace by a beautifully-preserved 16th-century cloister. ● *Daily 9am-noon & 2-7pm. Place Richelieu (tel: 02 51 56 36 52).*

➤**H. Vrignaud Fils**. Opposite the cathedral is an old-world shop selling the output of the Vrignaud family's local distillery, which manufactures—among other specialities—a famous coffee-based liqueur called Kamok, a pear-flavoured drink called Liqueur du Puy-du-Fou, and a blend of orange and brandy known as Liqueur des Vendéens. ● *Tues-Sat 10am-12.30pm & 2.30-7pm (1 July-31 Aug, Mon-Sat 9-11.30am & 2.30-7pm). 2 Place Richelieu (tel: 02 51 56 11 48).*

➤**Jardin Dumaine**. The shady green oasis in the town centre is well hidden behind the Hôtel de Ville (town hall). Inside, you can stroll among gravel paths (though not on the grass!), formal borders, collections of interesting trees and shrubs and an avenue of giant 150-year-old yew hedges (from which waft strains of recorded music in summer). There is a pretty Victorian-style bandstand for open-air concerts. Youngsters are bound to love the topiary animals on the north lawn that recall the fables of La Fontaine—mostly familiar to British children, as the 17th-century French writer cribbed them from Aesop. ● *Daily 9am-7pm (1 July-31 Aug, 9am-9pm). Access via Rue de l'Hôtel-de-Ville or Allée St-François (tel: 02 51 56 36 52). Free.* ♿

➤**Chapelle des Ursulines**. The austerity of the white-walled chapel in this former convent is softened by a decorative altar-piece and an astonishing 33-metre-long wooden ceiling entirely covered with 17th-century paintings of cherubs and musical instruments (to avoid a spinning head or a crick in the neck, it's best to sit down to look at them). A plaque on the end wall records the sad fate of the convent's nuns during the Vendée Wars; 11 of them died in the town's prison. ○ *1 July-31 Aug, Mon-Sat 2.30-6pm. Rue Clemenceau (tel: 02 51 56 36 52). Free.*

➤**Centre Boléro**. In an intimate café-theatre setting, the Boléro puppet company stages sophisticated shows on musical themes linked to individual composers, from Django Reinhardt to Johann Sebastian Bach. Currently undergoing renovation, the theatre reopens in autumn 2004 along with a charming little museum featuring Guignol, Punchinello and other types of marionette, from China, Turkey, Java and other countries. ● *2 Rue Traversière, off Rue du Port, S of the cathedral (tel: 02 51 56 89 97). Opening hours & ticket prices not available at time of writing.*

➤**Le Port**. If you drive south from the cathedral and turn left into Place du Port you come to a wide esplanade surrounded by imposing buildings, a

■ Luçon: topiary in the Jardin Dumaine.

legacy of Luçon's once-thriving port that was linked to the sea by a 20km canal. In the mid-19th century this was one of the largest ports in France for the export of cereals but, once the railways made water transport uneconomic, its fortunes declined and its basins were filled in. Various ideas have been put forward for breathing new life into this forgotten backwater, including a plan to re-excavate the basins and display in them a collection of old-fashioned river boats. ●

❯**Église des Magnils-Reigniers**. A light carpet of moss covers the stone-flagged floor inside a former priory church, in a village 3km north-west of Luçon. Three altars are ranged side-by-side at the east end; opposite, on the west wall, you can make out some misty-coloured 12th-century frescoes, discovered only in 1968, showing images believed to be of the resurrected Christ appearing to his disciples. ○ *1 July-31 Aug, Tues-Fri 3-6pm. Information from Les Magnils-Reigniers mairie (tel: 02 51 97 70 00). Free.*

MAILLEZAIS

ⓘ tel: 02 51 87 23 01 fax: 02 51 00 72 51
office.tourisme@cc-vsa.com

This village on the edge of the "Venise Verte", 30km east of Luçon, is famous for the set of ancient monastical ruins that tower over the countryside to the west. Pause first in the centre of Maillezais (pronounced "my-er-zay"), to admire the Romanesque church of St-Nicolas, its main doorway decorated with carved stone birds, serpents and acrobats. As you head towards the abbey, along Rue de l'Abbaye, look out for number 74: pieces of grey bone stick out high up in the walls—placed there, legend has it, to protect from sickness any animals kept inside.

Between April and October you can hire little boats at a pretty waterside spot just below the abbey, and explore the local waterways. If you engage the services of a guide, he will do the hard work—and may decide to astonish you by stirring up the mud of the canal bed and demonstrating how to set fire to gases that are released above the surface.

A cycle route links Maillezais with La Tranche, almost 60km to the west, via a network of towpaths, and from there to the rest of the Vendée's 150km of coastal cycleway.

❯**Abbaye St-Pierre**. West of the village, where the wind sweeps in exhilaratingly off the open marshes, rise the ghostly remains of an early 11th-century abbey, a dazzling example of Romanesque architecture. Some 200 monks lived here in the 13th century, undertaking the first draining of the area to create the productive fields that exist today. During this time, they suffered much harassment from Geoffroy la Grand'Dent ("Longtooth"), half-factual, half-fictional son of the powerful Raymondin de Lusignan and the fairy Mélusine (see page 127). Three hundred years later, the writer Rabelais (see page 115) spent three years within its walls. During the Wars of Religion, the abbey was seized and fortified by the Protestants—in 1589 the Calvinist writer Agrippa d'Aubigné turned it into a Protestant stronghold, and remained its governor for 30 years. After this relatively stable time, the abbey sunk into a long period of decline that continued after the Revolution in 1789, when its remains were confiscated by the state and much of the stone sold.

An excellent visitors' leaflet in English, translated by local resident Edwin Apps, who has also written an entertaining book on the abbey (details on page 170), describes the history of the buildings and the daily life of the monks who lived there. From excavations made in the uneven ground, you can make out the positions of the refectory, cloister and chapter house. Among more intact buildings are the octagonal kitchen, the monks' and visitors' refectories, and the dormitory that would have housed visiting pilgrims and other travellers. Worn stone steps lead down to underground storage areas that include a magnificently-preserved vaulted space called a cellarium.

During summer, groups of costumed actors plunge visitors into the abbey's turbulent history, popping out to play set pieces and bring to life its most signifcant characters during 50-minute promenade performances (in French) that are given six times daily. Occasional concerts and *son-et-lumière* shows are also held; watch the local press, or ask tourist offices in the area for details. ● *Mon-Sat 9.30am-12.30pm & 1.30-6pm; Sun & public holidays 10am-6pm (1 June-30 Sept, daily 10am-7pm; "promenades contées" performances, late June-mid Sept). Closed last three weeks of Jan. Rue de l'Abbaye (tel: 02 51 87 22 80). 4€, students 2€, children free.*

➤**Chapelle de Chalais**. Seek out this simple little church in a small agricultural hamlet 3km north of Maillezais for its delightfully primitive painting of St Roch, and of the dog that brought him food during the saint's self-imposed isolation while he was suffering from the plague. ● *Chalais.*

MARANS (Charente-Maritime)

ⓘ tel: 05 46 01 12 87 fax: 05 46 35 97 36
www.ville-marans.fr
office-de-tourisme.marans@wanadoo.fr

After the flat landscape and low-built houses of the marshes, it comes as a surprise to find dignified, three-storey, stone buildings and to look down from the traffic-laden N137 upon a calm, almost Venetian scene of fishing boats and pleasure craft moored alongside quays bordered by white-painted houses with coloured shutters (pictures on page 108).

Straddling the Sèvre Niortaise river, this port 23km north-east of La Rochelle was for more than two centuries—until rail transport superseded water—the focus of intense commercial activity. Today its narrow cobbled streets are still busy—especially when the market is in full swing in the pretty, glass-sided hall near the quay. It is worth pulling off the lorry-choked main road into a side street, and spending time walking around this attractive town. For a bird's-eye view in summer, you can climb the tower of the church. (With its extraordinarily modern metalwork spire, it's a landmark that's hard to miss.)

The name of Marans is synonymous with that of a breed of chicken renowned for its brown, speckled eggs—these appealed to no less a connoisseur than James Bond, who can be heard in *From Russia With Love* to order "Marans eggs" for breakfast.

➤**Embarcadères**. Easy to spot on the east side of the bridge are two pontoons offering rental of canoes or motorboats, so you can set off on exploratory trips up the Sèvre Niortaise and along some of the adjacent canals that iron out a few of the river's more eccentric meanders. Possible circuits range in duration from an hour to a whole day. ◑ *Easter-end Oct. Information from Le Thalassa restaurant, Quai Joffre (tel: 05 46 35 08 91). From about 15€ an hour for five people.*

■ **Maillezais Abbey: ghostly shell of a once-magnificent cathedral.**

MARANS EXTRAS

Market: *Tues & Sat (larger on first Tues).*
Marché nocturne. *Evening market, selling crafts & local produce, along quayside, Thurs (mid July-31 Aug).*
Speciality: *Marans eggs.*
Restaurant: **Crêperie Le Bilig**. *Savoury galettes (buckwheat pancakes) with a wide range of fillings make a tasty lunch by the river. 83 Quai Joffre (tel: 05 46 01 06 89).*

➤**Musée Capon**. On the first floor of the tourist-office building in the town's main street is a diverse collection of items, presented in two rooms. They include local pottery, head-dresses and archaeological finds, and even an ancient door saved from the town's now-renovated church. ● *Mon-Fri 9.30am-12.30pm & 2-5pm (1 Feb-mid Nov, Mon-Fri 9.30am-12.30pm & 2-5pm; Sat 9.30am-12.30pm. 1 July-31 Aug, Mon-Sat 9.30am-12.30pm & 2-5pm). 62 Rue d'Aligre (tel: 05 46 01 12 87). 1.60€.*

➤**Moulin de Beauregard**. The council has restored this 17th-century windmill, unused since 1935. Its wood-shingled roof stands proudly above some of Marans' newer houses, and enthusiasts have set the slatted sails turning again. After climbing up and down the steep wooden stairs for demonstrations of the machinery, you can buy stone-ground organic flour to take home. ◑ *15 Mar-30 Nov, Sat, Sun & public holidays 10am-12.30pm & 2.30-6.30pm (15 June-15 Sept, Tues-Sun 10am-12.30pm & 2.30-6.30pm). Avenue de la Gare (tel: 05 46 00 74 68). 3€, children 1.50€.*

MAREUIL-SUR-LAY

ⓘ **tel: 02 51 97 30 26 fax: 02 51 30 53 32**
www.paysmareuillaisvendee.com
ot@paysmareuillaisvendee.com

The small wine-producing town, dominated by the spire of its austere Romanesque church and by a picturesque 16th-century castle, overlooks the river Lay, 10km north-west of Luçon. (If the calm waters look tempting, you can enquire about boat rental from the hairdresser's shop in the square by the bridge).

A list of vineyards offering *dégustations* (tastings) around the area's signposted "Route des Vins" (wine route) is available from the tourist office. The village of Rosnay, 5km to the west, claims the highest wine output in France per head of population: more than 8 per cent of its 436 inhabitants are wine-producers.

➤**Boutique du Château Marie-du-Fou**. The Mourat family, among Mareuil's best-known wine-producers, who have recently restored the old castle, sell some of their reds, whites and rosés from a shop below it, alongside the bridge. In the charming little building that was once a tollhouse, enthusiastic staff discuss the finer points of their wines, and pour some for you to taste before you buy. ● *Tues-Sat 9am-12.30pm & 2.30-7pm (1 July-31 Aug, Mon-Sat 9am-12.30pm & 2.30-7pm). 2 Place Circulaire (tel: 02 51 97 20 10).* ♿

➤**Église de Dissais**. A 12th-century church 2km east of Mareuil has been restored as a memorial to 7,500 combatants who lost their lives during the Vendean army's three attempts to take the nearby town of Luçon from the Republicans in 1793, during the region's post-Revolution civil war. ◑ *Mid May-30 Sept, Sun & public holidays 3-6.30pm (1 July-31 Aug, daily 3-7pm). Signposted off D19 (tel: 02 51 97 26 91). Free.*

➤**Pont de Lavaud**. This simple iron bridge, 4km south-west of Mareuil, was designed by none other than the great engineer Gustave Eiffel in 1866, to carry traffic on chunky stone pillars across the river Lay. If you'd like to explore the river from here, you can rent canoes in summer from the waterside L'Aubraie bar and restaurant, beside the bridge. ●

➤**Parachute memorial**. A large granite slab on the D50, just to the west of Eiffel's bridge (see above), commemorates the first Allied parachute drop of arms to Vendean Resistance workers, on 14 July 1943. Once they picked up the poetical coded message "*Pourquoi me réveiller au souffle du printemps?*" (Why awaken me at the first breath of spring?) via the BBC from London, members of the *résistance* prepared to receive the precious consignment, which they hastily concealed from view in the house that stands beside the present monument. ●

MAREUIL EXTRAS

Market: Thurs (larger on last Thurs of month).
Marché de la Nature. Farmers' market, with changing seasonal themes. First Sun of month, St-Florent-des-Bois, 10km NW of Mareuil.
Specialities: Gâche vendéenne (sweet bread) from La Maligorne, 37 Rue Hervé-de-Mareuil. Wines of Mareuil & Rosnay.
Wine shops: **J. Mourat** (see main entry).
Festival: **Les Vignerons en Fête**. Local producers show off their wines, & offer tastings. Aug.

MOUTIERS-SUR-LE-LAY
ⓘ tel: 02 51 97 30 26 fax: 02 51 30 53 32
www.paysmareuillaisvendee.com
ot@paysmareuillaisvendee.com

This sleepy village on the river Lay, 10km north of Luçon, is clustered around a pretty square overlooked by several superb *maisons bourgeoises* (large houses), and a part-Romanesque church. From around the fifth century AD, a community of monks lived here (*moutier* means monastery). A former priory, just off the square, was once the residence of the bishops of Luçon.

■ The Tour de Bessay:
a sentry's-eye view.

❯ **Tour de Bessay**. Guided tours are given of a magnificent Renaissance tower attached to a traditional *logis*, or country house, 2km south of Moutiers. After watching a short video, you ascend via a series of big empty rooms towards the bell-shaped, lantern-topped roof, finishing at the *chemin de ronde*, or sentry-way. Pierced by holes through which muskets could be aimed at invaders, it offers panoramic views over the surrounding countryside. In the garden, a tumbledown dovecote reveals 3,000 nesting-holes, giving an idea of how many pigeons might have been needed in times gone by to feed family and staff. ⭘ *1 July-31 Aug, Wed-Mon 2.30-6.30pm. Bessay; information from tourist office (tel: 02 51 97 30 26). 3.40€, children 1.70€.*

LA ROCHELLE (Charente-Maritime)
ⓘ tel: 05 46 41 14 68 fax: 05 46 41 99 85
larochelle-tourisme.com
accueil@larochelle-tourisme.com

★ One of France's best known and most attractive ports, this historic city is within easy reach for anyone staying in the south Vendée. The most interesting shops, streets and sights are conveniently clustered around the picturesque Vieux-Port, where elegant yachts float beside the three ancient towers that once guarded the harbour entrance.

English, off and on, from the time of Eleanor of Aquitaine until the Hundred Years War, the great salt- and wine-trading port of La Rochelle was fiercely Protestant in the 16th century and was thus bloodily involved in the Wars of Religion. The city successfully resisted a long siege by the Duke of Anjou in 1573, but a subsequent one (1627-28) led by Cardinal Richelieu, who was determined to unify France by stamping out Protestantism, left only 5,000 survivors from a population of 28,000. Ruined for a time, La Rochelle later became prosperous again on the lucrative West Indian sugar and slave trades.

Principal shopping areas are neatly contained within the east and west boundaries of the old town: Grande-Rue des Merciers, full of half-timbered buildings, and Rue du Palais (which has a branch of the Galeries Lafayette department store). If you stroll through the streets around the fairy-tale-style Hôtel de Ville (town hall) be sure to take in the 16th-century Maison Henri II, the mirrored gilt splendour of the Café de la Paix, near Place de Verdun, the old arcades that line Rue du Minage, and the Porte de la Grosse Horloge that was formerly the gateway between port and city.

Devotees of the *Fort Boyard* television programme can take a two-hour boat trip that circles the 19th-century fortress lying off the coast. (Boats leave from near Tour de la Chaîne; landing at the fort is not permitted.) Built to protect the military installations of Rochefort, Fort Boyard was made obsolete by advances in technology before its full complement of guns was installed. You can also take excursions to the popular Ile de Ré, a low-lying island that can be reached by road across an elegantly curving bridge (toll

■ La Rochelle: a town of historic buildings and picturesque streets.

16.50€ each way for a car). For relaxation, La Rochelle has a couple of small beaches: one to the west of the Tour de la Lanterne, and another near Les Minimes yacht marina.

The town's layout is quite compact, so it's best to leave the car somewhere and explore on foot. There's a large underground car park on Place de Verdun, some pay-&-display spaces on the quayside around the Tour de la Lanterne, and more parking near the Aquarium. Wear comfortable shoes, though, as the cobblestones are hard on the legs. Watery areas intervene a good deal, but there are footbridges or little ferries here and there to enable you to cross. The tourist office, within a slightly bleak modern shopping precinct in the Le Gabut district, near the Tour St-Nicolas, organises tours of the old town on foot and also by horse-drawn carriage. Among the following selection of attractions, the first three are in the old town; the rest—including the Aquarium—lie to the south and south-west of the tourist office, and within walking distance of it.

➤ **Tour St-Nicolas/Tour de la Chaîne/Tour de la Lanterne**. Of La Rochelle's three famous 14th-century towers, the first two stand either side of the harbour entrance, one containing models and plans showing the port's history, and the other using a mini *son-et-lumière* show to explain the devastating 1627 siege. The Tour de la Lanterne—a little farther west, and topped with a gothic spire—is a former lighthouse and one-time prison. Its rooms are decorated with some amazing graffiti inscribed by captives, many of them English sailors who etched into the soft stone walls of their jail precise images of the ships in which they had served. Each tower has identical opening hours and admission charge. ● *Tues-Sun 10am-12.30pm & 2-5.30pm. Vieux-Port area (tel: 05 46 34 11 81). 4.60€, students 3.10€, children free; for all three towers 10€ & 6.50€.*

➤ **Musée du Flacon à Parfum**. Upstairs, above a perfume shop near the Grosse Horloge, are more than 1,000 scent bottles in designs from Lalique to Salvador Dali, plus miniatures, labels and powder-boxes: a fascinating and unusual collection. ● *Mon 1.30-7pm, Tues-Sat 10.30am-7pm (1 July-31 Aug, Mon 1.30-7pm, Tues-Sat 10.30am-7pm, Sun & public holidays 3-6pm). 33 Rue du Temple (tel: 05 46 41 32 40). 4.30€, students 3.80€, children under 10 free.*

➤ **Musée du Nouveau Monde**. A grand 18th-century mansion contains paintings, drawings, sculpture and maps relating the story of the town's links with the New World—America, Canada and, in particular, the West Indies. Covering the past 400 years, it deals with emigration, relations with American Indians, fur-trading, plantation-owning and the slave trade. ● *Wed-Sat & Mon 9.30am-12.30pm & 1.30-5pm; Sun 2.30-6pm (1 Apr-30 Sept, Wed-Sat & Mon 10am-12.30pm & 2-6pm, Sun 2.30-6pm). 10 Rue Fleuriau (tel: 05 46 41 46 50). 3.50€, children free.*

>★ **Aquarium**. Just a couple of minutes' walk from the main tourist office, La Rochelle's Aquarium provides an incredible experience. Though the admission charge may be high, you can look forward to a good two hours' entertainment viewing the thousands of sea creatures, from frail seahorses to large sharks, and to some superb presentation. Visitors enter through a glass tunnel entirely surrounded by tiny, translucent jellyfish swimming gracefully in all directions. Throughout the tour, the lighting and other effects are magical: shoals of sardines are transformed into shimmering silver hordes that rival any Christmas decorations; glowing knightfish are enhanced by specially dimmed lighting; waves are heard to break gently on a reconstituted coral reef. Items are labelled in English as well as French. It is understandably popular, so try and go mid-week, off-season or around noon, when the crowds may be slightly smaller. ● *Daily 10am-8pm (1 Apr-1 Sept, daily 9am-8pm; 1 July-31 Aug, daily 9am-11pm). Bassin des Grands-Yachts (tel: 05 46 34 00 00). 12€, students & children 9€ (audioguide in English 3.50€).* ♿

>**Musée Maritime**. Large, refreshingly old-fashioned museum of maritime history in La Rochelle's former fish-auction building, just south of the Aquarium. Displays of fishing techniques—particularly interesting are the models of trawlers, dredgers, drifters, lobster- and line-fishing boats—and navigation and sonar aids, plus reconstructed workshops showing the now defunct boatbuilding and coaling businesses of the adjacent La Ville en Bois district. Try to catch the excellent display of sailing (English explanation sheet available at reception), using a radio-controlled model yacht on an enormous indoor pool equipped with powerful wind machines. Afterwards, the demonstrator invites spectators to enter a wind tunnel on foot, and struggle against a force 9 gale (hold on to hats, glasses and scarves here). Outside is a variety of ships to visit—though you need to be pretty agile to cope with the steep stairs and uneven decks. ◐ *1 Feb-1 Nov, daily 2-6.30pm (1 Apr-30 Sept, daily 10am-6.30pm; 1 July-31 Aug, daily 10am-7.30pm). Place Bernard-Moitessier (tel: 05 46 28 03 05). 7.60€, children 5.30€.*

>**Musée des Modèles Réduits**. Scale models, from 1m-high square-rigged ships to small-gauge electric trains, are on display in an interesting museum across the basin from the Musée Maritime. There's a miniature version of La Rochelle railway station, and a huge Wild-West-style layout with dozens of trains criss-crossing on some 200 metres of track. In the museum's mini-theatre it's worth sitting through a slightly clunky little stage show about great sea voyages, from Erik the Viking to Captain Cook, to enjoy the wonderful sight of model ships sailing on real water, staging smoke-filled naval battles in front of your eyes. ● *Daily 2-6pm (1 Feb-31 May & 1 Sept-31 Oct, 10am-noon & 2-6pm; 1 June-31 Aug, daily 9.30am-7pm). Rue de la Désirée (tel: 05 46 41 68 08). 6.50€, children 4€; combined ticket for model museum & adjacent museum of automata (see below) 10€, children 5.50€).* ♿

>**Musée des Automates**. From the moment you enter this enjoyable museum of mechanical toys—passing a model cow that can swish its tail, flap its ears and chew the cud—you can't help laughing out loud at some of the sophisticated and bizarre actions of the automatic dolls and other characters. This amusing collection, next door to the model museum (above), features acrobats, dancers, musicians, fortune-tellers, butchers and doctors, many with animated lips and waggling eyebrows. There's also a sizeable recreation of a Montmartre street scene, its shop windows full of busy working models advertising the trades within. ● *Rue de la Désirée (tel: 05 46 41 68 08). Opening hours & admission charges as Musée des Modèles Réduits, above.* ♿

LA ROCHELLE EXTRAS

Markets: *Daily, Place du Marché. Sun, La Pallice, 2km W of town centre.*

Specialities: *Charentais melons. Pineau des Charentes (fortified wine, drunk as apéritif). Chaudrée (fish soup with white wine). Mouclade (mussels in curry sauce).*

Restaurants:

Café de la Paix. *Good brasserie food in splendid Art-Nouveau interior, near Place de Verdun. Menus from 14€. 54 Rue Chaudrier (tel: 05 46 41 39 79).*

Les Quatre Sergents. *Elegant restaurant near the Vieux Port, with some tables in a 19th-century conservatory. Menus from 15€. 49 Rue St-Jean du-Pérot (tel: 05 46 41 35 80).*

Festivals:

Carnival. *Mid-May.*

Francofolies. *A feast of popular French music & culture. July.*

Le Grand Pavois. *Large in-water boat show. Sept.*

Golf: *Golf de la Prée. An 18-hole course at Nieul-sur-Mer, 7km N of La Rochelle (tel: 05 46 01 24 42).*

ST-CYR-EN-TALMONDAIS

ⓘ tel: 02 51 30 82 82 fax: 02 51 30 88 29

ST-CYR EXTRAS

Restaurant: Auberge de la Court-d'Aron. Cooking of a high standard at a pretty, stone-built inn, alongside the village's château. Menus from 14€. 1 Allée des Tilleuls, beside the Parc Floral (tel: 02 51 30 81 80).

Small village 12km west of Luçon, at the southern limit of the woods and fields of the *bas-bocage*. On the east side of St-Cyr is a marvellous garden filled with luxuriant tropical and other plants. To the west is the village's other curiosity—a moving war memorial, with a statue of a soldier dramatically silhouetted against the sky.

> ★ **Parc Floral et Tropical de la Court-d'Aron**. In the grounds of a stately, 17th-century-style mansion (not open to the public) is a magnificent garden, with verdant lawns, woodland walks, spring bulbs, and summer colour from icelandic poppies and carpets of busy-lizzies. Families are well catered for, with picnic areas, children's playground, and giant tortoises, koi carp and other creatures to look at. The gardens' most famous feature, however, is the large lake that is covered, from June to September, in thousands of exquisite pink lotus flowers standing above the water on tall green stems. It's a surprising, and unforgettable, sight. ◖ *Mid Apr-31 Oct, daily 10am-7pm. On D949 (tel: 02 51 30 86 74). 8€, children & disabled 6€ (mid June-mid Sept 10€ & 8€).* ♿

> **Église de Curzon**. The pride of this simple church in Curzon, a drowsy village 3km south-east of St-Cyr, is its 11th-century crypt. Tug open the trapdoors in the floor, press a button on the right for five minutes' illumination and screw up your courage.... Down below, strange stone faces ogle you from the tops of the carved columns—a rather spooky experience that you'd never expect so close to the seaside razzmatazz of La Tranche, just 13km away. ●

STE-HERMINE

ⓘ tel: 02 51 27 39 32 fax: 02 51 27 39 32

STE-HERMINE EXTRAS

Market: Fri (larger on last Fri of month).

Factory shop: Relais des Marques. Huge selection of NewMan & other stylish casual clothes for women & men. Mon 2-7pm; Tues-Fri 10am-12.30pm & 2-7pm; Sat 10am-7pm. Parc Atlantique, Vendéopole business park; near junction 7 of A83 (tel: 02 51 28 82 17).

Festival: Théâtroscope. Five days of historical re-creations around the château. Early Aug.

If you arrive from the west at this small town on the edge of the plain, 12km north-east of Luçon, you almost have the impression of falling off the wooded *bocage* on to a carpet of fields of crops that roll away to the horizon like an undulating ocean. The main crossroads, on the N137, is dominated by an imposing World War I memorial (picture on page 39) featuring the politician Georges Clemenceau and several *poilus*—the affectionate nickname for French soldiers of 1914-18. Ste-Hermine's other small treasures are well hidden, but include a handsome, privately-owned château near the church and, worth seeking out on a Friday morning, an attractive 19th-century market-hall.

> **Aire de la Vendée**. It may seem bizarre to suggest a motorway service station as a tourist attraction but you could spend a happy couple of hours at this one on the A83. Located between junctions 6 and 7, about 4km west of Ste-Hermine, it offers three state-of-the-art museums as showcases for the region. "La Vendée en Images" is full of projected photographs and hands-on, multi-language computer screens. The "Théâtre du Marais" presents a 10-minute video (in French) about the ecology of L'Aiguillon Bay. The third experience, "La Vie du Marais Poitevin", plunges you into the beguiling green wilderness of the "Green Venice" marshes—right down to virtual duckweed under foot. The surroundings have been planted up imaginatively with marshland flora, and edged with fences of woven willow. In July and August you may even be offered a free go at some sport, like archery. It's all part of the French motorways' scheme to combat driver fatigue by encouraging motorists to take a break. You can also reach it on foot, through a back

entrance, without the need to pay a motorway toll. Head towards La Roche on the D948, turn left onto the D19, towards Mareuil, and then follow Aire de la Vendée signs off to the north. From the small parking area, you can walk in through a gate. ● *Sat, Sun & school holiday periods 10am-6pm (1 June-31 Aug, daily 10am-6pm). Aire de la Vendée (tel: 02 51 28 81 63). Free.* &

>St-Juire-Champgillon. This tongue-twisting *commune* (actually two separate, equally pictur-esque villages) 4km north-east of Ste-Hermine has turned itself into a summer artistic centre. A walk around the alleys and lanes of either village reveals distinguished-looking mansions of mellow local stone, plus other unexpected delights: in Champgillon, a Jardin Blanc and a Jardin Noir (gar-dens planted with white or dark-coloured plants, respectively); in St-Juire, fleeting glimpses of a couple of privately-owned châteaux and, behind the school, a small "Jardin des Cinq Sens", a garden designed to please each of our five different senses. There is also a summer-long series of art exhibitions held in a couple of converted barns near St-Juire's *mairie*. ○ *Exhibitions: July & Aug, Sun-Fri 3-8pm. St-Juire (tel: 02 51 27 82 04). Free.*

ST-MICHEL-EN-L'HERM

ⓘ tel: 02 51 30 21 89 fax: 02 51 30 21 89
ot.paysnedelamer@wanadoo.fr

Though it rises only 17 metres above sea level, this former island of whitewashed houses, 15km south-west of Luçon, seems almost imposing when seen across the flat marshland. From the tourist office, in the centre, you can take a 2.5km circular walk through the back lanes by following a series of green arrows. If you drive north along the Triaize road, look out on the right at the hamlet of Les Chaux; a farmhouse there is built on a centuries-old bank of oyster shells—thought to have been either a fortification against the sea or protection from invading Normans.

■ Monastic ruins: abbey at St-Michel-en-l'Herm.

>Abbaye Royale. Behind the tall boundary wall of a large house on the main square are the remains of a former royal abbey whose Benedictine monks were among those who undertook the draining of the marshes surrounding the village. First established in the seventh century, the abbey was reconstructed several times after the ravages of the Hundred Years-War, the Wars of Religion and, finally, the devastating Wars of the Vendée. Still intact are the 17th-century chapter house and the lofty refectory, while skeletal ribs of vaulting are all that remain of the *chauffoir* where the monks took exercise. Allow a good 45 minutes for this interesting visit. ○ *1 July-31 Aug, guided tours Tues, Thurs & Fri 10am-noon & 3-5pm. Closed on public holidays. Information from tourist office (tel: 02 51 30 21 89). 2.80€, students 1.80€, children 1€.*

ST-MICHEL EXTRAS

Market: Thurs.
Specialities: Eels.
Cheese (Petit-Vendéen, La Micheline).

LA TRANCHE-SUR-MER

ⓘ tel: 02 51 30 33 96 fax: 02 51 27 78 71
www.ot-latranchesurmer.fr
ot-latranchesurmer@wanadoo.fr

Its 13km of sandy beaches, and its dozens of campsites, have made La Tranche, 32km south-west of Luçon, a popular family resort that is also a paradise for surfers and wind-surfers. The influx of summer visitors—particularly young people—swells the population from its winter level of around 2,000 to between 80,000 and 100,000. When weather conditions are right, surfers escape to the rollers off La Terrière and the Pointe du Grouin beaches; the less sporty will find shady walks in the forest of holm oaks and fragrant pines to the west of the town, and plenty of temporary entertainments like paint-ball, amusement parks and street theatre to fill the summer days and evenings. La Tranche has a calmer side, too. Back in 1953, a couple of Dutch horticulturalists opened the eyes of the townspeople to the idea of using their sandy soil to start a bulb industry; you can see how successful they have been by visiting La Tranche's renowned Floralies gardens (see below) in spring or summer.

The town has been much rebuilt since World War II, during which many of its buildings were razed by the occupying Germans to improve sightlines for the defence of their submarine base at La Rochelle. However, there are still plenty of former fishermen's cottages to be found in the narrow side streets.

In more modern style, a new vista has been created in the town centre. At the end of Avenue de la Plage, the view of the sea is framed by an imposing Greek-style colonnade, flanked by the glass-sided Pavillon de l'Aunis—soon to become the town's casino.

If you crave a little relief from the level landscape, try heading north-west to hunt for prehistoric stones in leafier countryside around Avrillé and Le Bernard, or to enjoy some medieval fun at Talmont castle. Alternatively, go north in search of other curiosities, such as the bizarre stone animals on the churches of Angles and St-Benoist; north-east to look round the shops and cathedral in Luçon; or venture south-east to spend a day on the delightful waterways of the "Venise Verte" or in historic La Rochelle. (All these places are described in detail on other pages.) For some, however, the flat countryside surrounding La Tranche can be a positive advantage: 60km of signposted cycle routes lead eastward across marshes and alongside canals to Maillezais, in the "Green Venice" area; and the Vendée's 150km of smooth-surfaced coastal cycleway heads north-west to Jard-sur-Mer, and beyond towards Les Sables-d'Olonne and—ultimately—as far as Noirmoutier island.

■La Tranche: Pointe du Grouin lighthouse.

LA TRANCHE EXTRAS
Markets: Tues & Sat, Place de la Liberté. Wed (1 July-31 Aug), La Grière. Sun (1 July-31 Aug), La Terrière.
Specialities: Flowering bulbs. Garlic. Onions.

➤ **Parc des Floralies**. Gusts of perfume welcome you to an impressive garden, signposted to the west side of the town, where borders and leafy glades are ablaze with spring colour, dramatic formal patterns of crocuses and narcissi, and rivers of tulips of every shape and hue. The gardens remain bright in the summer months, too, thanks to the begonias, petunias, gladioli and sweet-scented carnations—with not a dead-head in sight. Good children's playground, and some pleasantly shady picnic spots. ◑ *1 Mar-30 Apr & 1 July-30 Sept (seasons may vary according to weather conditions), Mon-Fri 10am-12.30pm & 2-6pm; Sat, Sun & public holidays 10am-6pm. Boulevard de la Petite-Hollande (tel: 02 51 30 33 96). Spring: 5.20€, children 2.75€, disabled free. Summer: free admission for all.* ㅤ

TRIAIZE
ⓘ tel: 02 51 56 11 53 fax: 02 51 56 38 21

TRIAIZE EXTRAS
Festival: Fête de la Bouse. Cowpat day, & festival of old farming techniques. July.

Attractive marshland village 7.5km south of Luçon, grouped around a restored 12th-century church with an unusual spire that looks like a partially-inflated, wavy sausage-balloon. The lack of wood in this open landscape meant the inhabitants had to find other fuel for cooking and heating, and the village has perpetuated the once-widespread custom of making *bouses*. These were made from cowpats trampled into mud, then shaped, dried and stacked until needed for the fire. After burning, even the ash made a valuable fertiliser. At the annual festival of old customs the stuff is put to good use for cooking mussels, *mogettes*, eels and other local specialities, as well as for throwing, frisbee-style, in competitions. ≫➤ *page 109*

Green Venice

ⓘ tel:05 49 35 86 77
www.parc-marais-poitevin.fr
info@ parc-marais-poitevin.fr

★ This 35,000-hectare labyrinth of tranquil, duckweed-covered waterways nicknamed "La Venise Verte" ("Green Venice") is one of the region's most entrancing features, and the prettiest corner of the Marais Poitevin, or Poitou Marshes.

Slightly smaller in area than the Isle of Wight, the vast "wet" marshland drained by 12th-century monks and 17th-century Dutch engineers stretches from Marans in the west to Niort in the east, and from Maillezais down to Arçais. It is criss-crossed with tiny *rigoles*—canals, edged with rustling poplars or pollarded willows—that run into the Sèvre Niortaise river and then to L'Aiguillon Bay.

Although the name has a vaguely urban sound, "Green Venice" is actually entirely rural. The tree-lined waterways, which serve partly as drainage for little squares of green pasture and partly as avenues of transport for everything from wedding parties to cattle, are blissfully silent, except for the buzz of dragonflies, and the giggles of incompetent crews of tourists who, unlike the expert locals, zigzag inelegantly from bank to bank. You can fit from four to six people into one boat, so the hourly hire fee of about 25€ (15€ if you forego the guide) is quite a bargain.

If you prefer to stay on dry land, cycle rental is on offer in the larger villages, and there are signposted trails to explore on foot or by bike. Try the lovely waterside lane along the south bank of the Sèvre, just south of Maillé. However, as it was once the towpath, it's not too wide in places, and it could be difficult to turn a vehicle around, or for two cars to pass. For a dreamy aerial view, you can even be wafted by hot-air balloon over the area, from Fontenay-le-Comte (see page 116).

Because the Poitevin Marshes straddle three *départements*, or counties, it can be quite difficult to obtain information on the area as a whole. Look out in the region's tourist offices for the excellent free map called *Le Marais Poitevin: Carte Découverte*. Produced by the Parc Interrégional du Marais Poitevin, it indicates places to hire boats and bikes, and where to find everything from beauty spots and footpaths to churches and museums. In most villages you can rent canoes, electric boats or workaday *plates* (flat-bottomed metal boats) between April and October, with or without a guide.

Here, arranged roughly west to east, are some of the most attractive villages of the "Venise Verte". Larger places on the fringes, such as Marans, Maillezais and Chaillé, have fuller entries on other pages.

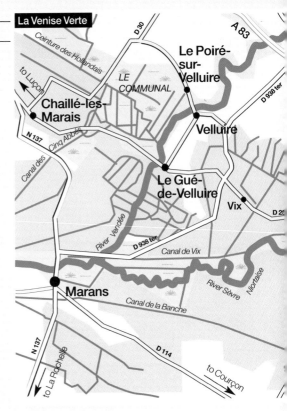

CHAILLÉ-LES-MARAIS
See main entry, page 91.

MARANS
See main entry, page 97.

LE GUÉ-DE-VELLUIRE
ⓘ tel: 02 51 52 52 52
At the site of a ford *(gué)* across the Vendée river, this pretty village (picture on page 108) has some beautiful old stone buildings in Rue de l'Église. Rent boats from Le Guétréen café, which also offers snacks and, from June to September, regular musical evenings.

VELLUIRE
See main entry, page 109.

VIX
ⓘ tel: 02 51 00 62 24
A large village strung out along the D25; look out for a riotously flowery private garden at the eastern end. A popular, *son-et-lumiere* is staged in early August, in odd-numbered years, on the Sèvre Niortaise river.

MAILLÉ
ⓘ tel: 02 51 87 05 78
Old-fashioned wells, with winding-handles, still stand

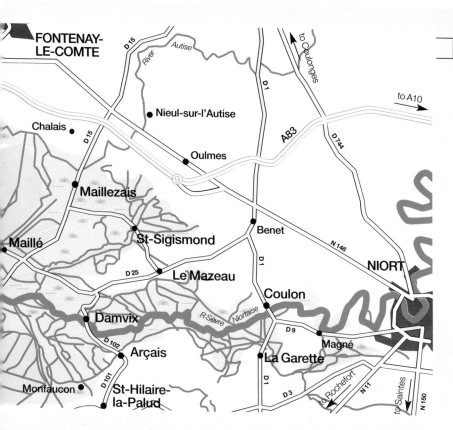

FONTENAY-LE-COMTE

in front of many of the houses, lending this village a frozen-in-time atmosphere. The Romanesque church features marvellous, carved stone acrobats—though slightly eroded by the centuries. Electric boats, for up to eight people, cost 30€-40€ an hour.

MAILLEZAIS
See main entry, page 96.

DAMVIX
ⓘ tel: 02 51 87 14 20

A delightful setting for this village, with its rows of houses overlooking a long stretch of river. Cycle and boat hire available. A small museum of fishing adjoins La Récré crêperie. Lunchtime cruises depart from near the bridge (see Extras, page 108).

ARÇAIS (Deux-Sèvres)
ⓘ tel: 05 49 35 43 44

A picturesque château overlooks the main slipway of this charming village. Craft and antique shops line the cobbled pavements; winding alleyways contain a selection of attractive *gîtes* and bed-&-breakfast establishments. Boat and cycle rental available.

ST-HILAIRE-LA-PALUD (Deux-Sèvres)
ⓘ tel: 05 49 35 32 15

There's an interesting bird park (see over) on the edge of the village. Boats can be rented on the shady canals at nearby Monfaucon.

VENISE VERTE EXTRAS

Markets: Fri, Vix. Fri (1 July-31 Aug) & Sun, Coulon. Sun (1 July-31 Aug), Maillé.

Specialities: Eels. Snails. Lamb & mogettes (haricot beans). Melons. Wine.

Wine producer: **Mercier Frères**. Fiefs Vendéens wines: reds, whites & rosés. 1 May-30 Sept, Mon-Sat, 9.30am-noon & 2.30-6.30pm. Domaine de la Chaignée, 2km NW of Vix (tel: 02 51 00 65 14).

Restaurants: **Ferme-Auberge du Montnommé**. Farm-restaurant serving regional dishes. Le Grand Montnommé, S of Vix (tel: 02 51 00 64 79; booking essential).

> **Les Oiseaux du Marais Poitevin: Parc Ornithologique**. The visit to this bird park begins with an excellent film about bird migration. Outside, a signposted trail takes you past enclosures of ducks, geese, and wading birds. ◐ *Late Mar-Easter, daily 2-7pm; Easter-14 Sept, daily 10am-7.30pm; 15 Sept-1 Nov, Wed-Mon 2-7pm. Le Petit Buisson (tel: 05 49 26 04 09). 6€, children 3.50€; family (2+2) 17.50€.* ♿

LA GARETTE (Deux-Sèvres)
ⓘ tel: 05 49 04 51 73
Pretty village, with a series of interesting craft shops, restaurants and boat-hire places in some of the ancient houses that line its half-mile-long, pedestrianised main street. Parking on outskirts.

COULON (Deux-Sèvres)
ⓘ tel: 05 49 35 99 29 fax: 05 49 35 84 31
www.ville-coulon.fr
ot@ville-coulon.fr
Officially one of "the most beautiful villages of France", the capital of the "Venise Verte" contains old streets full of craft shops, and many photogenic fishermen's houses reflected in the waters of the Sèvre Niortaise. Several companies rent out traditional boats; if you have brought a picnic, choose a hirer that owns a waterside site along the way, where you can stop off to eat on dry land.

> **Maison des Marais Mouillés**. In a stone Renaissance building you learn about the "wet" marshland: the reclamation of the land from the sea; the industries of eel-fishing and poplar-wood production; and the cultivation of *mogettes* (haricot beans), which are such an important part of the Vendean diet. A room-setting recreates a typical marshland interior, and film and photographs illustrate how the flat-bottomed boats are used even today to transport everything—including livestock—to and from the little green fields. Unsurprisingly, you also learn at least four different words for canal! ◐ *1 Feb-30 Apr & 1 Oct-30 Nov, Sat, Sun 10am-1pm & 2-7pm (school holidays, daily 10am-noon & 2-7pm); 1 May-30 Sept, daily 10am-noon & 2-7pm (1 July-31 Aug, daily 10am-8pm). Place de la Coûtume (tel: 05 49 35 81 04). 5€, students 3.80€, children 2.50€.*

VENISE VERTE EXTRAS

La Récré. Waterside pizzeria/crêperie in an old school building; menus are in the form of a school exercise-book. Damvix (tel: 02 51 87 10 11).

Le Collibert II. Lunchtime cruises aboard a glass-sided boat. Menus from 25€, children 15€. 1 July-31 Aug; Tues, Thurs, Sat, Sun 12.30-4.30pm. Damvix (tel: 02 51 87 19 16; booking essential).

Festival: La Nuit, le Marais, le Conte. Annual storytelling evening. The audience is conveyed by boat along illuminated canals. July. Damvix.

■ The Marais Poitevin: each town and village has a charm of its own. Top, boat-hire at Le Gué de Velluire; below, the pretty town of Marans.

>Réserve Naturelle de St-Denis-du-Payré. A thoroughly enjoyable introduction to bird-watching is provided at a 207-hectare marshland wildlife reserve, on open pastureland 3km north-west of Triaize—though an awkward lunchtime closing period means that a visit takes a bit of careful planning. You have to buy tickets first at the Maison de la Réserve (visitor centre), well signposted in the centre of St-Denis-du-Payré—a village 5.5km west of Triaize. Allow 45 minutes here, to enjoy an informative 15-minute film (in English if requested) on the marshes and their flora and fauna; the hands-on demonstrations upstairs about local ecology (many captions in English); and the rooftop observatory from which—if you have brought binoculars—you can look across to L'Aiguillon Bay and towards the distant curve of the Ile de Ré bridge.

At the reserve itself, along the Triaize road, you take a wooden boardwalk, often screened from wildlife by wooden walls, for 300 metres or so to a wood-built observatory. Inside is a comfortable space with 18 high-powered telescopes, and knowledgeable volunteers to point out (often in excellent English) the most interesting birds to be seen. Year-round residents include ducks, harriers, curlews, egrets and the rare Bonelli's eagle. Winter sees wigeon, teal and greylag goose arrive; in spring, when the wild orchids and irises are in flower, black-tailed godwits pause in their thousands; summer visitors include redshank, white storks and the occasional spoonbill; while migratory species like garganey and black tern may drop by in autumn. ◗ *Early Feb-early Mar & early Apr-early May, daily 9.30am-12.30pm & 2-6pm. I July-31 Aug, daily 9.30am-12.30pm & 3-7pm. Late Oct-early Nov, & Christmas holiday period, daily 9.30am-12.30pm & 2-5pm. Closed 1 Jan, 1 May & 24, 25, 31 Dec. Maison de la Réserve, 9 bis Rue de Gaulle, St-Denis-du-Payré (tel: 02 51 27 23 92). 5.35€ (includes access to observatory, 2km E on D25); students, children & disabled 3.80€; family (2+3 or more) 18.30€. ⓖ (except upstairs area at visitor centre).*

VELLUIRE

ⓘ tel: 02 51 52 31 04 fax: 02 51 52 37 05
www.cc-pays-fontenay-le-comte.fr

A prosperous-looking stone-built village 21km east of Luçon, located at a crossing-point on the Vendée river. A little way to the west is the *communal*, or common grazing land, of Le Poiré-sur-Velluire, last vestige of a tradition whereby local farmers turn their animals out together in spring, and round them up to reclaim them in December. Along the D65 south towards Le Gué-de-Velluire (see page 106) the road climbs to give you the strange impression of being on a cliff overlooking the ocean—indeed, the flat marshland that lies 40 metres below was once the sea bed.

>Communal. This 250-hectare nature reserve is run on a system of "commons". During winter the pastureland is flooded. Once it dries out and the grass shoots up in spring, farmers turn out their horses, cows and geese—each marked with an identifying number—and the new season is celebrated with a colourful festival. The *communal* is a haven for birds: storks nest here from early spring; little bustard gather in autumn; and spectacular numbers of lapwing and golden plover visit between September and March. An observatory 2km west of Velluire, on the straight, poplar-edged road linking L'Anglée and La Tublerie, provides an excellent vantage-point. ●

>Le Séchoir du Marais. A surprising discovery is this farm 7km south of Velluire, growing more than 50 varieties of flowers, which are dried on an industrial scale. Visitors are welcomed to the dark, 35-metre-long drying-shed where, amid upside-down bundles of stems hanging from the roof, you can watch a video about the way the flowers are harvested. A shop sells ready-made floral arrangements and bunches of dried flowers. ● *Mon-Sat 9.30am-12.30pm & 2.30-7pm. Les Gargouillasses, signposted off the D25 east of Le Gué-de-Velluire (tel: 02 51 52 57 39). Free.*

VELLUIRE EXTRAS

Restaurant: Auberge de la Rivière. Upmarket restaurant, overlooking the river Vendée, in a Logis de France hotel. Menus from 33€. Rue Fouarne, signposted from village centre (tel: 02 51 52 32 15). *Festival: Ouverture du Marais Communal.* Grand fête celebrating the new grazing season on the village's common. Le Poiré-sur-Velluire, 1km NW of Velluire. Late Apr.

Area 4

North

Le Boupère

St-Prouant

Prieuré de Grammont

Bo Tif

Lac de Moulin-Rochereau

Monsirei

to Nantes

Puybelliard

Sigournais

to Nantes

CHANTONNAY

River Grand Lay

Bazoges-en- Pareds

A83

D 949 bis

D 949 bis

D 106

D 31

Lac de l'Angle-Guignard

N 137

La Caillière

to La Roche

6

D 8

D 23

0   5   10km

7 Ste-Herminè

D 52

For explanation of symbols, see page 6.

L'Hermena

TH PL

A83

Pétosse

to Luçon

Fontenay-le-Comte, Pouzauges and the Haut-Bocage

This region contains the Vendée's largest forest, highest village and—from pre-Revolution days when the area was known as Bas-Poitou—its lovely former capital of Fontenay-le-Comte. Medieval wall-paintings adorn some ancient churches around Pouzauges. The charmingly unspoilt villages of Bazoges-en-Pareds and Vouvant wait to be discovered, as do the vestiges of the Vendée's once-important coal industry at Faymoreau. In more futuristic mode, not far off lie the state-of-the-art cinemas and video arcades of Futuroscope.

BAZOGES-EN-PAREDS

ⓘ tel: 02 51 51 25 19 fax : 02 51 51 21 60

★ You can easily spot Bazoges as you drive across the rolling green hills of the *bocage* on the D949bis; look out for a huge castle keep, crowned by a jaunty little pointed watch-tower. With its fortified stronghold, ancient church and old square overlooked by ancient stone buildings, this unspoilt village 12km south-east of Chantonnay retains a charmingly old-world atmosphere.

❯**Donjon**. The magnificent square tower dominating the village is the keep of a long-vanished castle that dates back to the 14th century. An English explanatory leaflet is available to guide you around the recently restored and furnished interior that includes a fascinating display of armour, and shows the order in which a man would put it on. Up the uneven spiral stone stairs are rooms decorated with tapestries, solid oak chests and four-poster beds. The reward at the top is wonderful panoramic views of the surrounding countryside from the covered sentry-way that runs round the entire summit of the building. Down below, across the courtyard, is a beautifully laid-out medieval-style garden, with fruit trees, herbs and fragrant old-fashioned roses growing in wattle-edged beds alongside a huge 16th-century *fuie*, or dovecote, once home to 2,000 pigeons. On summer nights the keep is beautifully illuminated. ◑ *15 Feb-15 Nov, Sun & public holidays 2.30-6pm (Easter-30 Sept, daily 2.30-6pm). 12 Cours du Château (tel: 02 51 51 23 10). 4€ (including garden), children 1.50€. ⅙ (garden only).*

❯**Musée d'Arts et Traditions Populaires**. Guided tours of Bazoges' excellent museum, housed in one of the buildings clustered round the *donjon*, give a glimpse of rural life in the region in former times (descriptive sheet available in English). Among intriguing facts that emerge: several generations of a family would share a bedroom; country people believed dirt prevented disease entering through empty pores, so washed only face and hands; babies old enough to crawl were tightly swaddled and placed upright with their legs in a hollow container during the day, to keep them out of danger while their mothers worked in the fields. ◑ *Details as above. 3€, children 1€.*

❯**La Ciste des Cous**. About 1km south-west towards La Jaudonnière, and signposted off to the right at a bleak and lonely site, is the Vendée's oldest megalithic monument, dating from 4000BC. Its roof has long disintegrated, leaving a circular, stone-flagged enclosure, with a low tunnel leading to a prehistoric burial chamber from which more than 100 skeletons were excavated in 1913. ●

CHANTONNAY

ⓘ tel: 02 51 94 46 51 fax: 02 51 46 99 30
www.ville-chantonnay.fr www.cc-deuxlays.fr
tourisme-chantonnay@wanadoo.fr

This market town in the centre of the Vendée, 21km south-west of Pouzauges, is known as "the gateway to the *bocage*". To the north and east the landscape is one of hills and valleys; Chantonnay also has three large lakes nearby, offering opportunities for boating, sunbathing, fishing and waterside walks.

Interesting old villages in the area include Puybelliard and Sigournais. From the latter, which is clustered around the remains of an ancient castle, some signposted walks lead through vineyards dotted with quaint stone buildings known as *cabanes de vignes*, built to store their tools by wine-growers of days gone by.

Restaurant: Auberge du Donjon. Sophisticated *food served in a prettily-restored stone house opposite castle. Menus from18€. 28 Rue de la Poste (tel: 02 51 51 20 07).*
Festivals:
Nocturnes au Donjon. *Atmospheric torchlit evenings around castle precincts. July & Aug (twice a year).*
Foire aux Marrons. *Chestnut festival. La Caillère-St-Hilaire, 3km S of Bazoges. Oct.*

Market: Tues & Sat.
Restaurants:
Le Clemenceau. *Popular for pizzas (6€-11€), plus steaks & grills. 44 Avenue Clemenceau, near Super U (tel: 02 51 46 83 81).*
La Morlière. *Good food overlooking lake, with play-space for children, 7km NE of Chantonnay. From Sigournais take Monsireigne road for 2km (tel: 02 51 40 41 98).*

❯**Les Cinq Fours**. Three giant stone lime-kilns (of an original five) stand incongruously in a housing estate to the south of town. You can look at them from the road, with a chance of a close-up view on the heritage days, (see page 9) in September. ● *Rue de la Carrière, off D31 La Caillière road.*

❯**Château de Sigournais**. High stone walls surround an imposing medieval castle keep, with slate-roofed turrets, in a village 4km north-east of Chantonnay. Guided tours of the interior feature coats of arms on display from 34 French provinces and 144 Vendean villages, and some before-and-after photographs showing restoration work on the castle. There are magnificent views from the covered *chemin de ronde*, or sentry-way, at the top. ○ *1 July-early Sept, daily 2.30-6.30pm. Sigournais village centre (tel: 02 51 40 40 71). 3.50€, children 2€; under 12s free.*

❯**Puybelliard**. Although this village lies just 20 metres south of the busy D949bis, 2km north-east of Chantonnay, it produces a strong feeling of having stepped back in time. The fortified church has slit openings through which defenders could fire to protect the villagers gathered within; opposite is a venerable prison tower; behind that are narrow lanes and alleys, particuarly Rue des Dames, near the *mairie,* lined with buildings that display arches, Renaissance porches and other ancient features. ●

■ Chantonnay: old kilns, above left. Puybelliard: former prison, above.

CHANTONNAY EXTRAS

*Wine: **Domaine de la Barbinière**. Good-value Fiefs Vendéens wines from producer Philippe Orion. Sat 9am-12.30pm & 2-7pm (1 July-31 Aug, Mon-Sat 2-7pm). On D31, 8km SE of Chantonnay (tel: 02 51 34 39 72).*

Festival: Quatre Jours en Chantonnay. *Four-day walking festival, open to all. May (over the Ascension Day weekend).*

LA CHATAIGNERAIE

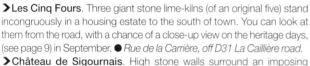

ⓘ tel: 02 51 52 62 37 fax: 02 51 52 69 20
tourisme@paysdelachataigneraie.org

If you approach this little hillside town from the south-east, by the D19, you see a rocky outcrop supporting a stone viaduct that is a popular spot for country walks, and also the location of a bungee-jumping enterprise. More surprises are in store if you arrive from the west, by the D949bis; a local horticulturalist has lined the road with a riot of miniature trees trimmed into spirals and pyramids.

❯**Elastic Bungee**. Anyone crazy enough to contemplate taking a 52-metre plunge above the valley of the river Mère should head for the disused viaduct, 5km east of La Châtaigneraie. ◑ *Mid Apr-early Nov, most Sats & Suns. Viaduc de Coquilleau, on D19, Route de Coulonges (tel: 05 65 60 00 45). 45€ first jump (includes certificate & T-shirt).*

❯**Église de Cheffois**. Push open the door of the soberly-designed forti-fied church that towers above a picturesque village 4km north-west of La Châtaigneraie to see a surprising multitude of statues within. ● *Cheffois.*

LA CHATAIGNERAIE EXTRAS

*Restaurant: **Ferme-Auberge du Moulin Migné**. Delicious home-produced meat & vegetables, in a restored watermill. (Vegetarian meals may be ordered 24 hours in advance.) Menus from 14.50€. 5km W of La Châtaigneraie, signposted S of D949bis at Cheffois (tel: 02 51 69 68 76; booking essential).*

❯**St-Pierre-du-Chemin**. This large village 6km north-east of La Châtaigneraie is known for its special greyish-pink stone, called *pierre des Plochères*, outcrops of which can be seen in surrounding fields, and which has been used in the construction of several large buildings. The village's best claims to fame, however, are the relics of third-century martyr St Valentine that have been held in the church—on the left of the nave—since the mid-19th century. For obvious reasons, in mid-February the village is the focus of a "Fête des Amoureux", or Festival of Love. ●

FAYMOREAU-LES-MINES

ⓘ tel: 02 51 87 23 01 fax: 02 51 00 72 51
office.tourisme@cc-vsa.com

Village on the eastern border of the Vendée, 16km north-east of Fontenay-le-Comte, in an area rich with memories of the French industrial revolution. Coal was mined in the region from the early 19th century, the industry reaching its peak between 1913 and 1958, when labourers imported from Czechoslovakia and Poland were producing up to 60,000 tonnes of coal a year to fuel a local power station and a glassworks. At the pit village of La Verrerie, 3km north of Faymoreau itself, miners and mine-masters had their homes in three parallel streets known as *corons*, the poorest houses being at the top of the valley and the smartest (along the *coron* known as "Bas de Soie", or "silk stockings") at the bottom. All can still be seen at La Verrerie today. A few other relics of the mining days remain, notably an evocative pit-head tower at Épagne, 8km to the north-west.

❯**Centre Minier**. A mining museum installed in the old glassworkers' hostel tells the history of the local industry. Visitors are transported in a rickety lift down (actually rather less far than it seems!) to a re-creation of a mine in a series of illuminated tableaux. (Don't hang back politely at these, otherwise by the time you move in for a close look you'll miss the short-lived lighting effects.) Back upstairs there are displays of mining lamps, tools and documents, a "*salle des pendus*"—a room where work-clothes were hung to dry at the end of the day—plus plenty to read (in French) about the area's coal industry and about the East European miners who worked here. ● *Sun 2-6pm (1 Apr-30 June & 1 Sept-1 Nov, Tues-Sun & public holidays 2-7pm; 1 July-31 Aug, daily 11am-7pm). Closed 1 Jan & 25 Dec. La Cour, La Verrerie (tel: 02 51 00 48 48). 4.60€, children 3.10€.* ♿

❯**Chapelle des Mineurs**. Walk down the hill to the newly-restored chapel, built in 1875 by the mine director of the time to keep the workers more attuned to Catholicism than Communism. Nineteen modern stained-glass windows were installed in 2001, designed by French artist Carmélo Zagari—himself the son of a miner—to evoke the hard life of miners everywhere. ● *Opening hours as for museum, above. Free.*

❯**Église de Foussais-Payré**. Visitors come from afar to marvel at the sculpted façade of the 11th-century church in a village 6km west of Faymoreau. Sadly, though, the depredations of the region's various wars mean that some of the statues have lost their heads. Beautifully-carved panels either side of the doorway show a Crucifixion scene, and the risen Christ with his disciples at Emmaus. Over the doorway you can make out fantastical animals, and the figure of Jesus between the symbols of the four Evangelists. Concerts are often held inside the church during summer. Among the Renaissance houses around the picturesque village centre, look for the Auberge Ste-Catherine (St Catherine's Inn), which was the family home of 16th-century mathematician François Viète (see page 115), and for a tiny, open-sided building that was once a market-hall. ●

■ **Foussais-Payré: Bible scenes set in stone.**

FONTENAY-LE-COMTE

(i) tel: 02 51 69 44 99 fax: 02 51 50 00 90
www.ville-fontenaylecomte.fr
www.cc-pays-fontenay-le-comte.fr
www.tourisme-sudvendee.com
ot.paysdefontenay.le.comte@libertysurf.fr

★ Ancient streets lined with Renaissance houses—once the haunts of poets, scientists, philosophers and lawyers—indicate the former importance of a town that, until the French Revolution of 1789, was the capital of Bas-Poitou (as the Vendée region was formerly known). Lying near the south-eastern corner of the *département* at the junction of the rolling plain and the wooded hills of the *bocage*, Fontenay was much damaged by the English in the Hundred Years War. Later, having a large Protestant population, the town saw considerable turmoil during the Wars of Religion. But its status was overturned for good after the Vendée Wars, when Napoleon deemed it too far from the geographical centre of the *département* to quell any new peasant uprisings, and picked on the then small village of La Roche-sur-Yon as his new capital.

The writer François Rabelais (c1494-1553), who created two legendary giants of French literature, spent more than 15 years in Fontenay as a monk, before moving to the abbey of Maillezais (see page 96) in 1524. In a series of bawdy, satiric allegories with touches of local *patois* he told of Gargantua, who rode on a mare as big as six elephants, and of his son, Pantagruel, who shattered a mighty ship's chain that bound him into his cradle with one blow of his infant fist, learnt all knowledge and every language, and once sheltered a whole army from the rain beneath his tongue.

The town is laid out on both sides of the Vendée river. The leafy Place Viète, at the top, is called after François Viète—a 16th-century mathematician, born in Fontenay, who is credited with the creation of modern algebra. This side of the river buzzes with activity on Saturday mornings, when the market is in full swing—the food-hall is by the river, not far from arcaded Place Belliard and Rue du Pont-aux-Chèvres, both lined with interesting old houses. The elegantly-sculpted 16th-century spring, the Fontaine des Quatre-Tias (from which the name "Fontenay" derives) is a little to the north of the market-hall. Above it, on the site of the town's long-vanished feudal fortress, is a tree-filled park known as Parc Baron. Across the river, don't miss the ancient Rue des Loges, and several imposing, once-grand houses.

A walking route is marked around the old quarters—brochure available from the tourist office, which also arranges regular guided tours on foot, including some around the town's Renaissance cellars. A special trail in July and August features contemporary works of art installed in the town's streets and squares.

As a refugee from war-torn Belgium, writer Georges Simenon, lived in Fontenay during World War II, and used the town as a setting for several of his detective novels. In *Maigret a Peur*, for example, his fictional policeman tracks a serial killer through its old streets.

Market: Sat.

Restaurants:

Le Fontarabie. Good-value lunches in slightly old-fashioned hotel on Fontenay's main street. 57 Rue de la République (tel: 02 51 69 17 24).

Crêperie Le Pommier. Eat salads, or sweet & savoury pancakes, on a shady terrace in summer; or cheese fondue, by the log fire, in winter. 9 Rue des Gélinières, Pissotte, 4km N of Fontenay (tel: 02 51 69 08 06).

Ferme-Auberge de Mélusine. Excellent food at a classily-converted barn in the centre of a village 6km NE of Fontenay. Menus around 15€; try the "grillée de mogettes" (garlic-rich beans on toast). Place de la Maison-Neuve, St-Michel-le-Cloucq (tel: 02 51 51 07 61).

Brocante: Emmaüs. Large treasure-trove of furniture & other household items. Tues, Wed, Fri 2.30-6pm; Sat 10am-noon & 2.30-6pm. Rue de la Meilleraie, St-Michel-le-Cloucq, 6km NE of Fontenay, on D104 (tel: 02 51 51 01 10).

Festivals:

Festival de Terre-Neuve. Classical French plays, acted out in front of the elegant Château de Terre-Neuve (see main entry). July & Aug.

Les Ricochets. Street theatre throughout the town, with music & storytelling. July & Aug.

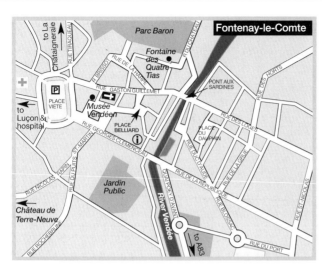

■ **Fontenay: old arcades in Place Belliard.**

❯**Musée Vendéen**. You should come here to get a feel for Fontenay's history before walking around its streets. Ground-floor rooms contain locally-discovered antiquities and some beautiful Gallo-Roman glass. Upstairs are examples of furniture typical of the southern Vendée and displays on the region's bird and animal life, including the sure-footed Vendean mule, a cross between the large *baudet du Poitou* donkey and a sturdy female horse. These beasts were much sought after up to World War I by the French army. The second floor contains works by 19th-century painters Paul Baudry and Charles Milcendeau (see page 59), and wood-engraver and etcher Auguste Lepère. ● *Wed-Sun 2-6pm (15 June-15 Sept, Tues-Fri 10am-noon & 2-6pm; Sat, Sun 2-6pm). Rue du 137e RI, near Place Viète (tel: 02 51 69 31 31). 2.20€, students & children free.* ♿

❯**Château de Terre-Neuve**. Nicolas Rapin, 16th-century poet and magistrate, created this exquisite, fairy-tale-style stately home which he trimmed with pinnacles and turrets and adorned with terracotta statues of the Muses. Today it is a private home, but 50-minute guided tours are given of some of the beautifully-furnished rooms. The visit features magnificent fireplaces—one depicting the search for the "philosopher's stone" (familiar to Harry Potter fans as the mineral that alchemists believed would turn base metals into gold)—and some mellow wooden panelling from the château of Chambord, in the Loire valley, plus collections of keys, ivory, costumes and Old Master paintings. A section is devoted to the etching-plates of artist Octave de Rochebrune, who was responsible for restoring the château in the 19th century, and there are collections of gothic keys, flintlock pistols and hundreds of pestles-and-mortars. Georges Simenon, lived here with his family between 1940 and 1942. ◐ *1 May-30 Sept, daily 9am-noon & 2-7pm. Off Rue de Jarnigande (tel: 02 51 69 99 41). 5.60€, children 1.80€.*

❯**Rue des Loges**. On the east side of the river, across the Pont aux Sardines, you can stroll along the oldest street in Fontenay. Now pedestrianised, the town's former main thoroughfare is a little run-down today, but still has many picturesque shop-fronts and ancient houses of stone or half-timbering, some with plaques outside giving a résumé of their history. Don't hesitate to explore the small covered alleys that lead off it, sometimes to hidden-away inner courtyards. ●

❯**Auzay**. A small village, 7km south-west of Fontenay that has been a rich source of neolithic discoveries. Its more recent historical treasure is an iron bridge designed by Gustave Eiffel. ●

❯**Montgolfière du Bocage**. When weather conditions are right, you can take a morning hot-air balloon trip from Fontenay and drift above the silvery waterways of the Marais Poitevin, or "Green Venice" (see page 105). ● *Times & take-off location by appointment (tel: 05 49 80 10 45). 220€ per person per hour (four people 210€ each; five people 200€ each), children 130€.*

>**Parc du Château de l'Hermenault**. A sober-looking country house stands on the site of a building that was, until the 17th century, the summer residence of the bishops of Maillezais (see page 96). François Rabelais (see page 115) is said to have planted the seeds of some of the mighty plane trees in its grounds. You can visit the parkland—at present being painstakingly restored—which contains a *pigeonnier*, or dovecote, a 17th-century barn with some magnificent roof timbers, a watermill, and a *lavoir*, or washing-place. ○ *Grounds only: 1 July-31 Aug, Tues-Sun 2.30-6.30pm. L'Hermenault, 11km NW of Fontenay (tel: 02 51 00 15 37). 3.50€, children free.*
>**Pétosse**. A quiet village 8km west of Fontenay, strung out along a main street rejoicing in the name of Rue des Chats-Ferrés ("Street of Iron-shod Cats"). Local legend says that witches, disguised as cats, clattered along in metal-soled clogs to attend their sabbaths. Whatever the truth, if you go into the church you will find near the north-east corner of the central cupola a strange little feline figure, set to pounce from the ceiling. Beneath the village is a warren of *souterrains* (underground passages), thought to have been a refuge for local inhabitants from marauding Vikings a thousand years ago; there are occasional guided tours of them in July and August. ● *Information from L'Hermenault tourist office (tel: 02 51 00 15 37).*

MERVENT

ⓘ tel: 02 51 00 20 97 fax: 02 51 00 03 34
www.cc-pays-fontenay-le-comte.fr
www.tourisme-sudvendee.com
otsi-mervent@wanadoo.fr

At this hillside village in the heart of the large forest of Mervent-Vouvant, 7km north of Fontenay-le-Comte, you can gaze out across the valley from a viewpoint on the site of Mervent's former castle. In summer, the series of lakes created by dams across the Mère and Vendée rivers are good places for bathing, canoeing and windsurfing; the most popular swimming area is below Mervent, at La Vallée, near the bridge where the D99 crosses the water. The leafy D99A takes you on a winding route for 6km through the woods; there are also many signposted walks and rides among the 5,000 hectares of oak and chestnut—shady in summer and colourful in autumn—that are home to red deer and wild boar.

The forest still has an active industrial side too, its 35m-tall sessile oaks being particularly sought after for cabinet-making, carpentry, wood flooring and the production of wine-barrels.

>**Parc de Pierre-Brune**. A beautiful drive through the forest on the D99A brings you to a large, shady, pleasantly unsophisticated amusement park in the heart of the forest, 2km north of Mervent. Once you get used to the razzmatazzy music, you'll find plenty to entertain the children in the way of adventure playground, train-rides, mini-golf, chair-o-planes, bumper-boats and mini-karting, as well as the Vallée Enchantée, full of colourful swings, slides, roundabouts, crazy bikes, bouncy castle and seesaws. ◖ *Apr, daily 11am-7pm; 1-31 May, Sat, Sun & public holidays 11am-7pm; 1-30 June, daily 11am-7pm; 1 July-31 Aug, daily 10am-8pm; 1-15 Sept, daily 11am-7pm; 16-30 Sept, Sat, Sun 11am-7pm; 1-31 Oct, Sun 11am-7pm. Off D99A (tel: 02 51 00 20 18). 10€.* ♿
>**Grotte du Père Montfort**. Candles burn inside a little cave some 4km north-west of Mervent village, in which St Louis-Marie Grignon de Montfort lived for a time in 1715 during a mission to convert the region's many Protestants to Catholicism. It's halfway-down a precipitous slope in the forest, overlooking the river Mère, signposted to the east off the D938ter. After a—literally—rocky start, the steep path is replaced by a sturdy boardwalk with steps and handrails. Père Montfort founded several religious orders, and is buried at St-Laurent-sur-Sèvre (see page 148). ●

■ Mervent: stylish B&B, Logis de la Cornelière.

>Château de la Citardière. A curiously low, solid, moated Renaissance castle, its top decorated with impressive stone spouts that look like cannons, stands in the woods 2km north-east of Mervent. On the pretext of visiting the excellent *crêperie* or one of the château's temporary exhibitions, you can go inside one or two of the vaulted rooms; one contains an excellent example of a *potager*, or stone cooking-range formerly heated by hot embers. Concerts and other cultural events take place in summer.
● *Sat 5-8pm; Sun & public holidays noon-7pm (1 June-15 Sept, Thurs-Sun noon-7pm; 1 July-31 Aug, daily noon-7pm). Closed late Dec-late Jan. Les Ouillères, off D99 (tel: 02 51 00 27 04). Free.* ⅊

>Aventure Parc. Activity-packed treetop challenges among the stately oaks of Mervent Forest, with routes at varying levels of difficulty strung out across taut wires and swaying bridges. ❶ *From June 2004. 1km NW of Mervent village, near Le Chêne Tord campsite. Telephone number, opening hours & ticket prices not available at time of writing.*

>Maison des Amis de la Forêt. A small museum beside a lake, 2km north-east of Mervent, which uses displays of mushrooms and stuffed birds, boar and deer, to show the woodland's wildlife. It also demonstrates the uses made of forest materials to create wheels, clogs and other items. Outside is a mini-golf, each hole designed to represent a different local tourist attraction. ● *Thurs-Tues 2.30-5.30pm. 127 Route de la Bironnière, La Jamonière (tel: 02 51 00 00 87). 2.50€, children 1.70€.* ⅊ *partial.*

>Parc Zoologique et Paysager. Exotic birds, farmyard animals, monkeys and meerkats welcome visitors to this small, agreeably shady zoo park in the heart of Mervent forest. A 3D film on animals is projected in one building; ask at reception for special viewing glasses. ● *Daily 10am-7pm. Le Gros Roc, on D65 (tel: 02 51 00 07 59).* ⅊

MONCOUTANT (Deux-Sèvres)

ⓘ tel: 05 49 72 60 44 fax: 05 49 72 84 76
www.terre-de-sevre.org/sicm/
sicm@terre-de-sevre.org

On the edge of this small town, 15km north-east of La Châtaigneraie, the largest fishing centre in Europe (see Pescalis, below) has opened its waters to anglers. The installation of this enormous project has encouraged the development of other tourist attractions in the area, so it's worth crossing the Vendée border into the neighbouring county of Deux-Sèvres to sample a few of them.

>Pescalis. This huge fishing centre provides year-round sport in a series of lakes, each stocked with a different range of fish, from trout to carp, black-bass to pike. Tuition available for beginners (in English; booking recommended). Equipment hire and sales on site, and holiday accommodation available in campsite and hotels—plus walking, riding, tennis and other activities for determined non-fishers. An "underwater experience", the *Spectacle sous les Eaux de Pescalis*, gives the impression of touring the depths, providing a fish's-eye view of hooks and floats, and including a film show (subtitled in English) about the centre and its philosophy. ● *Sun 2-6pm (15 June-15 Sept, daily 10am-7pm). 2km S of Montcoutant on D744 (tel: 05 49 72 00 01). Site admission free. Spectacle: 8€ for first adult (7€ for additional adults in same party), children under four 2€. Whole- & half-day fishing available: prices range from 9€ (half-day) to 44€ (24-hour session, including night carp-fishing). www.pescalis.com/*

>Musée d'École de la Tour Nivelle. A brilliant concept, this "museum" of school life actually provides you with the experience of sitting in a French classroom scrawling a *dictée* (dictation) in the kind of scratchy, old-fashioned pen that has to be dipped in ink. Visitors—adults or children—have to don beret, overall and clogs, and file into the 1920s-style schoolroom to sit at wooden desks under the eye of a "teacher" (or guide). It's hugely entertaining if you speak reasonable French; perhaps a bit inhibiting if you don't (though the guides do speak some English). You can also go upstairs to see the living accommodation once allocated to the village teacher. Alongside the reception area are displays of work by Ernest Pérochon, a 1920s novelist who was born in the nearby town of Courlay. ● *1 Jan-30 June & 1 Oct-30 Nov, first & third Sun of month, 2.30-6.30pm; 1 July-31 Aug, Thurs-Sun 2.30-6.30pm. La Tour Nivelle, on D938ter 8km N of Moncoutant (tel: 05 49 80 29 37). 4€, children 2.50€.* ⅃

❯ **Jardin des Chirons/Rocher Branlant**. In a valley deep in the countryside, 12km south-east of Moncoutant, five million years of erosion have left a chaotic legacy of enormous rocks, sprinkled as if by a giant hand beside the Sèvre Nantaise river. (In spite of the "*jardin*" signposts, don't expect a garden!) Look for the 30-tonne *rocher branlant*, a granite stone that can be made to rock fairly easily when pressed in the right place. You can rent headsets with an interesting commentary in English on the different stones and the legends associated with them. Near the visitor centre are a children's playground and mini-golf. ● *Site accessible at all times.* ◑ *Visitor centre open mid Apr-early May, daily 3-6pm; early May-30 June, Sun & public holidays 11am-6pm; 1 July-31 Aug, daily 11am-9pm; 1 Sept-15 Oct, Sun 11am-6pm. 1km N of D949bis at Vernoux-en-Gâtine (tel: 06 81 17 28 33). Site access free; varying charges for activities, map & audioguide.*

MOUILLERON-EN-PAREDS

ⓘ tel: 02 51 00 32 32
tourisme@paysdelachataigneraie.org

In Mouilleron's main square around noon, the 13 bells from the Romanesque church play *Ave Maria* before the midday chimes. Incredibly, this unspoilt village, 16km east of Chantonnay, is the birthplace of not just one, but two of France's most famous wartime heroes: Georges Clemenceau (1841-1929), who was born above a former shop on today's Rue Clemenceau; and Jean de Lattre de Tassigny (1889-1952), who drew his first breath in a more prosperous-looking house (see below) in the street that now bears his name.

❯ **Maison Natale du Maréchal de Lattre de Tassigny**. Cosy, 19th-century middle-class house, home of the maternal grandparents of distinguished French soldier Jean de Lattre, and still furnished in comfortable bourgeois style. Decorated eight times in World War I, de Lattre became a general at the start of World War II but was imprisoned by the Vichy government in 1943. He later escaped, took command of a unit in north Africa, led the French First Army that landed in Provence in August 1944, liberated Alsace, crossed the Rhine and the Danube rivers, and accepted the surrender of Germany in Berlin on 8 May 1945.

The three floors of the house are filled with family furniture and mementoes, and details of the Marshal's career, including his later service as commander-in-chief of the French forces in Indo-China during the early 1950s. Part of the display is devoted to de Lattre's son, Bernard, who was killed in Indo-China in 1951 and who lies buried beside his father in the village cemetery. Guided tours of the house in English are offered during the summer, and special events are held on occasional Sunday afternoons ● *Daily 10am-noon & 2-5pm (15 Apr-15 Oct, daily 9.30am-noon & 2-6pm). Closed 1 Jan & 25 Dec. Rue de Lattre (tel: 02 51 00 31 49). 3€ (Sun, 2.30€; first Sun of month free), students 2.30€, children free. Admits also to Musée des Deux Victoires (see below).*

❯ **Musée National des Deux Victoires: Clemenceau-de Lattre**. Personal relics, photographs and documents draw parallels between these two famous sons of Mouilleron, especially relating to the signing by Georges Clemenceau of the Treaty of Versailles on 28 June 1919, and to Jean de Lattre's signature in Berlin on behalf of France at the conclusion of World War II. Look for a large stone eagle that once stood in the Reichstag, in Berlin, and for a piece of used blotting-paper kept by Clemenceau as a souvenir of the 1919 treaty—Hitler later had the original document destroyed, so this collection of "mirror-image" signatures is all that survives. ● *Admission details as above.*

> **Rochers de Mouilleron**. From the ancient village pump and washing-place you can take the Sentier des Meuniers (the Millers' Path), once busy with donkeys carrying bags of corn up through the woods. On a windy ridge at the top stand three majestic windmills, one now an oratory to the memory of Maréchal de Lattre de Tassigny and his son Bernard, and an imposing memorial showing the Marshal's troops in Indo-China. You can also reach the ridge by road; signposted off the D949bis, on the east side of the village. Like those on the Mont des Alouettes (see page 137), these mills and 11 others that stood here played an important signalling role during the Wars of the Vendée. ●

> **Manoir des Sciences de Réaumur**. A 17th-century manor house 7km north-east of Mouilleron contains a permanent exhibition on the life of René-Antoine Ferchault de Réaumur (1683-1757). Born in La Rochelle, this versatile French scientist spent holidays here, at his family's country mansion. As well as inventing the thermometer that bears his name (on which freezing-point is 0 and boiling-point 80 degrees), Réaumur developed a method of making steel, invented the first coach-springs to make travel more bearable, attempted to cross rabbits with chickens, and carried out studies of insect life that earned him a reputation as the father of French entomology.

Sadly, the story of this fascinating career is not put over well for non-French-speakers, relying on artfully-filmed talking heads, on lengthy passages to read, and on mundane items such as a piece of coal "just like Réaumur would have used". Best features are the boxes into which you put your hand to feel different temperatures, and the "*théâtre optique*" in which actors have been magically reduced to 10cm in height by 21st-century technology, and appear in a miniature 18th-century room-setting. The exterior and grounds are delightful, planted with flowers to encourage the bees that the scientist so admired, and there are interesting temporary exhibitions in the outbuildings on themes related to Réaumur's work. ◐ *1 Feb-30 Nov, Sun & bank holidays 2-7pm; 1-30 Apr, Thurs-Sun 2-7pm; 1 May-30 Sept, daily 2-7pm (1 July-31 Aug, daily 11am-7pm). 8 Rue Ferchault, Réaumur (tel: 02 51 57 99 46). 4.70€, children 3.20€.* ♿

NIEUL-SUR-L'AUTISE

ⓘ tel: 02 51 87 23 01 fax: 02 51 00 72 51
www.nieul-sur-lautise.fr
office.tourisme@cc-vsa.com

The surviving group of monastic buildings in the heart of Nieul (pronounced "n-yerl") is the most intact in the whole region. The village, 10km south-east of Fontenay, has close connections with Eleanor of Aquitaine (1122-1204), who is said to have been born at her father's castle that once stood here. Known as Aliénor to the French, she was Queen of France through her first marriage to Louis VII and later Queen of England after becoming the wife of Henry Plantagenet (King Henry II). A pretty watermill is the focus of a biennial festival during which old crafts and activities bring to Nieul's streets a flavour of days gone by.

NIEUL EXTRAS

Restaurant: **Crêperie du Moulin de l'Autise**. *Sweet & savoury pancakes & other snacks, near the village watermill. 15 Rue du Moulin (tel: 02 51 50 47 13).*

Festival: **Fête de la Meunerie**. *Old-time milling festival. Whitsun in odd-numbered years.*

> **Abbaye Royale St-Vincent**. Founded in 1068, this abbey was home to Augustinian monks involved in the draining of the marshland to the south, particularly in the digging of the Canal des Cinq Abbés (see page 91) around 1217. Wonderful designs of biblical characters and of strange animals decorate the façade of the abbey church (binoculars would be useful, to study the higher ones); representations of the Seven Deadly Sins adorn the pillars flanking the front porch. Push open the door to view the lofty nave, with its high ceiling and its tall, rather alarmingly-inclined columns.

For the cloisters and the rest of the abbey buildings, pass through a pretty herb garden to the right of the church and follow signs to the *accueil* (reception) building. On its first floor is a series of touch-screens on which—if you press the Union Jack quickly enough—you can obtain commentaries in English on various topics. (If your reactions are too slow first time, press the "back" arrow and try again.) Subjects include monastic orders, the hard life of the monks, the building of the abbeys and the draining of the marshes. As each screen has a different bank of information, you could be standing listening for some time. However, though it's a lot to absorb at one session it is both comprehensive and fascinating.

A long attic room contains examples of early musical instruments—hurdy-gurdy, bagpipes, horn, harp—as illustrated in the carvings from this and other nearby churches, and you hear snatches of their music. In the Canons' Dormitory, more examples of stone-carving portray scenes from the Bible—some shown in a horseshoe-shaped arrangement reproducing the west front of Benet church, 10km south-east of Nieul (worth a visit, later, to see the reality). From the dormitory, a flight of steps leads down to the abbey's pride—the magnificently complete cloister of white stone. On your way round it, you come across an exquisitely-lit slab from the grave of a 14th-century abbot, and the tomb of Aénor of Chatellrault, mother of Eleanor of Aquitaine.

Information on the abbey's history is given in an excellent leaflet handed to all visitors (available in English). In summer there are often plays, concerts and *son-et-lumière* performances. ● *Mon-Sat 9.30am-12.30pm & 1.30-6pm; Sun & public holidays 10am-6pm (1 July-31 Aug, daily 10am-7pm). Closed last three weeks of Jan. Rue de l'Abbaye (tel: 02 51 50 43 00). 4€, students & disabled 2€, children free. ♿ except dormitory.*

> Maison de la Meunerie. With its chickens and rabbits, and a series of outbuildings clustered around the outside, this picturesque 18th-century watermill has a homely feel. Flour is produced all year round and bread baked on the site each morning from mid-July to mid-August. You can also visit the miller's former living-quarters, furnished in traditional Vendean style. Keep an eye on small children outside, as the edges of the deep millpond are surprisingly unprotected. ◑ *Easter holidays & Oct half-term, daily 3-6pm; 1-31 May, Sat, Sun 3-6pm; 1 June-30 Sept, daily 10.30am-12.30pm & 2-7pm. 16 Rue du Moulin (tel: 02 51 52 47 43). 3.50€, children 2€. ♿ partial.*

NIORT (Deux-Sèvres)

ⓘ tel: 05 49 24 18 79 fax: 05 49 24 98 90
www.niortourisme.com
info@niortourisme.com

The large, flower-decorated town straddling the lovely Sèvre Niortaise river is dominated by three features from different ages: a pair of sturdy castle keeps, the twin spires of the Église St-André,

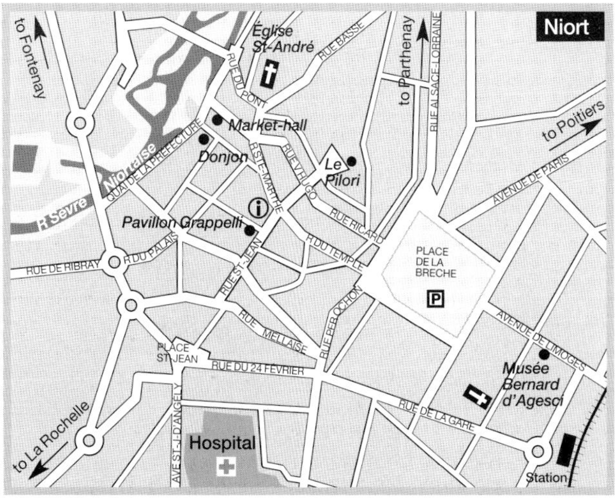

NIORT EXTRAS

Market: *Food-hall, Tues-Sun; plus outdoor stalls Thurs & Sat.*

Specialities: *Angelica. Chabichou (goat's cheese). Tourteau fromagé (cheesecake). Beurre d'Échiré (butter).*

Restaurants:

André Perrier. *Busy bar inside the market-hall, with hearty portions of excellent lunchtime plats du jour (daily specials).*

Les Deux Chèvres. *A Belgian-American couple serve tasty dishes just NE of the market-hall; menus from 13€. 19 Rue Basse (tel: 05 49 05 10 44).*

Shops: ***Huvelin***. *Top chocolate shop, selling many angelica-flavoured specialities. 24 Rue Ste-Marthe (tel: 05 49 28 33 52).*

and a delicate, 19th-century glass market-hall. It's best to park in the huge square called Place de la Brèche, to the east of the old centre, and then to begin exploring its streets—several of them with quaint half-timbered buildings—on foot.

Along Rue Ricard, off the west side of the square, the sinuous bodies of four bronze dragons snake along the pavements, performing the useful function of keeping cars to the centre of the street and pedestrians to the side. The smartest shops are a block south, on Rue du Rabot and Rue Ste-Marthe. At right-angles is Rue St-Jean with, at its north end, the intricately-decorated 14th-century Pilori building—home to a changing series of exhibitions—and, to the south, many interesting craft, home-interiors and food shops.

Chamois-leather-making and the manufacture of gloves were Niort's major industries, until France's main supply of pelts dried up with the loss of Canada in 1763. Leather-workers scrubbed the skins in the river, on the sloping pavement along today's attractive waterside walk north of the market-hall. They hung them to dry in airy lofts nearby, still recognisable from their slatted wooden sides.

■ **Niort: fortress built by English kings.**

These days Niort is known throughout France as the centre of the nation's insurance industry. The town has also become the official focus for the region's crafts. If you want to see some of them, the tourist office can provide a map of studios and workshops within the town, and a brochure showing the location of others elsewhere in the Poitou-Charentes region.

Angelica is grown on a large scale in the area. Many local shops sell sweets and pastries made from the crystallised green stalks of the plant, as well as a liqueur reputed to have staved off infection in Niort during a 17th-century bout of the plague. Another gastronomic heritage is butter from the small town of Échiré, 10km north-east of Niort, which is presented at the smartest tables worldwide. Like the best French wines, the delicately-flavoured *beurre d'Échiré* enjoys an *appellation d'origine contrôlée*.

NIORT EXTRAS

La Ferme Ste-Marthe. Hundreds of cheeses, ripened to the peak of perfection. 19 Rue St-Jean (tel: 05 49 24 06 97). Établissements Thonnard. Angelica in all its forms can be sampled & bought from the main angelica-grower. Avenue de Sevreau, 4km SW of Niort on D9, direction Magné (tel: 05 49 73 47 42). Festival: Biennale d'art sacré. Biennial show of religious art. Jan, in even-numbered years. Golf: Golf de Niort-Romagné. An 18-hole course, 2km S of city centre. Chemin du Grand-Ormeau, off N150 (tel: 05 49 79 91 73 / 05 49 09 01 41).

❯**Musée du Donjon**. The vast, grey, Romanesque keep looming above the river, was constructed by the English kings Henry II and Richard I. It contains a museum of archaeological discoveries—among them a bronze chariot wheel found recently in the marshes near Coulon, and a beautiful gold necklace dating from 2000BC. Steep flights of stone spiral steps lead upward to rooms full of local costumes, furniture and an authentic-looking 1830-style Poitevin interior, plus descriptions of the tanning and glove-making industries. From the roof you can enjoy panoramic views of the town. ● *Wed-Mon 9am-noon & 2-5pm (2 May-15 Sept, Wed-Mon 9am-noon & 2-6pm). Closed on winter & spring public holidays. Rue Duguesclin (tel: 05 49 28 14 28). 2.67€, children free (everybody free on Wed).*

❯**Musée Bernard d'Agesci**. After renovation, the municipal museum is due to reopen in 2005 with a permanent display of three collections. The Beaux-Arts (fine arts) section is strong on Spanish and Dutch 17th- and 18th-century paintings, plus ivories, enamels and tapestries. The second part covers the region's birds and animals, but also has a section devoted to work by local sculptor Pierre-Marie Poisson, who created decorative pieces for the great French ocean liners of the 1920s and 30s. Appropriately, since the building was once a girls' school, the final area will bring together in the former classrooms a huge range of teaching aids spanning more than 100 years, from magic-lantern slides to CD-ROMs. ● *From 2005. 28 Avenue de Limoges, E of Place de la Brèche. Opening hours & ticket prices not available at time of writing.*

❯**Pavillon Grappelli**. Bearing the title of "Ville et Métiers d'Art ", Niort is a focus for some 1,000 craft-workers living in the Poitou-Charentes region. This elegant 19th-century building is a shopfront for their cabinet-making, sculpture, jewellery, ironwork and other skills. ● *During exhibitions: Wed 2-7pm; Thurs-Sat 10am-1pm & 2-7pm. 56 Rue St-Jean (tel: 05 49 17 10 55).*

POITIERS (Vienne)

ⓘ tel: 05 49 41 21 24 fax: 05 49 88 65 84
www.ot-poitiers.fr
accueil@ot-poitiers.fr

Although this city is some 80km from the eastern edge of the Vendée, visitors are drawn here from far and wide for the theme park of Futuroscope, just 8km to the north, off the A10 autoroute. However, in case you want to make a detour into the old part of Poitiers, almost encircled by the Clain and the Boivre rivers, the main architectural and artistic highlights to look out for are: the Romanesque church of Notre-Dame-la-Grande, with its intricately-sculpted façade; the gothic cathedral of St-Pierre, decorated with 12th-century stained glass in vibrant reds and blues; and the series of Romanesque and gothic wall-paintings in the Baptistère St-Jean.

❯**Parc du Futuroscope**. In contrast to the medieval splendours of Poitiers, the architecture of this "European cinema park" is a riot of glass and strangely-angled buildings. You really need more than a day to visit everything here—not so much because of its size (the site is surprisingly compact), but because of the time spent queuing for the most popular attractions. (Take snacks to eat while you wait; not only will you save time, but they'll be better in quality than the on-site ones.) On spring and summer evenings, the day is rounded off with a spectacular laser show.

The latest in screen entertainment includes Imax, 3D, 360-degree cinema, and Europe's largest flat screen. Newest additions are Digital City, an area devoted to video games—with sections for beginners as well as for experts—and a 3D film where you feel you are floating with astronauts 400km above Earth. You can "take off" on a space mission, "ride" an out-of-control coal wagon, try a "magic carpet", with images projected simultaneously in front of your eyes and beneath your feet, or experience virtual reality behind a pair of special electronic spectacles. Among family attractions outside are bumper-boats, remote-controlled cars, slides, adventure playgrounds and a maze with "paths" delineated by jets of water, while indoors you can watch animated Lego models, create harmony in the "musical house" or influence the outcome of interactive cinema shows.

The tourist office just inside the entrance can help arrange overnight accommodation, either in adjacent modern hotels or in local *chambres d'hôte* (B&Bs). You can also borrow headsets for simultaneous translation here (but must leave a passport as a deposit). The site has little shade, so take sun protection—particularly sunglasses, to counteract the glare that reflects off the many shiny surfaces around when you emerge from the cinemas. Note that children less than 1m 20cm in height are not allowed into the shows where seats move with the action. ◗ *1 Apr-mid Nov, daily 10am-6pm (until dusk on days with an evening show, which are approximately: early Apr-31 Aug, daily; 1 Sept-mid Oct, Sat; Oct half-term & Nov Armistice weekend, daily; but double-check to avoid disappointment). Jaunay-Clan, exit 28 from the A10 motorway (tel: 05 49 49 30 80). 21€ (two-day ticket 40€), children 16€ (29€); from mid Apr-31 Aug, then Sat, Sun & public holidays from 1 Sept to mid Nov, 30€ (57€); children 22€ (40€); under-fives free. www.futuroscope.com/* ♿

LA POMMERAIE-SUR-SEVRE

ⓘ tel: 02 51 92 81 80 fax: 02 51 92 82 43
www.paysdepouzauges.fr
tourisme@paysdepouzauges.fr

Seemingly caught in a time-warp, this sleepy village 9km north-east of Pouzauges is at the extreme edge of the Vendée. There are some attractive picnic and fishing spots at Les Ilots, where the D43 crosses the Sèvre Nantaise river.

❯**Église St-Martin**. La Pommeraie's pretty little church is known for a series of Renaissance frescoes that depict in witty style, along the south wall, the Seven Deadly Sins. The procession of colourfully-clad people, mounted on life-sized animals and being carted off towards Hell by an extravagantly-horned demon, was intended to remind the village's inhabitants to attend confession. Press a button on the wall opposite the painting to start up a free mini sound-and-light show that explains the sequence. ●

❯**Château de Deffend**. The owners of this charming private home open its doors to visitors for a few weeks each summer. Built in 1864 of white stone and pink brick, it stands just outside the Vendée, 1km to the east of La Pommeraie as the crow flies. During a 40-minute guided tour of the reception rooms, you are shown elegantly-carved woodwork, imposing family portraits, comfortable-looking furniture and some wonderful views across the Sèvre Nantaise. The wooded grounds are planted with 50,000 trees and criss-crossed with leafy paths. ◯ *1 July-31 Aug, daily 2.30-6pm. Le Deffend, near Montravers, on S side of the D34 (tel: 05 49 80 53 63). 5€, children 3€.*

LA POMMERAIE EXTRAS

Festival: Fête de l'Été. Folk dancing & fun on the banks of the Sèvre Nantaise. Late July.

■ **La Pommeraie: to Hell with the sinners.**

POUZAUGES

ⓘ tel: 02 51 91 82 46 fax: 02 51 57 01 69
www.paysdepouzauges.fr
tourisme@paysdepouzauges.fr

You need to be extremely adept at hill-starts to drive around the narrow streets in the centre of this attractive town nicknamed "the pearl of the *bocage*". Even the buildings seem to have difficulty clinging to Pouzauges' rocky slopes.

A better idea is to park near the church and wander round on foot following the "fil vert", a painted green line that leads you on a roughly 90-minute trail via shops and major points of interest. The tourist office can provide an accompanying leaflet for this circuit; it also stocks maps showing some of the interesting *sentiers pédestres* (footpaths) in the undulating countryside around.

POUZAUGES EXTRAS

Market: Thurs (larger on first & third Thurs).
Restaurant: Auberge de la Bruyère. Marvellous view over the countryside from the terrace; menus from 13.50€. 18 Rue Dr-Barbanneau (tel: 02 51 91 93 46).
Festival: Les Côtes Pouzaugeaises. A gruelling annual running race over 14km of hilly terrain. Late June.

➤**Château de Pouzauges**. Occupying the highest point in the town is the ruined, 13th-century stronghold that once belonged to the notorious Gilles de Rais (see page 148). The remaining towers of the 12 that formerly surrounded the castle are gradually being revealed from beneath thick coverings of vegetation. You can visit the imposing, square keep—which is now home to just a few pigeons—and share their bird's-eye view of the countryside if you climb the steep wooden steps to the top. ○ *15 June-15 Sept, daily 2.30-6.30pm (1 July-31 Aug, daily 2.30-7.30pm). Pouzauges (tel: 02 51 57 01 37). 2.45€, children 0.82€.*

➤**Église Notre-Dame du Vieux-Pouzauges**. Well signposted, about 1km south-east of the town centre, the church of Notre-Dame (completed in around 1066) is a real gem. Once inside it, you can't miss the magnificent wall-paintings on the north side of the nave—press a button nearby for a seven-minute *son-et-lumière* display, with French commentary, highlighting this medieval strip-cartoon. A symphony of terracotta and ochre, the frescoes are thought to date from the 13th century and were discovered in 1948 under layers of paint. Five scenes on the lower level depict episodes in the the the life of the Virgin Mary and her parents. Above are friezes of grotesque animals, and illustrations representing different months of the year; over the west door, some more-recently uncovered paintings show Cain and Abel. ●

➤**Bois de la Folie**. Druids once worshipped the mistletoe at this mysterious, distinctively-shaped clump of trees, reputed to be inhabited by the fairy Mélusine (see page 127) as well as by numerous pixies and goblins. You can reach the hilltop wood by footpath from an exposed ridge1km north of Pouzauges, off the Les Herbiers road, near the two privately-owned windmills of Terrier-Marteau, which peep tantalisingly over the treetops. ●

➤**Puy Crapaud**. Signposted from the roundabout off the eastern side of the Pouzauges bypass, 269-metre "Toad Hill" is one of the highest points in the Vendée—the locals claim that on a clear night you can see the beams of coastal lighthouses, 80km to the west. At the summit, an old windmill emerges incongruously from the roof of a restaurant; if you climb the precarious steps to the top, you are rewarded with a superb view of the Vendean hills and *bocage*. ● *Viewing platform open Thurs-Tues.*

➤**Château de St-Mesmin-la-Ville**. A small-scale, partly-ruined, 14th-century fortress overlooks a tributary of the Sèvre Nantaise river at the hamlet of La Ville, just beyond St-Mesmin and about 8km east of Pouzauges. Its walls and five towers seem to grow from the very rock, giving an idea of how impregnable the building would have looked to attackers. Off its six-sided inner courtyard are several rooms—some dilapidated, some gradually being restored. You can climb the long flight of spiral stone steps through a series of lofty chambers to reach the ramparts, with their panoramic views. In July and August the château bursts into life with exhibitions on historic themes and a programme of medieval-style entertainment that ranges from markets to banquets, fire-eating to atmospheric evening tours. ◑ *1 May-14 June, Sun & public holidays 3-7pm; 15 June-15 Sept, daily 10.30am-12.30pm & 2.30-6.30pm. La Ville, off D960bis (tel: 05 49 80 17 62). 5€, children 3€; extra charges for some events.*

ST-MICHEL-MONT-MERCURE

ⓘ tel: 02 51 57 20 32 fax: 02 51 57 76 04
www.paysdepouzauges.fr
tourisme@paysdepouzauges.fr

Its relatively dizzy elevation of 290 metres qualifies this lofty spot 14km north-west of Pouzauges as the highest village in the Vendée. A massive copper statue of St Michael, patron saint of high places, crowns the late-19th-century church—you can climb 194 steps inside for a 360-degree panorama on a clear day across five *départements*. The altitude gives St-Michel its own microclimate, with a tendancy to be several degrees colder than villages below.

❯**Chapelle de Lorette**. In the pretty village of La Flocellière, 2km east of St-Michel, is an unusual small church. Its interior is modelled exactly on the Santa Casa—the "holy house" in Nazareth that was the birthplace of the Virgin Mary, and was said to have been transported by angels in 1294 from there to the Italian town of Lorette. La Flocellière's streets are especially charming. Try and sneak a look into some of the walled gardens and through the gates of the village's privately-owned château. ●

❯**Maison de la Vie Rurale**. Farm museum 1.5km south-east of St-Michel, with geese, chickens, rabbits and other birds and animals of the barnyard. There are explanatory panels about styles of farm buildings, and an area devoted to vegetables, flowers and other plants, such as wil-

■ Rural life: goose at St-Michel's farm museum.

low, that were once an important part of rural life. Concerts and events on countryside themes are held in summer. ❍ *1 May-14 June, Sun & public holidays 2.30-6.30pm; 15 June-14 Sept, daily 10.30am-6.30pm. Ferme de la Bernardière, off D752 (tel: 02 51 57 77 14). 5€, children free.* ♿

ST-PROUANT

ⓘ tel: 02 51 66 40 60 fax: 02 51 64 00 42
www.cc-deuxlays.fr

The small village 10km south-west of Pouzauges, is best known for the charming little priory that stands in the countryside nearby (see below). Just to the north is the forest of La Pélissonnière, where summer sunlight filters through the trees alongside the D23 and illuminates the shady walks. In autumn, the woods are a favourite haunt of mushroom-hunters searching among the fallen leaves for all sorts of delectable fungi.

❯**Prieuré de Chassay-Grammont**. This diminutive, but extraordinarily well preserved priory was founded by Richard the Lionheart in 1196 for some 10 monks of the Grandmontine order (seemingly, the more austere the religious régime, the more good points its benefactor notched up for the afterlife). The mini-monastery, standing in the fields 3km south-west of St-Prouant, fell into disuse long before the Revolution but, having been used as farm buildings until as recently as 1983, it escaped the usual wartime destruction of religious buildings. Today, the tall chapel, the chapter house and the restored refectory with its elegantly vaulted Plantagenet-style ceilings, still form a complete, harmonious group enclosing the small cloister. The abbey contains changing exhibitions on this order of hermit-like monks, who took vows of poverty, humility and chastity, and existed on a near-vegan diet of fruit, vegetables and bread. Prestigious classical concerts are held in the chapel between spring and autumn. ❍ *Mid June-mid Sept, daily 10am-7pm. Off D960bis (tel: 02 51 66 47 18 or 02 51 50 43 10). 2.50€, students & disabled 2€, children free.*

❯**Musée de la France Protestante de l'Ouest**. Guided tours of a museum and research centre, in a country house 4km east of St-Prouant, explain three centuries of Protestantism in western France. Historic items on show include photographs, documents and such objects as the metal tokens that admitted clandestine worshippers to secret services during times of religious intolerance.

Jean Calvin (1509-64), the French Reformist and disciple of Martin Luther, spent some time in Poitiers spreading his doctrine, giving western France a strong Huguenot (as Calvin's brand of Protestantism was described) tradition. The Wars of Religion (1562-98) pitched Catholics against Protestants, causing death and the destruction of religious buildings on a grand scale.

The French king Henri IV (who had been himself a Protestant) converted to Catholicism on his accession to the throne in 1589 and nine years later issued the Edict of Nantes, allowing French Protestants freedom of worship. This was revoked by Louis XIV in 1685, causing more than 400,000 Huguenots to flee overseas (many to Britain). Only with the Revolution in 1789 were their political and civil rights restored. Many Protestants still live in this area, and in St-Prouant, Fontenay, Pouzauges, Mouilleron, Mouchamps, and other towns and villages, you come across small churches (known as *temples*) of the *église réformée,* as the Protestant church is known in France. ○ *15 June-15 Sept, Tues-Sat 10am-1pm & 2-7pm, Sun 2-7pm. Le Bois-Tiffrais, Route de Réaumur, Monsireigne (tel: 02 51 66 41 03). 2.50€, children 1.50€.*

VOUVANT

ⓘ tel: 02 51 00 86 80 fax: 02 51 87 47 92
office.tourisme.vouvant@wanadoo.fr

★ With its postern gate and cobbled streets, this attractive fortifed place 12km north of Fontenay-le-Comte could almost be a film set, and deserves its title of one of the most beautiful villages in France. High on a promontory in a crook of the river Mère, Vouvant is surrounded by stout defensive walls from which you can look down on the meandering waterway below, and is filled with allusions to the region's most famous inhabitant, the mythical Mélusine (see below). Crowds throng here in the summer to drink in the medieval atmosphere, to admire the façade of the church, to attend prestigious exhibitions in the adjacent Nef Théodelin gallery and to look for interesting crafts. Across the river, pedalos may be rented at the Pic Vert *crêperie,* and mountain bikes at nearby La Girouette.

➤ Tour Mélusine. The ancient watch-tower dominating the village and surrounding countryside was built—according to folklore—in 1242 by the fairy Mélusine. This legendary creature, who had been sentenced by a curse to become half-serpent each Saturday, has been credited with the construction of several castles in the region, each within the space of a single night. Some say her name is a corruption of "Mère Lusignan", and that she married into a powerful local family of that name. Before agreeing to marriage, however, she made it a condition that her husband, Raymondin, should never see her on Saturday. He agreed. But one day, mad with jealousy, he spied on his wife as she was bathing naked and saw to his horror that she had a serpent's tail. Realising that her secret was out, the distraught Mélusine flew through the window on leathery wings, never to be seen again, and all her works crumbled . . . though enough of the stone steps remain in this case to allow you a spectacular view from the top. If closed, the key to the tower is available from the nearby Café du Centre. ● *Place du Bail (tel: 02 51 00 86 80). 1.50€, children 0.70€.*

➤ Église Notre-Dame. The richly-sculpted decoration on the north front of the 11th-century church (see picture, page 34) is one of the marvels of the Vendée. Fantastical animals surround the twin doorways; above them is a series of magnificent, life-sized statues dating from the 15th century. Inside the church the ornamentation is simpler, and you can have a closer look at some stone carvings that repose in the ancient crypt. In the south aisle, a stone slab commemorates Geoffroy la Grand'Dent, or Geoffrey Longtooth, son of Mélusine and her human husband, who repented from his violent warmongering (see page 96) in time to ensure a Christian burial. ●

➤ Maison de Mélusine. Inside the tourist office near the Tour Mélusine you can view a short film about Vouvant and the legend of its famous Vendean fairy. In the basement, some artistic representations include a copy of the Mélusine sculpture by the Martel brothers (see page 45) that decorates the huge dam on the nearby Mère river. ● *Tues 10am-12.30pm & 1.30-6pm (1 July-31*

Aug, Mon-Sat 10am-12.30pm & 1.30-6.30pm; Sun & public holidays 10am-noon & 3-6pm). Place du Bail (tel: 02 51 00 86 80). Video & exhibition 2€, children 1€.

➤ Cour des Miracles. Behind the Bar de la Tour café is a pretty courtyard. Its name alludes to a story that one December day in 1715 a sick child begged visiting missionary, and future saint, Père Montfort (see page 148) for some cherries. The priest told the boy's grandmother to pick some. The old lady opened the door and, to her surprise, saw a tree in this little yard laden with fruit. ●

■ **Vouvant: old well in Cour des Miracles.**

Area 5

0   5   10km

For explanation of symbols, see page 6.

to Ancenis

to Nantes

★ **CLISSON**

● **Gétigné**

● **Cugand**

N 149

to Nantes

Château de la Preuille

River Sèvre Nantaise

River Maine

D 763

D 755

Tiffauges

● **La Bruffière**

St-Hilaire-de-Loulay

to Nantes

D 54

D 753

D 755

D 37

to Nantes

MONTAIGU

D 23

D 62

Les Landes-Génusson ●

to Challans

D 753

to Nantes

④

St-Georges-de-Montaigu

River Grande Maine

Lac de la Bultière

● **Rocheservière**

D 7

D 84

N 1137

River Petite Maine

D 6

Bazoges-en-Paillers

Legé

←

St-Sulpice-le-Verdon

★ *Logis de la Chabotterie*

D 937

Chavagnes-en-Paillers

D 39

● *Chêne-Chapelle*

Les Brouzils

Refuge de Grasla

N-D de Salette

● *Mémorial*

Forêt de Grasla

St-Fulgent

Lac de la Tricherie

A 87

D 18

● **Les Lucs-sur-Boulogne**

D 763

St-Denis-la-Chevasse ●

A 83

Vendrenn

⑤

D 6

River Boulogne

D 37

A 87 (opens 2005)

Ste-Florence

N 137

Belleville-sur-Vie

to La Roche

Les Essarts

North

↑

River Yon

to La Roche

N 160

D 52

Château de la Grève

to Niort & Fontenay

Les Herbiers, Clisson and the Vendée Wars

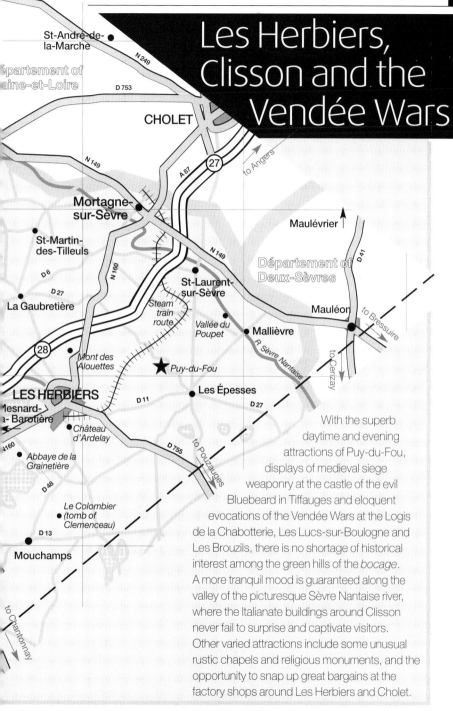

St-André-de-la-Marche

Département of Maine-et-Loire

N 249

D 753

CHOLET

to Angers

N 149

A 87

(27)

Mortagne-sur-Sèvre

Maulévrier

St-Martin-des-Tilleuls

N 149

Département of Deux-Sèvres

D 6

N 160

D 27

St-Laurent-sur-Sèvre

D 41

La Gaubretière

Steam train route

Vallée du Poupet

Malliévre

Mauléon

to Bressuire

(28)

Mont des Alouettes

Puy-du-Fou

R. Sèvre Nantaise

to Cerizay

LES HERBIERS

Les Épesses

Mesnard-la-Barotière

D 11

D 27

N 160

Château d'Ardelay

D 755

to Pouzauges

Abbaye de la Grainetière

D 48

Le Colombier (tomb of Clemenceau)

D 13

Mouchamps

to Chantonnay

With the superb daytime and evening attractions of Puy-du-Fou, displays of medieval siege weaponry at the castle of the evil Bluebeard in Tiffauges and eloquent evocations of the Vendée Wars at the Logis de la Chabotterie, Les Lucs-sur-Boulogne and Les Brouzils, there is no shortage of historical interest among the green hills of the *bocage*. A more tranquil mood is guaranteed along the valley of the picturesque Sèvre Nantaise river, where the Italianate buildings around Clisson never fail to surprise and captivate visitors. Other varied attractions include some unusual rustic chapels and religious monuments, and the opportunity to snap up great bargains at the factory shops around Les Herbiers and Cholet.

LES BROUZILS

ⓘ 02 51 42 27 75 fax: 02 51 42 79 30
www.les-brouzils.fr
otsaintfulgent@wanadoo.fr

On the edge of one of the Vendée's rare forested areas, this small village 12km south of Montaigu is one of the centres of cultivation for the *mogette*, the white haricot bean that has for so long been the staple food of the Vendeans. At the annual October beanfeast 200 kilos of them are simmered in cauldrons over wood fires, and then spread on toast to create *grillée de mogettes*—a popular local snack.

If you want to experience the sensation of life in the time of the Vendée Wars, don't miss the marvellous reconstruction in Grasla Forest of an 18th-century woodland village (see below), where soldiers and farmers hid from marauding Republicans.

➤Refuge de Grasla. During 1794—the worst year of the Vendée Wars—almost 2,500 people from local families would seek safety each night from the *colonnes infernales* (see page 37) at a site in the heart of a forest in which the Vendean leader Charette often concealed his troops. Today, signposts guide you from the D7, 2km south-east of the village, to an area where the atmosphere of those times has been brilliantly recaptured. As the lookout's horn toots from the treetops, you experience the surprise felt by the Republican General Terrand when he stumbled upon an empty encampment after eventually venturing into this dangerous area that was then still roamed by wolves as well as by hostile Vendeans.

In a brushwood-camouflaged visitor centre, maps and videos explain the causes of the Vendée Wars and describe the way a typical Vendean family lived in the forest. Outside, in the woodland glades, you step back in time among rough shelters improvised from branches and bracken similar to those that met the eyes of the Republicans. Typical of an 18th-century community, they include chapel, smithy, saw-yard and workshops—complete with appropriate sound effects—and even a gently-smoking charcoal kiln. At cleverly-disguised information points you can press buttons to hear additional commentary on aspects of the refugees' lives (explanatory sheets available in English).

You could easily spend a couple of hours in this lovely spot—especially on a hot day when the leafy glades and picnic areas provide welcome shade. Combined with a visit to the Chabotterie (see page 147), it makes an ideal way of getting to grips with the Vendée Wars. On summer Sundays (and occasional Thursday evenings) theatrical promenade performances provide atmospheric living-history sessions. Actors and volunteers playing "Amandine" and her fellow "refugees" lead spectators around the woodland encampment. ○ *1-31 May, Sat, Sun & public holidays 2-6pm; 1 June-mid Sept, daily 11am-6pm; mid Sept-mid Oct, Sun 2-6pm. Forêt de Grasla (tel: 02 51 42 96 20). 5€, children 3€, family (2+2 or more) 16€. "Sur les Pas d'Amandine" performances: 1 June-mid Sept, Sun 3.30pm & 5.30pm (1 July-31 Aug, also Thurs 8pm); 6€, children 3€, family (2+2 or more) 16€.* ♿

■ **Refuge de Grasla: rustic shelters, as used in the Vendée Wars.**

> **Musée des Ustensiles de Cuisine**. France's only museum devoted to kitchen utensils is managed with charm and enthusiasm by the ladies of a village 8km south-west of Les Brouzils. Beautifully presented on two floors are domestic items used between 1850 and 1960. You can see the evolution of everything from cooking stoves to potato-peelers, coffee-roasters to yoghurt-makers—plus some lethal-looking pressure-cookers. ○ *1 May-end Oct, Sun & public holidays 2.30-6.30pm (1 July-31 Aug, Wed-Mon 2.30-6.30pm). 25 Place Georges-Clemenceau (opposite the post office), St-Denis-la-Chevasse (tel: 02 51 41 39 01). 3€, children 1€.* ⎈ *ground floor only.*

■ **Kitchen history, St-Denis.**

CHAVAGNES-EN-PAILLERS

ⓘ 02 51 42 27 75 fax: 02 51 42 79 30
www.mairie-chavagnes-en-paillers.fr
otsaintfulgent@wanadoo.fr

A profusion of bell-towers and churches indicates that this small town 12km south-east of Montaigu is one of the Vendée's "holy places". In 1801 a local priest, Father Baudouin, founded its imposing seminary and two convents. One seminary building—opposite the church—has now become an English-language Catholic boarding school for boys.

> **Sanctuaire de Notre-Dame-de-Salette**. Some 20 towers and turrets of stone and brick teeter at the top of an impossibly steep slope about 5km south of Chavagnes (see pictures, page 141). Built in 1889, they are interspersed with colourfully-painted figures representing visions that appeared to two children in eastern France 43 years earlier. A simple chapel built like a castle keep stands at the highest point; you can scramble up the grassy slope to it, past the Stations of the Cross; it's safer to descend by the steps that lead back down to the road, past the statues. A shady picnic area by a pretty, tree-lined stream awaits you at the bottom. Notices remind visitors to respect this holy place so, however tempting the idea, children should not make unseemly noise or climb on the monuments. ● *Off the D17, between La Rabatelière & St-Fulgent.*
> **Chapelle de la Sainte Famille du Chêne**. Another extraordinary religious structure is this little stone chapel grafted onto an ancient oak tree, 2km south of Chavagnes. Built in 1874 by the same zealous priest who erected the sanctuary above, it has a large bell dangling outside. Push open the chapel door to see an altar in the hollow of the tree, its wooden surrounds worn smooth by countless hands and knees. ● *Signposted off the D6 at La Haie, just before the junction with the D17.*

CHOLET (Maine-et-Loire)

ⓘ tel: 02 41 49 80 00 fax: 02 41 49 80 09
www.ot-cholet.fr
info-accueil@ot-cholet.fr

Although lying outside the Vendée's eastern boundary, the town of Cholet, 48km south-east of Nantes, has a claim to be the *"capitale de la Vendée militaire"* (capital of military Vendée), since the Vendée Wars also involved much of the *département* of Maine-et-Loire. The valiant Vendean leader Henri de la Rochejaquelein—remembered for his command: "If I advance, follow me; if I retreat, kill me; if I die, avenge me!"—is commemorated at the spot where he fell to a sniper's bullet at Nuaillé, 7km north-east of Cholet, aged just 22.

Sacked and burnt three times during the troubled post-Revolution years, the town centre still retains some picturesque mansions with ironwork balconies, once the homes of wealthy cloth merchants. *Toiles* (textiles) made the city's fortune in the 18th century.

■ Local hero: Henri de la Rochejaquelein stone.

Today, ready-to-wear garments and shoes are turned out from Cholet's factories, many of which have good-value factory shops.

The curious additional claim to be France's *"capitale du mouchoir"* ("handkerchief capital") comes from a time when this item was among the specialities manufactured here. The humble product shot to prominence in 1900 when Théodore Botrel, a Breton cabaret artist, created a stirring romantic song called *Le Mouchoir Rouge de Cholet* ("The Red Handkerchief of Cholet"), in which he sang of a soldier who bought three white Cholet handkerchiefs as a present for his true love. Before he could give them to her, they were requisitioned by the Vendean General Charette—one to wear on his head, one to hold his sword, and the third to pin over his heart to staunch the blood from a wound. Such was the song's success, that the town began to turn out blood-red handkerchiefs bordered with white—still on sale in many of Cholet's shops.

Principal shopping streets are clustered around the twin-spired 19th-century church of Notre-Dame on the rather bleak main square; the tourist office is one block to the west, in Place Rougé.

❯ **Musée d'Art et d'Histoire**. Ultra-modern museum, devoted largely to the Vendée Wars and the city's role in them—more than 50 per cent of its population was killed in the four years of fighting. A good explanatory leaflet about the wars is available in English. Among some fascinating exhibits are weapons, objects, and a series of dramatic 19th-century paintings commissioned by Louis XVIII of both Republican and Vendean leaders. Other displays feature 18th- and 19th-century sculpture, and a large collection of contemporary abstract works. The museum, up a rather precipitous flight of steps, is not too well indicated but is on a boulevard immediately south of the town centre, just beyond the gardens of the Palais de Justice; some parking possible in the little streets across the river. ● *Wed, Sat, Sun & public holidays 10am-noon & 2-6pm; Thurs, Fri 2-6pm. Closed 1 Jan, 1 May & 25 Dec. 27 Avenue de l'Abreuvoir (tel: 02 41 49 29 00). 3.20€, students & children free.* ♿

❯ **Musée du Textile**. The brick chimneys of this former bleaching-house 1.5km north of the town centre on the D752, are visible from afar. The building, dating from 1881, is now beautifully restored as a museum, showing stages in the manufacture of Cholet's famous textiles. A new, glass-roofed section contains some huge *métiers*, or looms, which the guide sets going into clattering motion. In an old engine-shed nearby you can feel the texture of cotton, linen and hemp; outside is a garden full of plants used for dyeing (such as woad) or for carding (teasels). ● *Wed, Sat, Sun & public holidays 10am-noon & 2-6pm; Thurs, Fri 2-6pm. Closed 1 Jan, 1 May & 25 Dec. Route de Beaupréau (tel: 02 41 75 25 40). 1.60€, children free.* ♿

❯ **Factory shops**. As you would expect for a place at the heart of French clothing and footwear manufacturing, Cholet has an excellent clutch of factory outlets. The main area, near La Séguinière, 5km west of Cholet, has a collection of 15 shops selling discounted Naf-Naf, Nike, Puma, Adidas, Kickers, Levis, Mat de Misaine & other top brands. A smaller area is located at Le Cormier, 3km south-west of Cholet, with two shops selling fashion for adults and children, and household linens. ● *Mon 2-7pm; Tues-Sat 10am-7pm. La Séguinière, signposted just S of D753, Noirmoutier road; Le Cormier, near roundabout at junction of N249 with the N160, La Roche-sur-Yon road.*

❯ **Musée de la Chaussure**. A place with the name of St-André-de-la-Marche (*marche* means "walk" or "step") seems a highly appropriate location for a museum devoted to Cholet's footwear

CHOLET EXTRAS

Market: Wed, Place Travot. Sat (8am-5pm), Place du 8 Mai 1945 (off Boulevard Delhumeau, near the Musée d'Art et d'Histoire).

Restaurant: Brasserie Grand Café. On W side of main square; menus from 12.50€. 1 Place Travot (tel: 02 41 65 82 41).

Factory shops: Le Circuit des Marques. See main entry.

Festivals: Carnaval. Colourful daytime carnival parade; a spectacular night-time procession takes place six days later. Mar or Apr.

Golf: Golf de Cholet. 18-hole course. Allée du Chêne-Landry, 3km N of Cholet on D752 (tel: 02 41 71 05 01).

industry. A disused shoe factory in the centre of a village 11km north-west of Cholet is home to a collection of old shoe-making equipment—including machines for cutting, stitching, pressing, adding heels or making holes for shoelaces—and for an exhibition of shoes from around the world.
◑ *1 Mar-1 Dec, Sun 2.30-6.30pm (1 Apr-31 Oct, Sun-Fri 2.30-6.30pm; 1 July-31 Aug, daily 2.30-6.30pm). 6 Rue St-Paul, St-André-de-la-Marche (tel: 02 41 46 35 65). 4.50€, children 2.50€.*

CLISSON (Loire-Atlantique)

① tel: 02 40 54 02 95 fax: 02 40 54 07 77
www.clisson.com
ot@clisson.com

★ Your first impression on arriving at this captivating town on the banks of the Sèvre Nantaise river, some 25km west of Cholet and on the northernmost border of the Vendée, is of having somehow strayed into a corner of Tuscany—an unexpected side-effect of the Vendée Wars.

The Republicans' remorseless fire-and-sword policy ruined the castle in 1794 and flattened Clisson, leaving just two ancient bridges across the Sèvre and its tributary the Moine. Rebuilding was started in Italian style by wealthy brothers Pierre and François Cacault, with Frédéric Lemot, a sculptor whom they had known in Italy. The idea caught local imagination and from the early 19th century all kinds of Italianate buildings—including factories—grew up along and above the two rivers. Today, on summer nights when they are floodlit, Clisson's steep cobbled streets and flights of steps take on a truly magical quality.

Friday mornings are fun, because of the busy market (try to avoid visiting between Sunday and Tuesday, though, as either castle or shops are closed). There are restaurants to suit every taste and pocket, and shady picnic places near the Moulin Plessard watersports base, about 500m south-east. Signposted footpaths lead along the banks of the Sèvre north towards Le Pallet or south towards Tiffauges. The tourist office arranges guided tours of the town or of the surrounding vineyards (in English if requested), or you could strike off on your own by car to follow the "Route Touristique du Vignoble Nantais," a signposted trail through the local wine-producing area famous for its Muscadet and for its Gros-Plant du Pays Nantais. (Note that you may need cash for any wine purchases, as the smaller producers are not generally equipped to take credit cards.) Wine-sampling can begin even before you leave the tourist office, as the premises are shared with an association of 28 producers, and tastings are offered on the spot.

It's a little-known fact that 1km or so along the river bank, in nearby Cugand, is the home of *The Magic Roundabout*. Eric Thompson's laconic style and English scripts were a perfect match for the drily witty French commentaries written by the late Serge Danot, creator of these much-loved children's programmes. From 1966 onwards, all the episodes of *Le Manège Enchanté,* as the television series is known in France, were filmed in a former tannery—one of the large waterside Italianate buildings on the path south-east of Clisson. More recently, Margote and Zébulon (sorry: Florence and Zebedee!) and the heavily English-accented Pollux (Dougal) have been brought out of retirement to make their big-screen début in a new, digitised, 3D feature film.

CLISSON EXTRAS

Market: Tues, Les Halles. Fri, throughout the streets. Wed, La Trinité, on E side of river.

Specialities: Muscadet de Sèvre-et-Maine & Gros-Plant wines.

Restaurants:
La Bonne Auberge. Gastronomic dishes for a special treat; menus from 35.50€ to 56.50€. 1 Rue Olivier-de-Clisson (tel: 02 40 54 01 90).
La Vallée. Waterside restaurant with great views & some excellent Muscadets. Menus from 18€. 1 rue de la Vallée (tel: 02 40 54 36 23).

Festivals:
Les Mediévales. A weekend of medieval street entertainment. Aug.
Festival de Danses et Musiques du Monde. Traditional music & dance from around the world. Cugand, 4km SE of Clisson. Late Aug.

🏵 route touristique
🏵 du vignoble nantais

➤**Château de Clisson**. Successive enclosures and improvements carried out between the 12th and 16th centuries have made this impregnable-looking stronghold a fascinating example of different styles of military architecture. Set on a rocky spur overlooking the town, it is today a dramatic ruin with defences that range from early arrow-slits to the much wider openings required for the firing of cannon. ● *Wed-Sun 10am-noon & 2-6pm (1 Apr-30 Sept, Wed-Mon 10am-noon & 2-6pm). Town centre (tel: 02 40 54 02 22). 2.20€, children 1.50€.*

➤**Les Halles**. Wander inside the town's market-hall, tucked away between the castle and the nearby church, and look up at the intricate arrangement of 15th-century wooden beams that support its roof. The building—still in use on market days—survived the town's destruction only because of its usefulness as a temporary barracks during the Vendée Wars. ● &

■ **Clisson: a deliciously unexpected flavour of Italy.**

➤**Garenne Lemot**. Large, steeply sloping park studded with follies, statues, temples and grottoes on the east bank of the Sèvre, designed as his own country retreat by the sculptor Frédéric Lemot (1771-1827), whose vision is so indelibly stamped on the town. The woodland is carpeted with bluebells in April. ● *Daily 9.30am-6.30pm (1 Apr-30 Sept, daily 9am-8pm). Free.* & *part.*

➤**Villa Lemot**. The elegant mansion that Frédéric Lemot (see above) built for himself inside the park is open for temporary art exhibitions. From the villa's terrace you look straight across the river towards the Temple de l'Amitié, Lemot's burial place. ● *During exhibitions. Times & address as for Maison du Jardinier, below. Admission charges vary.*

➤**Maison du Jardinier**. Charming, Italian-style, rustic building near one of the park entrances containing an exhibition showing the influences of Italian ideas on the town's architecture. ● *Tues-Fri 10am-noon & 2-5pm; Sat, Sun 2-5pm (1 Mar-31 Oct, Tues-Sun 10am-noon & 2-6pm; 1 June-30 Sept, Mon 2-7pm; Tues-Sun 10am-noon & 2-7pm). Closed 1 May. Garenne Lemot (tel: 02 40 54 75 85). Free.* &

➤**Moulin à Foulon**. From the Middle Ages, the Sèvre Nantaise was extremely important to local industries, at one time powering more than 100 watermills doing everything from grinding corn to tanning leather. This small, water-powered mill 4km south-east of Clisson was used until 1955 for "fulling" (hammering woollen fabric to produce weatherproof felt). The mill and its adjacent dye-house have now been restored, with panels to illustrate dyeing and fulling processes; a guide sets some of the noisy hammers in motion so you can appreciate what a din they must have made. ● *Site all year.* ○ *Visits: 15 June-15 Sept, Tues-Sun 10am-noon & 3-7pm. Gaumier, 1km N of Cugand, signposted from the D77 linking Cugand & Gétigné (tel: 02 51 43 70 70). Free.*

LES ÉPESSES

ⓘ tel: 02 51 57 31 30 fax: 02 51 57 39 76
www.les-epesses.com
mairie@les-epesses.com

This small village in the *haut-bocage*, 10km north-east of Les Herbiers, is the focus for some of the *département's* best-known entertainment. The ruined granite-and-brick Renaissance castle of Le Puy-du-Fou, 2km north-west of Les Épesses, which was

LES ÉPESSES EXTRAS

Market: Fri.

***Factory shop: France Mode**. Women's shoes.* Tues-Fri 2-6.30pm, Sat 10am-12.30pm & 2-7pm. Rue de l'Industrie, signposted on S edge of town (tel: 02 51 57 30 58).

burnt down by Republicans in 1794, has become synonymous with the dazzling "Cinéscénie" sound-and-light show staged in the château's grounds on two nights a week during the summer months. On an adjoining part of the same site—though totally separate—is an excellent daytime attraction called Le Grand Parc, a "historical theme park" that is open every day in summer. Though there is plenty to entertain the whole family here by day or by night, it's probably too exhausting to try and cram visits to both into a single day. (Full description of both attractions on pages 142 and 143.)

There are wonderful panoramas over the undulating landscape of the *bocage* from many points, including from the D11 between Les Épesses and Les Herbiers. Those with a head for heights can enjoy even more elevated views from a hot-air balloon (see below).

> ★ **Le Puy-du-Fou**. Special feature on Cinéscénie and Grand Parc on pages 142-143. O
> **Montgolfière du Bocage**. Hot-air balloon trips, when weather conditions are right, carry Damien Merceron and his passengers high up over the hills and valleys of the *bocage*. ● *Morning & evening flights from Puy-du-Fou area. Times & pick-up location by appointment (tel: 05 49 80 10 45). 220€ per person per hour (four people, 210€ each; five people, 200€ each), children 130€.*

LES ESSARTS

ⓘ tel: 02 51 62 85 96 fax: 02 51 62 85 96
www.ville-les-essarts85.fr
www.ot-paysdesessarts.fr
info@ot-paysdesessarts.fr

This industrial and market town 20km south-west of Les Herbiers possesses an ancient church crypt and a romantically-ruined feudal castle. A more modern claim to fame for Les Essarts is its position 5km from the crossroads of two *autoroutes,* the Nantes-Niort-Bordeaux A83 and the new A87 Angers-Cholet-La Roche (due to reach La Roche in 2005). The complex rural "spaghetti junction" is France's fifth-largest motorway intersection.

■ **Les Essarts: war-torn.**

> **Château des Essarts**. Henri of Navarre (later King Henri IV) is said to have stayed at this now-crumbling castle in 1588. Of the *logis*, or main house, destroyed during the Vendée Wars, little remains but a Renaissance fireplace hanging precariously at second-floor height and an elegant "barley-sugar"-style column now exposed to the elements. On the perimeter stands the square, 11th-century Tour Sarrasine that gave defenders a good view over the surrounding countryside and, near a religious statue on the edge of the grounds, you can see an earth-covered tumulus thought to be an ancient Gallic burial mound. O *1 July-15 Sept, daily 2.30-6.30pm. On N160, on N side of town (tel: 02 51 62 85 96). 3€, students & children 1.50€, under 12s free.*

> **Église des Essarts**. Beneath the floor of the large, twin-spired 19th-century church at the hub of the town's one-way system is a Romanesque crypt, a vestige of an ancient priory that once stood on the site. Enter the church through the south door, turn right and then go down a little stone stairway. (Press a button to light the steps, and another to illuminate the crypt.) A French commentary tells you the crypt's history while you admire the sculpted pillars and a few vestiges of wall-paintings. ●

> **Château de la Grève**. At St-Martin-des-Noyers, 8km south-east of Les Essarts, is an interesting, domestic-scale castle, built in the 12th century

Market: Wed (larger on third Wed of month) & Sat.

Restaurant: Le Pinier. Popular "relais routier", or French transport café. Hearty five-course meal, including wine & water, 10.40€. On N160, 4km NE of Les Essarts, near junction 5 of A83 (tel: 02 51 62 81 69).

Brocante: Emmaüs. Large junk shop in countryside. Wed, Fri, Sat 2.30-6pm. Bois-Jaulin, off N160, 2km SW of Les Essarts (tel: 02 51 06 06 85).

and fortified during the Hundred Years War. For the past 150 years the château—which has changed hands only three times in eight centuries—has been used as farm buildings. Today it is gradually being restored; a guided tour features the moat, turrets, mullioned windows and granite fireplaces, as well as the castle's vaulted cellars—once used as a prison. ○ *1 July-31 Aug, daily 3-7pm; 1-30 Sept, Sun 3-7pm. On D60, 2km W of St-Martin-des-Noyers (tel: 02 51 07 86 36). 3€, students 2.30€, children free.*

❯**Gaston Chaissac paintings**. The most improbable listed building you could imagine is the run-down outdoor lavatory block at a little school in Sainte-Florence, 7km north-east of Les Essarts. The artist Gaston Chaissac (1910-64), who lived here during the years that his wife was the village schoolteacher, daubed one or two of his characteristically primitive designs inside a couple of the playground toilets. There are plans to set up displays about Chaissac's life inside one of the redundant schoolrooms—probably by 2005. In the meantime, if you're passing this way you can ask the staff of the *mairie* to allow you into the loos for a peep at the two small, faded pictures. (To view some of Chaissac's more sophisticated output, visit the Abbaye Ste-Croix museum in Les Sables-d'Olonne, see page 83). ● *Mairie, Ste-Florence, S of N160 (tel: 02 51 66 01 01).*

LA GAUBRETIÈRE
ⓘ tel: 02 51 67 10 21
www.cc-canton-mortagne-sur-sevre.fr
tourisme@cc-canton-mortagne-sur-sevre.fr

Known as the "Pantheon of the Vendée", the graveyard of this village 9km north-west of Les Herbiers is the last resting-place of many who fought in the 18th-century Vendean uprising. During the long series of battles and reprisals, La Gaubretière lost 1,200 of its 1,700 population. The village's château (see below) has associations with two Vendean leaders, both of whom also lost their lives. Another—General Charles-Henri Sapinaud— miraculously survived the troubles and died in 1829 after having been La Gaubretière's first mayor; he is commemorated on a memorial near the church.

❯**Église de La Gaubretière**. Inside the church is an altarpiece dedicated to St Bartholomew, whose expression of terror in front of the executioners who are flaying him alive has earned him the nickname in local *patois* of "St Épourail" ("scary saint"). Mothers used to bring young children here to cure them of fearfulness—though you would imagine the sight of the statue might have produced a totally opposite effect. ●
❯**Cimetière/Panthéon de la Vendée**. Local victims of the Vendée Wars, with some of the counter-revolutionary Vendean leaders, are buried either in family tombs or in a mass grave beneath a large granite obelisk. The cemetery is in Rue du 11 Novembre, off the D9 Tiffauges road. Pedestrians can reach it shortly after the church; for drivers, it is signposted from the roundabout by L'Entrepôt (see below) on a small road that leads round into Rue du 11 Novembre from the other end. ●
❯**Château de Landebaudière**. This somewhat austere 18th-century mansion, now municipal offices, is surrounded by a park of peaceful, tree-lined avenues. The Duc d'Elbée (see page 51) was married here in 1788, and the château also sheltered the Marquis de Bonchamps (see page 37) after he had been wounded in battle. ● *Park only. Rue du Commandant Sauvageot, on the Tiffauges road, north-west of the village.*
❯**L'Entrepôt**. The brightly-painted exterior of this factory shop selling jazzy fashion footwear for men, women and children strikes a distinctly upbeat note. The interior is full of the zaniest modern shoes, as featured in *Vogue*, *Elle* and other glossy magazines. Even if you can't see yourself teetering about the Vendée in their way-out designs and impossibly high heels, it's worth visiting the place just to admire the trendy clientele, and such items as patchwork suede boots and leopardskin-patterned kids' wellies. ● *Mon-Fri 10am-noon & 2-7pm; Sat 10am-6pm. 38 Rue du Commandant Sauvageot (tel: 02 51 66 36 65).*

LES HERBIERS
ⓘ tel: 02 51 92 92 92 fax: 02 51 92 93 70
www.ot-lesherbiers.fr
contact@ot-lesherbiers.fr

Busy manufacturing town overlooking the Grande Maine river, at the north-west end of the Vendean hills and 25km south-west of Cholet. Among its many industries are several internationally-known clothing manufacturers and the Jeanneau boat-building company (now part of Bénéteau, see page 54). Les Herbiers' disused station building, now a fashionable bar and restaurant, is the southern terminus for the steam train that runs in summer from Mortagne-sur-Sèvre (see page 145).

Vendrennes, on the N160, 10km south-west of Les Herbiers, is the supposed birthplace of the fluffy Vendean brioche (a sweet, delicately-flavoured bread, available in the UK today at Tesco, Sainsbury's and other stores). Its bakery is a hallowed stopping-place for everyone—from individuals to coach-parties—anxious to take home a taste of the real thing. You can't miss the shop, with its vast car park, though be very careful if you have to cross the main road to reach it.

❯Mont des Alouettes. This windy ridge, at a high point (231 metres) on the Cholet road 3km north of Les Herbiers, was considered in pre-motorway days the gateway to the Vendée. The three windmills that stand on "Lark Hill" today (along with four others, now demolished) were important semaphores for the Vendean forces during the 18th-century uprising. Hidden in the leafy *bocage* below, the Vendée's royalist guerrillas could be told of their Republican enemy's movements through the position in which the mills' sails were parked: signals included x for "all clear" and + for "alert". One of the mills has been restored, and is once again grinding corn. A chapel completed in 1823 by the Duchesse de Berry (see page 39) commemorates the wars (though you have to take your life in your hands crossing the busy N160 if you want a close-up look). ● *Site open all year.* ◐ *Windmill: Early Apr-31 May, Sat, Sun & public holidays 10am-12.30pm & 2-6.30pm; 1 June-15 Sept, Wed-Mon 10am-12.30pm & 2-6.30pm (1 July-1 Aug, daily 10am-7pm). On N160 (tel: 02 51 67 16 66/06 14 41 62 40). 3€, children 2€.*

❯Château d'Ardelay. A striking, square tower with a distinctive, red-tiled, pointed roof dominates the village of Ardelay, 3km south of Les Herbiers. You can tramp into the walled courtyard over a wooden drawbridge spanning the dry moat. During temporary exhibitions you can also visit the elegantly-restored 15th-century rooms inside, empty but for some magnificent granite fireplaces, and climb the stairs to view the impressive array of timbers supporting the steeply-pitched roof. ● *Site open all year. Interior, during exhibitions: Sat, Sun 2.30-6.30pm. On D23 (tel: 02 51 66 95 41). Free.*

❯Vieille Église St-Christophe. On the edge of Mesnard-la-Barotière, a village 8km west of Les Herbiers, is a pretty 11th-century church that contains some interesting medieval wall-paintings—best seen in broad daylight, since there is no electric lighting in the church. Even the most bloodthirsty child may flinch at the depictions of poor St Lawrence being barbecued over blazing logs, or at the beheading of John the Baptist. Less gruesome panels include the Annunciation, the Nativity and the Last Supper, and a scene thought to show

■ **Mont des Alouettes: mill in full sail.**

■ Religious revival: the Abbaye de la Grainetière has a new community of monks.

the paintings' wealthy 13th-century sponsors. Tops of columns around the chancel are decorated with primitive stone carvings of leaves and roughly-hewn beasts. Some descriptive notes lie on the altar (from 2004, new lighting and interactive screens should provide more sophisticated explanatory aids). ● *Off D11, E of village centre.*

➤**Abbaye de Notre-Dame de la Grainetière**. Founded in 1130 by Benedictine monks, this rural abbey 8km south-west of Les Herbiers was fortified, and withstood an English seige in 1372. (Students of French literature may like to know that Abbé Prévost wrote several chapters of his sentimental novel *Manon Lescaut* here, around 1731.) The abbey's fortunes declined, and after being severely damaged by Protestants during the Wars of Religion the building was further ruined in the aftermath of the Revolution and the Vendée Wars, and then sold off for use as a farm and a quarry. Today partially restored, it is a peaceful place. One side of its stone-flagged cloister, supported on graceful twin columns, remains intact; another surviving feature is a magnificent vaulted *salle capitulaire* (chapter house). Since the late 1970s, the abbey has been home once again to a small group of Benedictine monks who offer guided tours by appointment, though you may also walk around by yourself. ● *Tues-Sun 2.30-5.30pm. Signposted off N160 (tel: 02 51 67 21 19). 2€, children free.* ⑁

➤**Grand Labyrinthe**. Visitors to this large maze made of towering maize plants (what else!), 9km south-west of Les Herbiers, are in for some surprises. Emerging from the foliage-screened pathways at various places along the route they find small, immaculately-groomed gardens in which actors perform short playlets on some French literary theme, which is different each year. On August Saturdays there are atmospheric night-time visits of the maze by moonlight. O *1 July-31 Aug, Sun-Fri 10am-7.30pm, Sat 2-7.30pm (1-31 Aug, also Sat from 9pm). Off N160, 1km NE of Vendrennes (tel: 02 51 66 15 32). 7.50€, children 6€.*

LEGÉ (Loire-Atlantique)

ⓘ tel: 02 40 26 30 49
www.ville-lege44.fr
contact@ville-lege44.fr

A tall cyclindrical water-tower dominating the skyline proclaims the name of this town, 25km west of Montaigu and mid-way between Nantes and Les Sables-d'Olonne, long before you arrive at it. For several centuries, Legé enjoyed prosperity as part of the "Marches of Brittany", a free-trade zone between the former dukedom of Brittany and the kingdom of France. However, as the Vendean leader Charette made his base here in 1793 (at 2 Rue Madame de la Rochefoucauld, behind Legé's massive 20th-century church), the town suffered greatly at the hands of the *colonnes infernales* (see page 37). The general's admirers later commemorated him with the lofty little chapel near the town centre.

➤ **L'Enclos de la Colonne**. This strange garden behind the car park of Super U, laid out in the late 19th century, is full of grottoes and religious statues. A place of pilgrimage, it is located just off the Rocheservière road; turn left immediately after Legé's modern, open-air shopping centre. ●

➤ **Château du Bois-Chevalier**. This charming, moated house, hidden in woods 3km north-east of Legé, is a rarity—a stately home that has emerged unscathed from the troubles of the late 18th century. Built in 1655, the château has slate roofs and brick chimneys, which are mirrored in the serene waters surrounding it. During the Wars of the Vendée it belonged to royalist supporters, and General Charette used to hold parties in the drawing-room. It is still a private family home, but in summer you are allowed to view the exterior from the courtyard. ○ *1 July-early Aug, daily 10.30am-4.30pm. Signposted N of D753 (tel: 02 40 26 30 49). 3€, children 2€.*

LES LUCS-SUR-BOULOGNE

ⓘ tel: 02 51 46 51 28/02 51 31 21 29   fax: 02 51 46 51 20
www.ville-leslucssurboulogne.fr
mairies.lucs.boul@wanadoo.fr

On 23 February 1794 the Republican *colonnes infernales* (see page 37) wiped out 564 women, children and old people by setting fire to a hilltop chapel in which they had sought sanctuary. The village, 23km north of La Roche-sur-Yon, has become a shrine not only to the local victims but to all who fell in the post-Revolution civil war. The church, the rebuilt chapel, the memorial building, and even an art installation on a traffic island tell the story in different ways; from 2005, a new historical museum will add its own version.

LES LUCS EXTRAS

Restaurant: L'Auberge du Lac. Excellent food, in a lakeside setting; menus from 14€. 250 Rue du Général Charette, off D18, 500m NE of village (tel: 02 51 46 59 59).

➤ **Église St-Pierre**. The church on the crossroads at the centre of Les Lucs is really the place to start visiting the evocative sites about the Vendée Wars. Its 20th-century stained-glass windows tell the tale of the tragic events that took place in the chapel on the hill above Les Lucs (see page 140), as related by the *curé* Barbedette, a local priest who noted the names and ages of all the dead. To hear an in-depth French commentary on the Vendée Wars, look behind the organ for a set of coloured buttons: press the yellow one, wait five seconds, and then press the green. ●

➤ **Mémorial de Vendée: Chemin de la Mémoire**. Russian writer Alexander Solzhenitsyn performed the opening ceremony for this hall of memory, 1km north-east of the village centre, in 1993—the bicentenary of the Vendée Wars. Situated at the foot of the hill crowned by the Petit-Luc chapel, the low, slab-sided building arouses mixed reactions.

Think of it less as a museum, though, and more as somewhere that sets a mood. Small, knee-high panels identifying some of the wars' principal figures line the path to a wooden footbridge leading to the main door. Inside, a few exquisitely-chosen items are spotlit—though you need a torch to read the tiny labels that lurk in the dark beneath them, and certainly would find it helpful to know something about the characters and events beforehand (see page 31). However, once you let the hypnotic music seep in, the overall effect is extremely moving. Roughly-crayoned abstract sketches are projected, suggesting murders, fire and pillage. Real examples of the menacing weapons that the peasants improvised from their farming tools, re-angling the blades to create lethal bayonets, look as chilling now as they did two centuries ago. After you emerge into the daylight, blinking and somewhat subdued, you can climb a steep slope to the chapel of Petit-Luc. ● *Mon-Sat 9.30am-6pm; Sun & public holidays 10am-7pm (1 July-31 Aug, daily 10am-7pm). Closed last three weeks of Jan. On D18, 1km NE of Les Lucs (tel: 02 51 42 81 00). Free.* &

➤**Chapelle du Petit-Luc**. At the top of the hill above the memorial building stands a chapel built on the site of the 1794 massacre, using the stones of the original church. It contains marble panels bearing the names and ages of each of the 563 who died there. The 564th victim—Abbé Voyneau the village priest—is commemorated by a simple stone column. To find it, walk down the lane from the chapel to the D39, go straight across and past the old presbytery; the memorial marking the place where the cleric was put to death stands in a tree-shaded spot near a little stream. ● & *(To reach the chapel by car from the village centre, drive out on the D39 St-Denis-la-Chevasse road, & turn left where indicated.)*

➤**Historial de la Vendée**. Due to open alongside the Mémorial de Vendée, is a state-of-the-art museum that will present the entire history of the *département* from prehistoric times to its 21st-century agricultural, fishing, manufacturing and other industries. A living grass roof will ensure the building blends into the landscape alongside the Boulogne river. ● *From summer 2005. On D18, 1km NE of Les Lucs. Opening hours & ticket prices not available at time of writing.* &

MALLIÈVRE

ⓘ tel: 02 51 65 11 32 fax: 02 51 65 56 68
www.cc-canton-mortagne-sur-sevre.fr
tourisme@cc-canton-mortagne-sur-sevre.fr

With an area of just 17 hectares, the attractive, granite-built village of Mallièvre, 15km north-east of Les Herbiers, has the distinction of being the Vendée's smallest *commune*. Its steep, narrow streets are bordered by large houses, once inhabited by rich weaving-masters who installed their workers in cellars beneath their homes. Later, water-power was harnessed on a large scale and mills and factories grew up alongside the river Sèvre. A walking trail, the "Circuit des Fontaines," leads you past points of interest marked with blue plaques; the route is punctuated by occasional bollards on which you can press a button to hear a French commentary about the village and its industrial past.

MALLIÈVRE EXTRAS
Restaurant: Auberge du Poupet. Pretty riverside setting for some gastronomic meals. Menus from 17€. Poupet, 2km W of Mallièvre (tel: 02 51 92 33 25).
Festival: Le Festival du Poupet. Open-air music & comedy. Poupet, 2km W of Mallièvre. Aug.

➤**La Cave du Tisserand**. Near Mallièvre's small market square, you can peer into a tiny cottage that has been equipped with a loom, and learn about a weaver's life a century or more ago through sound and lighting effects—a sort of mini *son-et-lumière*. ◑ *1 Mar-30 Apr, Sat, Sun 10am-7pm; 1 May-14 Sept, plus Oct half-term, daily 10am-8pm; 15-30 Sept, Sat, Sun 10am-8pm. Free.*
➤**Vallée du Poupet**. A lovely place to picnic is this idyllic grassy valley on the banks of the river Sèvre 2km north-west of Mallièvre, with its old watermill, canoe-hire and, in summer, a well-known festival of open-air entertainment. ● *Signposted from D72, St-Malo-du-Bois road.*

MAULÉVRIER (Maine-et-Loire)

ⓘ tel: 02.41.55.06.50 fax: 02.41.55.06.50
www.maulevrier.monclocher.com
officedetourisme.maulevrier@wanadoo.fr

This village on the River Moine, 12km south-east of Cholet, has a few unexpected points of interest in addition to its internationally-famous Japanese garden (see page 144). Château Colbert, a grand hotel and restaurant, is a stately 17th-century mansion built by the brother of Louis XIV's great minister Jean-Baptiste Colbert. And (not surprisingly perhaps, since the French word *lévrier* means greyhound), Maulévrier has a *cynodrome*, or dog track. ⫸➤ *page 144*

■ **Religious heritage, opposite: towers and statues, top, of Notre-Dame-de-Salette; angels at St-Laurent; and oak-tree chapel near Rocheservière.**

LES ÉPESSES

Le Puy-du-Fou

Famous for night-time *son-et-lumière* and daytime historical entertainment throughout the summer, this site, set amid the green hills of the Vendée's *bocage,* enchants all ages.

➤★ Le Puy-du-Fou by day: Le Grand Parc. A whole day will hardly be enough to take in all the entertainment on offer at this impeccably organised "historical theme park" 10km north-east of Les Herbiers (see also page 134). Arrive as early as possible, and plan your day around the various performance times. The falconry ("Le Bal des Oiseaux Fantômes"), the storming of the medieval keep ("La Bataille du Donjon," pictured on page 35), the attack by Vikings ("Le Drakkar") and the dramatic chariot-racing ("Les Gladiateurs") are the most spectacular, and it's essential to be at the gates for each show at least 30 minutes before the advertised start.

The rest of the time there will never be a dull moment. You will wander round a reconstructed 18th-century Vendean village (including passing through a spookily gloomy tunnel with re-creations of scenes from the Vendée Wars), pass through the "medieval" township (pictured above) full of costumed entertainers and

wandering pigs, poultry and even a tame bear, and look around a fort and thatched village typical of the year 1000. Everywhere you look, there are immaculately-kept gardens.

New for 2004 is "Le Bourg 1900"; a turn-of-the-last-century village, complete with café and display of mechanised models. Future projects include demonstrations of *haute école*, the pinnacle of 18th-century horsemanship, and the construction of a lake-dwellers' village.

Don't forget sunhats and other protective clothing. Though many of the paths meander through shady woodland, the main shows are in the open, with little shelter.

There are two atmospheric restaurants on site, offering meals with period entertainment thrown in for around 20€, children 10€. (Reserve the moment you arrive at the park.) Elsewhere, drinks and rather disappointing snacks are on sale. You are not allowed to bring picnics into the grounds; however, you may leave to eat

■ Puy-du-Fou: the medieval village, opposite, and falconry display, top, from the Grand Parc; dazzling spectacle at the night-time Cinéscénie, above.

your sandwiches by the car park, and then be readmitted later. ○ *1 May-late Sept, Sat, Sun & public holidays 10am-7pm (1 June-early Sept, daily 10am-7pm). 2km NW of Les Épesses (tel: 02 51 64 11 11). 24€, children 13.50€ (under-fives free); two-day pass 36€ & 20.25€.* &

>★ Le Puy-du-Fou by night: Cinéscénie: *Jacques Maupillier, paysan vendéen.* Some 200,000 spectators a year come to witness this incredible open-air, night-time show, first performed in 1977. More than 800 local people and 50 horsemen act out the history of the Vendée through the life of "Jacques Maupillier", an archetypal Vendean, to the accompaniment of lasers, fountains, fireworks and the most sophisticated of sound and lighting techniques.

The commentary, using the voices of Philippe Noiret and other famous actors, is entirely in French. Foreign-language, partial translations are available through special headsets, though these do tend to cut you off from the shared atmosphere of the event. Anyway, after a slightly slow start the overall visual effect is so breath-taking that total understanding of the story hardly matters. Galloping horses thunder out of the castle to fall over at your feet, ballet dancers pirouette seemingly upon the very surface of the lake, and sudden bursts of light reveal hundreds of actors who have composed themselves into living tableaux in the darkness. The picturesque castle and its lake provide the backdrop to this thrilling spectacle, the ultimate in *son-et-lumière* performances, which has been described as "the Oberammergau of France."

As two-thirds of the seats tend to be sold by January, you do need to apply early (reservation-office staff speak English, and it's possible to book by credit card) since there are only about 20 performances a year. Note, however, that the show continues whatever the weather and that absolutely no refunds are made. Once the sun sets, night breezes can whistle across the lake even on the balmiest evening, so dress warmly and take rugs or sleeping-bags to cover legs. Rain-capes, or even large plastic bin-liners, for each member of the family are a wise standby if it looks at all like rain. Arrive at the box office at least one hour before the start, to find your places in the vast grandstand.

If you are desperate for tickets at the last minute, it's still worth turning up on the night, and presenting yourself at the box office at the starting time of the show (*not* an hour before-hand, in this case). By then, the ticket-holders are seated and staff can often squeeze a few extra folk in; you might even be lucky enough to catch some group organisers standing alongside the box office hoping to sell tickets that some of their party are unable to use.

Stewards organise the parking efficiently, but there can be delays after the show when every-one is trying to leave. If you pack a flask of coffee, you can sit and drink it by your car while the other vehicles are queuing for the exit; once you have finished it, you should have a clear run out onto deserted country roads. ○ *Late May-early Sept, mostly Fri & Sat. June/July starts 10.30pm; Aug/Sept starts 10pm; the show runs about 1hr 40 mins. 2km NW of Les Épesses (tel: 02 51 64 11 11). 22.50€, children 12€. www.puydufou.com/* &

■ Oriental tranquillity: Maulévrier's Japanese garden miraculously encapsulates the spirit of Edo Japan.

❯**Parc Oriental**. Created in 1900 by a Paris architect who adored the Far East, this amazing Japanese-style garden fell into oblivion during the 1940s until local horticultural enthusiasts launched a rescue project 20 years ago. Good explanatory panels (in English as well as French) give background information on the layout. Symbolising the four seasons of life, it is inspired by Edo designs of 16th to 19th centuries; its sculptures and Khmer temple were recycled from the 1900 Paris Exposition Universelle. Around the lake an oriental effect is created by the pagoda, the curved, red-painted bridges and the 120 species of trees and shrubs—including magnolias, acers and pines—complemented by delicate, Japanese-inspired pottery on sale in a studio within the grounds.

Though lovely at any period of the year, the garden is at its absolute best in April, at the time of the cherry blossom, and on sunny autumn days when the colours of the maple leaves are at their most vibrant. For evening openings in summer, visitors are handed a lantern to guide them round the illuminated pathways. The experience is enhanced by recordings of appropriate words and music. (Allow at least an hour for the complete tour.) ◗ *1 Mar-15 Nov, Tues-Sat 2-6pm, Sun & public holidays 2-7pm (1 July-31 Aug, daily 10.30am-7.30pm). Jardin de Nuit evening visits: early May-30 Sept, Sat & public holidays (14 July-15 Aug, Sat & Wed), 9.30pm or 10pm according to season. Beside Château Colbert hotel (tel: 02 41 55 50 14). 5€, disabled 3.10€, children under 12 free. Jardin de Nuit 10€, children free. ♿ (except one small area).*

MONTAIGU

ⓘ tel: 02 51 06 39 17 fax: 02 51 06 39 17
www.ville-montaigu.fr
office.tourisme.montaigu@wanadoo.fr

This attractive town overlooking the confluence of the Maine and Asson rivers, 52km south-west of Cholet, is still partly surrounded by solid medieval ramparts—atmospherically illuminated at night. Apart from the square Pavillon des Nourrices in one corner, little remains of the 12th- to 15th-century castle. Fortified and moated

MONTAIGU EXTRAS

Market: Second Wed & last Thurs of month, Champ de Foire. Sat, Place Pont-Jarlet.

Restaurant: *La Digue*. Good meals beside the river; menus from 11€. 9 Rue des Abreuvoirs (tel: 02 51 06 34 48).

by Louis XI, it was dismantled on orders from Henri III, to prevent it becoming strategically useful to Protestants. Today, the gardens around the walls provide pleasant pathways and shady picnic spots. Though the town's small museum is currently closed, you can get a feel for Montaigu's heritage by walking around the narrow, winding streets off Rue Clemenceau (the main shopping area), which are lined with ancient walls and picturesque old houses. A leaflet describing points of interest is available from the tourist office.

> Maison de la Rivière. In an old watermill 4km south of Montaigu is a museum devoted to freshwater fish, plants and insects. The visit gets off to a rather slow start, while you stand and listen to a lengthy recorded commentary about life at the mill, but things pick up once you climb the spiral stairs and can press buttons to call up clips of film about bird- and river-life. A final section gives a dream-like presentation of romantic watery images. Outside, you can experience the world of nature for real, exploring the Grande Maine river on foot or by canoe. ◗ *1 Apr-30 Sept, Tues-Sun 2-7pm (15 June-31 Aug, daily 11am-7pm); 1 Oct-2 Nov, Sun & public holidays 2-6pm. St-Georges-de-Montaigu (tel: 02 51 46 44 67). 4.50€, children 3€.*

> Château de la Preuille. This vineyard, located beside a pretty, moated 15th-century castle deep in the countryside 8km north of Montaigu, contains a small wine museum displaying a huge wine-press, and other wine-making equipment ancient and modern. Visitors can sample—and buy—some of the château's highly-rated Muscadet-sur-Lie, Gros-Plant, Gamay and Chardonnay. ● *Tues-Sat 9.30am-12.30pm & 2-6pm (15 June-15 Sept, daily 9.30am-12.30pm & 2-6pm). Near St-Hilaire-de-Loulay, 3km NW of Montaigu; turn NE off N137 towards St-Hilaire-de-Clisson, on D93, then take D54 from which La Preuille is signposted (tel: 02 51 46 32 32). Free.* ♿

MORTAGNE-SUR-SEVRE

ⓘ tel: 02 51 65 11 32 fax: 02 51 65 56 68
www.cc-canton-mortagne-sur-sevre.fr
tourisme@cc-canton-mortagne-sur-sevre.fr

Quiet town on the Sèvre Nantaise river, at the eastern boundary of the Vendée and 15km north-east of Les Herbiers, that was in English hands for half of the 14th century. Today it is dominated by the ivy-covered ruins of a fortress, said to have been built by the brother of William the Conqueror and which includes the remains of a circular tower still called the Tour des Anglais. The castle was torn down on the orders of Cardinal Richelieu in 1626, but the town centre still contains shady squares, steep little alleys and a few historic houses. A scenic segment of the railway line, that carried passengers between Cholet and Fontenay-le-Comte from 1914 until 1939, has been reawakened by local enthusiasts and now offers popular steam-hauled train rides in summer.

> Chemin de Fer de la Vendée: Train à Vapeur. For a ride on the Vendée's last steam train (see picture, page 146), follow signs for the tourist office, located in the old railway station near the level-crossing on the Cholet road. The three-hour excursion takes you, at a leisurely 40kph, along a 22km section of track between Mortagne and Les Herbiers and back, past green fields, across dizzying viaducts, over rivers and through the Vendean hills. During a 30-minute halt at Les Herbiers you can watch the engine being manoeuvred to face in the opposite direction; on the way back the train stops at Les Épesses station—now a bar—so you can cool down with a drink. Advance booking essential; arrive at Mortagne station well before departure time. ○ *1 June-14 Sept, Sun 3.30pm (1 July-31 Aug, Wed, Fri, Sun 3.30pm). Mortagne station (tel: 02 51 63 02 01). Single Mortagne-Les Herbiers: 9€, children 6€, family (2+3 or more) 35€; return: 11€, 8€ & 45€.*

> **Chapelle des Martyrs**. The victims of a Republican massacre in 1793 are commemorated by a little chapel in a village 13km south-west of Mortagne. Built in 1925, it contains two stained-glass windows depicting episodes from those tragic times and—most poignantly—framed extracts from 18th-century registers giving the names and ages of the 53 who were put to death. ● *St-Martin-des-Tilleuls, on the D72, just to the E of the village centre.*

Aller Retour Nº 849

■ Just the ticket: puff along Mortagne's scenic railway.

MOUCHAMPS

ⓘ tel: 02 51 92 92 92 fax: 02 51 92 93 70
www.mouchamps.com www.ot-lesherbiers.fr
contact@ot-lesherbiers.fr

The steep streets of this picturesque small town clinging to a hillside above the river Lay, 13km south of Les Herbiers, drop away to reveal endless misty views of the hills beyond. Resist the temptation to explore it by car, though; some lanes are so twisty and precipitous that you could easily get stuck fast. The famous French politician Georges Clemenceau is buried 5km away at his family's simple country manor house (see below).

> **Église de Mouchamps**. Inside the stocky Romanesque church is a memorial to Vendeans who died during the post-Revolutionary wars, meticulously categorised according to whether they were guillotined, massacred or shot. ●
> **René Guilbaud memorial**. A sleekly elegant monument, by sculptors Jan and Joël Martel (see page 45), commemorates aviator René Guilbaud (1890-1928). Born in Mouchamps, he disappeared with Norwegian explorer Roald Amundsen over the North Pole while on a mission to rescue the crew of an Italian airship. ● *Avenue des Marronniers, off D48, Les Herbiers road.* ♿
> **Le Colombier**. The body of French politician Georges Clemenceau (1841-1929) is buried next to that of his father in the grounds of the family's mellow 16th-century manor house (not open to the public). Born in the Vendée, at Mouilleron-en-Pareds (see page 119), Clemenceau became an MP in the 1870s and soon earned a reputation as a ferocious left-wing politician—dubbed "le Tigre" ("the Tiger"). After losing his seat in 1893 he turned journalist, before returning to politics in 1902. Prime Minister from 1906-09, and called on again in 1917, he successfully negotiated the Treaty of Versailles after the end of World War I, for which he received the affectionate nickname of "Père la Victoire" ("Father of Victory"). He returned to the Vendée to spend his retirement years in his seaside home at St Vincent-sur-Jard (see page 71). His grave may be visited in the wood just before the house and its outbuildings. Go through a little wooden gate, and follow a short path to the spot where the distinguished statesman lies under a cedar overlooking the Petit-Lay river, with his father's grave beyond. ● *Signposted off the D13, 5km E of Mouchamps.*

ROCHESERVIERE

ⓘ tel: 02 51 94 94 05 (July/Aug)/02 51 94 94 28 fax: 02 51 94 94 29
www.cc-canton-rocheserviere.fr
tourisme@cc-canton-rocheserviere.fr

This attractive village in the valley of the Boulogne 15km west of Montaigu is easily missed, since the D937 sweeps past it over an enormous viaduct. Today, the spruced-up square around the *mairie* gives due prominence to a few 16th- and 17th-century houses. The ancient packhorse bridge across the river was the site of a fierce battle between Republicans and royalist Vendeans in 1793, and of a further round of bitter fighting in June 1815. The stained-glass windows of the church illustrate another bloody episode of the Vendée Wars, a massacre on 27 February 1794.

The end of the long-drawn-out civil war came in 1796 with the capture of General Charette (see picture, page 36) in woods near the country house of La Chabotterie (see below and picture, page 33), 12km south-east of Rocheservière and now an understandably important point on the Vendée's historical map.

>Musée des Outils des Métiers du Bois. A restored watermill near the old bridge at the bottom of the town contains an evocation of the woodworking trades of the village, from carpentry and joinery to clog- and barrel-making. More than 600 tools on display, in different "shops" along an indoor "street". English leaflet available. O *Easter-30 June, Sun & public holidays 2.30-6.30pm; 1 July-31 Aug, Wed-Mon, 2.30- 6.30pm. Moulin du Bourg (tel: 02 52 94 92 38). 3€, children free.*

>Tract'Expo. Around 75 tractors dating from between 1938 and 1960—Massey-Harris, Ferguson, Fordson Major, even Porsche—are shown off by two enthusiasts, who have painstakingly restored most of the vehicles. This interesting agricultural collection is split between two sites in a village 9km south-east of Rocheservière. ◑ *1 May-31 Oct, Sat, Sun 3-6pm (1 June-30 Sept, daily 3-7pm). Rue de l'Église (Mormaison road), St-Sulpice-le-Verdon (tel: 02 51 42 84 98); & Ferme du Badreau, 2km NE of St-Sulpice, on D7 (tel: 02 51 42 81 92). Free.*

>★ Logis de la Chabotterie. To get the most out of your visit to this exquisitely restored manor house, the history of which is inextricably linked to that of the revered Vendean leader Charette, you need to allow a good couple of hours, and to have done a bit of homework on the Vendean uprising (see page 31). The *logis*, or country mansion, 12km south-east of Rocheservière, has been totally refurbished, its rooms ingeniously lit and furnished in impeccable 18th-century style, with murmuring voices and background sounds making you feel you have actually only just missed seeing the occupants. The kitchen contains the very table on which General Charette was laid to have his wounds dressed after his capture on 23 March 1796 by General Travot's exultant Republican troops; in another room you can watch a 12-minute video about the arrest and execution of the charismatic leader. An English leaflet available at the desk describes the self-guided tour.

Afterwards you embark on a 16-minute "Parcours", an automated history trail in and out of a series of rooms that display episodes from the events of the 1790s. The tableaux and models are excellent and the semi-animated waxworks that tell the story are realistic-looking. However, the quality of the French commentary—delivered as if spoken by Charette himself—often suffers from poor acoustics, and can be hard to understand, even for French-speakers. In the adjoining hall are serious, well-documented exhibitions on a different Vendée-related theme each year.

The immaculately-planted garden features flowers and vegetables in geometric borders and an arbour of deliciously perfumed old-fashioned roses. You can walk and picnic in the wider grounds, and follow the "Chemin de Charette" trail to a granite cross at the spot where the Vendean leader was taken. Events with appropriately period flavour are organised on summer afternoons, and a prestigious annual festival of baroque music is held in July. ● *Mon-Sat 9.30am-6pm, Sun & public holidays 10am-6pm (1 July-31 Aug, daily 10am-7pm). Closed last three weeks of Jan. On D18, 12km SE of Rocheservière & 2km SE of St-Sulpice (tel: 02 51 42 81 00). 6€, children free.*

>Chêne-Chapelle. Sandwiched between the roadside and the front garden of a house is a tiny chapel grafted onto a hollow oak. This fairyland-scale place of worship (see picture, page 141) was erected in the early 19th century; the tree is supposed to be 800 years old. ● *3km SE of St- Sulpice, & 1km SE of La Chabotterie; signposted from roundabout at La Grande Chevasse.*

ROCHESERVIERE EXTRAS

Market: *First Wed of month, L'Herbergement, 13km SE of Rocheservière.*

Restaurant: **L'Orée de la Chabotterie**. *Strong on offal & rustic specialities; menus from 14€. La Chevasse, on D18, 13km SE of Rocheservière (tel: 02 51 42 81 70).*

Brocante: **Dépôt-Vente Brocante et Loisirs**. *Tues-Sat 10am-12.30pm & 2-7pm, Sun 3-7pm. Route de Cholet, just E of D937 (tel: 02 51 31 07 47).*

ST-LAURENT-SUR-SEVRE

ⓘ tel: 02 51 65 11 32 fax: 02 51 65 56 68
www.saintlaurentsursevre.fr
www.cc-canton-mortagne-sur-sevre.fr
tourisme@cc-canton-mortagne-sur-sevre.fr

■ **Louis-Marie Grignion de Montfort.**

Since the death here in 1716 of St Louis-Marie Grignion de Montfort, St-Laurent has become a place of pilgrimage and a spiritual centre for 430 religious groups descended from those founded by the Breton missionary priest. Located 11km south of Cholet, this "holy town" of the Vendée lies in a curve of the Sèvre Nantaise river, on the eastern edge of the *département*. A monument on the La Verrie road, its steep steps lined with life-sized white angels (see picture, page 141), affords a wonderful view of the town's church towers and spires.

Apart from the basilica (see below), notable buildings include the Maison du St-Esprit, home to an order of missionaries, and the headquarters of the Filles de la Sagesse—an order of nuns who care for the sick, and who are happy to allow visitors to stroll around their convent's peaceful grounds. The saint also founded the Frères de St-Gabriel, a teaching order whose members work in underprivileged schools around the world. On their home ground, in St-Laurent, the brothers run the Vendée's top educational establishment, the 2,500-pupil Institution St-Gabriel.

➤**Basilique**. Among a forest of marble columns inside the huge 19th-century basilica church is the tomb of St Louis-Marie Grignion de Montfort, alongside that of Marie-Louise Trichet, the nun who founded the Filles de la Sagesse. Born in 1673 in Brittany, the newly-ordained Montfort became a chaplain at a hospital in Poitiers in 1700 and three years later founded, with the young Marie-Louise Trichet, a nursing order of nuns. Keen to rekindle religious ardour in a world he saw as full of vice and materialism, he took his missionary fervour to the countryside, visiting the poor and the sick and training others to spread the word. In Rome, he asked Pope Clement XI to send him to Japan as a missionary. The pontiff refused, and instructed him instead to evangelise his own region. The zealous Grignion de Montfort returned to France but met with hostility from the bishops of Normandy, Brittany and Saintonge. Made more welcome in this area, he based himself at St-Laurent, and in 1715 spent time living as a hermit at Mervent (see page 117). He was canonised in 1927. The saint's writings were a favourite source of inspiration to Pope Jean-Paul II, who came to the basilica to pay homage to his hero in 1996. ● *Daily 8am-7pm. Free.*

TIFFAUGES

www.cc-canton-mortagne-sur-sevre.fr
tourisme@cc-canton-mortagne-sur-sevre.fr

The ruined fortress looming over this little town 20km south-west of Cholet belonged to the sadistic Gilles de Rais (1404-40), whose evil doings inspired the fairy-tale of *Bluebeard*. You can spend a good half-day exploring the castle, hearing its gruesome history and watching the various entertainments given there. For a change of mood, stroll through Tiffauge's narrow streets and alleys, or take a walk beside the lovely Sèvre Nantaise river.

➤★ Château de Barbe-Bleue. "Barbe-Bleue", or "Bluebeard", was in reality the infamous Gilles de Rais, or Retz (different spelling, but both pronounced "ray") on whom the monster of Charles

Perrault's fairy-tale is loosely based. Having fought alongside Charles VII and Joan of Arc against the English in the Hundred Years War and reached the rank of field-marshal at the age of only 25, Gilles de Rais seemed set for a glittering military career. But after the English burnt Joan at the stake for witchcraft in 1431 he retired to his castle at Tiffauges and squandered his fortune on high living. He turned to alchemy and, believing gold could be made from the blood of young children, seized and murdered more than 200 from around his many properties, that included the castles of Pornic and Machecoul in the neighbouring Pays de Retz (see page 156). Justice finally caught up with him, and he was tried, and hanged, in Nantes.

You need two or three hours to get round all of the castle, which was reduced to its present state largely on orders from Cardinal Richelieu more than 300 years ago. Tours by guides in medieval garb take in the Romanesque crypt (site of many terrible deeds) supported by rows of sturdy columns, the *oubliettes* (secret dungeons below the round tower, in which prisoners could be "forgotten") and, near the top of the Vidame's Tower, a whispering gallery with 37 half-moon machicolations (the semi-circular holes in the floor through which missiles could be dropped on invaders). Hold on to small children here, if you don't want them to fall on later arrivals! In the tower's basement is an eerie, reconstructed laboratory of alchemy, complete with entertainment from a costumed magician and his assistant. A shadow-puppet show in another building tells the well-known fairy-tale version of Bluebeard, in which a young bride discovers her murdered predecessors.

Children can try out knightly activities, such as "jousting" on wooden rocking-horses in a medieval-style adventure playground. However, the most popular entertainment is the fantastic display of full-sized working reconstructions of 15th-century siege machinery by "warriors" in medieval costume. To the accompaniment of a witty French commentary and some deafening bangs they fire stone cannonballs and large bags of water over 150-metre distances, and offer goggle-eyed children the chance to cross (wooden) swords with them, fire a crossbow or be put in the stocks. (Performances at noon and 3.30pm from May to September, plus an extra 5.30pm one during July and August.) ◗ *1 Apr-late Sept, Mon-Fri 10am-12.30pm & 2-6pm (ticket re-admits after lunch); Sat, Sun & public holidays 2-7pm (1 July-31 Aug, daily 11am-7pm). On D753 (tel: 02 51 65 70 51). 7€, children 5€; family (2 + 2 or more) 21€.* ⚹ *part.*

■ **Gilles de Rais: soldier and sadist.**

Restaurant: Crêperie du Vidame. Savoury & sweet pancakes, served in a small café in the village centre. 25 Grande Rue (tel: 02 51 65 76 40).

Factory shop: Mulliez. Luxury household linen, sold from a large old industrial mill in a beautiful riverside setting. Tues-Sat 9.30am-12.30pm & 2-7pm. Route de St-Aubin, Le Longeron, 6km E of Tiffauges, signposted off the D111 N of the Sèvre (tel: 02 41 63 78 10).

➤ **Cité des Oiseaux.** This ornithological site 6km south of Tiffauges is based around 35 hectares of water that are home to ducks, coots and moorhens. Warblers and golden orioles arrive in spring; grebes and cormorants take up residence in summer; quantities of waders stop by in autumn; and smew and goosander take refuge in cold weather. On the west side of the reserve there's a museum in a two-storey stone house, with videos and models to explain bird evolution, migration and habits—though trendily-low lighting means you often cannot read the labels, so educational value is limited. Near the car park, a more realistic visitor centre shows lists of the birds seen recently. ● *Lakeside visitor centre: daily 8am-noon & 1.30pm-dusk (best to take your own binoculars). Free.* ◗ *Museum: 1 Apr-31 May, Sun-Fri & public holidays 2-6pm. 1 June-30 Sept, Mon-Fri 10am-12.30pm & 2-6pm; Sun & public holidays 2-7pm (1 July-31 Aug, daily 11am-7pm). Étangs des Boucheries, Les Landes-Génusson (tel: 02 51 91 72 25). 4.50€, children free.* ⚹

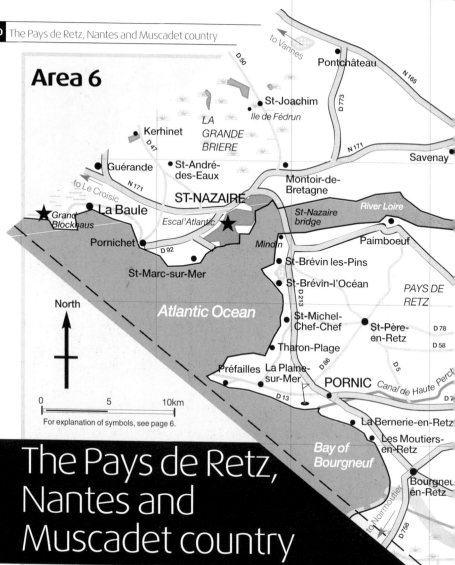

Area 6

to Vannes

Pontchâteau

D 50

N 165

St-Joachim

D 773

Ile de Fédrun

Kerhinet

*LA
GRANDE
BRIERE*

D 47

N 171

Savenay

Guérande

St-André-
des-Eaux

Montoir-de-
Bretagne

to Le Croisic

N 171

ST-NAZAIRE

★ Grand
Blockhaus

La Baule

Escal'Atlantic

★ St-Nazaire
bridge

River Loire

Pornichet

D 92

Mindin

Paimboeuf

St-Marc-sur-Mer

St-Brévin les-Pins

St-Brévin-l'Océan

*PAYS DE
RETZ*

D 213

North

Atlantic Ocean

St-Michel-
Chef-Chef

St-Père-
en-Retz

D 78

D 58

Tharon-Plage

Préfailles

La Plaine-
sur-Mer

D 86

D 5

PORNIC

Canal de Haute Perch

0   5   10km

D 13

D 7

For explanation of symbols, see page 6.

La Bernerie-en-Retz

Les Moutiers-
en-Retz

*Bay of
Bourgneuf*

Bourgne
en-Retz

to Noirmoutier

D 758

The Pays de Retz,
Nantes and
Muscadet country

The charms of the Pays de Retz, the area sandwiched between the Vendée and the River Loire, are often overlooked. Family resorts are strung out along the "Route Bleue" coast road; inland, villages and countryside wait to be explored, little car-ferries ply back and forth across the Loire, and wild animals roam Planète Sauvage safari park. North of the river, near the elegant seaside town of La Baule, the Grand Blockhaus conveys vivid memories of World War II, while the former German submarine base at St-Nazaire contains an imaginatively-created simulation of life aboard an ocean liner. All the places in this chapter fall within the *département* of Loire-Atlantique, whose capital city of Nantes offers plenty of sophisticated shopping. South-east of Nantes, in Muscadet country, wine-lovers can sample the output from hundreds of vineyards.

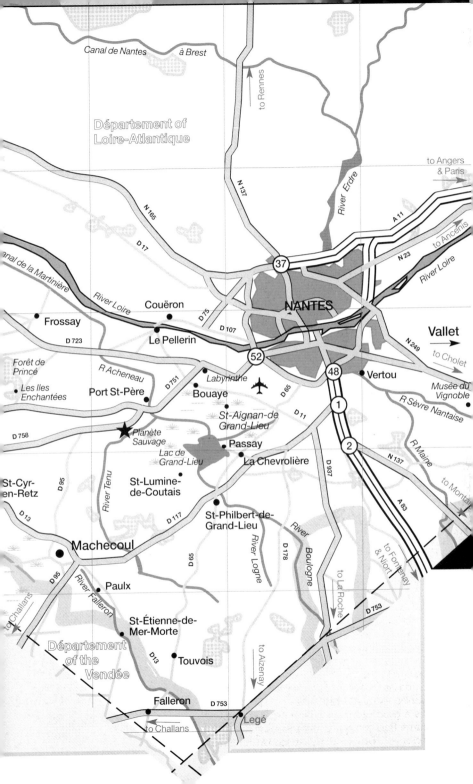

LA BAULE

ⓘ tel: 02 40 24 34 44 fax: 02 40 11 08 10
www.labaule.fr
tourisme.la.baule@wanadoo.fr

Its superb houses and hotels, built between the 1890s and the 1930s, and its 9km-long crescent-shaped sweep of beach made this large resort 25km west of St-Nazaire one of the most glamorous destinations in France before the last war. Today, modern apartment blocks and signs of mass tourism have somewhat marred La Baule's seafront, but just a couple of blocks inland the elegant villas of days gone by still nestle among the pine woods.

Avenue de Gaulle, linking the beach to the railway station, is the principal shopping street; live jazz is performed there each evening in July and August. Some of the other avenues ramble in slightly eccentric directions, following the lines of paths in the grounds of the resort's original grand houses. Riding, sailing and golf are the chic pastimes on offer, along with sessions of pampering in the town's two thalassotherapy centres (sea-water treatment spas).

> **Océarium du Croisic.** A modern aquarium stands near the sea on the south side of a picturesque fishing port, 8km west of La Baule. The interior is divided into tropical, Atlantic, Pacific and Arctic zones, with everything from penguins to Australian sharks, plus touch-tanks where children can handle less dangerous specimens. A glass tunnel within one aquarium gives you the feeling of walking across the sea bed alongside eels, skate and glittering sea-bass. ● *Daily 10am-noon & 2-6pm (1 June-31 Aug, daily 10am-7pm; mid Nov-late Dec, daily 2-6pm). Closed 1-31 Jan. Avenue de St-Goustan, Le Croisic (tel: 02 40 23 02 44). 10€, children 7€.* ♿

> **Musée des Marais Salants.** Aerial pictures in La Baule's tourist literature reveal salt-marshes behind the resort's elegant buildings, stretching north for 8km towards Guérande (see page 155). The method of transforming sea-water into crystals of salt is explained at this museum in a village 5km west of La Baule. A video shows the process of evaporation, due to wind and sun, and the way the "white gold" is harvested from June to September by the *paludier* (as a salt-maker is called in this region). Attractively-presented pictures, tools and clothes give an insight into the life of the salt-workers and their families. Much of their furniture was treated with a traditional ox-blood-coloured paint known as "Guérande red", a treatment that helped to preserve the timber. ● *Sat, Sun 10am-noon & 3-6pm; school-holiday periods, daily 10am-noon & 3-6pm (1 July-31 Aug, daily 10am-12.30pm & 2.30-7pm). Closed 1 Jan, 1 May & 25 Dec. 29 bis Rue Pasteur, Batz-sur-Mer (tel: 02 40 23 82 79). 4€, students, over-65s & over-13s 3€, younger children free.* ♿

> ★ **Le Grand Blockhaus.** Everyday items, from toothbrushes to phrase books, lent by American, British, French and German war veterans, form part of the collection amassed in this fascinating building 6km west of La Baule. Inside an unassailable-looking World War II German artillery and observation post, over three levels, you visit dormitories, as well as radio, weaponry and machine rooms. English leaflet provided, plus a good explanation of the 1942 St-Nazaire Raid and details of the St-Nazaire Pocket—the German forces' last toehold in

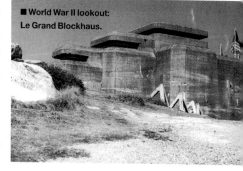

■ World War II lookout: Le Grand Blockhaus.

Europe (see page 166). Some bizarre *trompe-l'oeil* windows painted outside were part of the building's wartime camouflage, designed to convince Allied reconnaissance planes that the blockhouse was an innocent seaside villa. ◑ *Feb school holidays, Wed-Mon 10am-6pm; 1 Apr-11 Nov, Wed-Mon 10am-7pm (1 Apr-early May & 15 June-15 Sept, daily 10am-7pm). On coast road, between Batz-sur-Mer & Le Pouliguen (tel: 02 40 23 88 29). 5.50€, children 4€.*

➤**World War II cemeteries**. Allied and German war dead are buried in two immaculately-cared-for graveyards. The white headstones provided by the Commonwealth War Graves Commission can be seen in the Cimetière Anglais (British cemetery) at Escoublac, near the south-east corner of La Baule's airport, 1km east of the town centre. The 4,800 German troops who died in the Vendée, Loire-Atlantique and Maine-et-Loire are remembered in a more sombre setting. At the Cimetière Militaire Allemand, on the north side of the D92, just to the east of Pornichet and 5km south-east of La Baule, their names are marked on flat slabs set into the ground, among weeping cedars. ●

BOURGNEUF-EN-RETZ
ⓘ tel: 02 40 21 93 63 fax: 02 40 21 90 52
bourgneufenretz.otsi@wanadoo.fr

This large village, 33km south-east of the St-Nazaire bridge and just inland from the Bay of Bourgneuf, stands on the northern frontier of the Vendée. The muddy sea-bed is an excellent habitat for shellfish—particularly oysters, which are raised here in vast numbers.

Shellfish attract birds, too. If you make your way towards the shore, beyond the quaint little Port du Collet 2km west of Bourgneuf, you can watch thousands of egrets and other waders moving inshore when the tide is rising, poking in the mud for choice morsels.

➤**Musée du Pays de Retz**. Housed in an 18th-century convent building opposite the church, this interesting museum shows the history of the region: from fossils to folk traditions and from salt-production to shopping, plus local costume (including head-dresses) and some typical room-settings. A good video is shown (in French) on the region; some excellent English notes on the museum's collection are available on request. ◑ *Late Mar-early Nov, Tues-Sun 10am-noon & 2-6pm (1 July-31 Aug, daily 10.30am-1pm & 2-6.30pm). 6 Rue des Moines (tel: 02 40 21 40 83). 4€, students 2.50€, children 2€.* ♿

➤**Table d'orientation.** At a viewpoint on a ridge above the Machecoul marshes, a ceramic table identifies the steeples and other features spread below. Turn north off the D13, 4km south-east of Bourgneuf, and follow "*point de vue*" signs through the village of St-Cyr-en-Retz. ●

➤**Les Iles Enchantées**. In a delightful woodland, 13km north-west of Bourgneuf and a little way north of Chéméré, you can make out the vestiges of an 18th-century pleasure garden. Sunlight filters through the foliage and illuminates a series of recently-restored concentric canals, spanned by newly-built wooden bridges, encircling the "enchanted islands". Here and there you can make out some of the original box-hedging and the foundations of former pavilions. Spring is the best time to visit, when the leaves are on the trees and the canals should still have water in them. The entrance is hard to spot, but is signposted on the east side of the D66, opposite a farm. ●

FROSSAY
ⓘ tel: 02 40 39 72 72 fax: 02 40 39 78 35
www.mairie-frossay.fr
mairie-frossay@wanadoo.fr

As you drive across the rolling green countryside on the northern side of the Pays de Retz, there is no way you can miss this village 20km north-east of Pornic—Frossay's vast 20th-century church dominates the landscape for miles around. It's worth stopping for a look inside the cavernous building to view the brilliant modern stained glass. Set within a tracery of concrete, the windows are a curious marriage of the flamboyant-gothic style familiar from more traditional churches, and the techniques and materials of the 1930s.

Follow signs north from Frossay to the hamlet of Le Migron for a look at the Canal de la Martinière. This once-important waterway was used between 1892 and 1913 to provide a straight, deep-water channel alongside the Loire, enabling large vessels to reach the city of Nantes. More efficient dredging of the river made the canal obsolete, and today it is dedicated to fishing, boating, bird-watching and other peaceful pleasures. You can rent canoes here, or cross a bridge to visit a nature reserve on a grassy island.

➤Escal'arbres. Allow at least three hours to try out the treetop trails through the mighty oaks in the grounds of a 19th-century stately home, signposted off the D78 2km south-west of Frossay. The staff set you up with harnesses and give instruction on the safe use of the wires, platforms and walkways strung high up among the branches. ◐ *1 Apr-30 Sept, daily 9.30am-8pm; last starting-time 6pm (dates, days & times subject to change). Château de la Rousselière (tel: 02 40 39 79 59). 17€; children: nine-16 years 16€, five-eight years 14€; spectators 3€.*

➤Sentier des Daims. Well-signposted a little farther along the D78 is this large collection of different breeds of deer. As well as walking round the enclosures or climbing the observation tower to admire the elegant animals, you also learn about the relationship of man and deer. Life-sized models show how valuable the beasts were to cave-dwellers; another display illustrates the legend of St Hubert—patron saint of hunters—who is said to have been converted to Christianity on seeing before him in the forest a weeping deer with a cross between its antlers. Allow about two hours to see it all. The farm also has a well-respected restaurant (see page 153). ◐*1 Apr-31 Oct, daily 2.30-7pm (1 July-31 Aug, daily 10am-7pm); last admission 5.30pm. La Poitevinière, 3km SW of Frossay (tel: 02 40 39 75 06). 6.50€, children 4.50€.*

➤Paimboeuf. The former importance of this town on the Loire, that was the main port for Nantes until the development of St-Nazaire, is indicated by the 18th-century houses that still stand along its quays. The tourist office organises guided walks in July and August around streets that once thronged with shipowners and slave-traders, whaling-men and cod-fishermen. The winter months see flotillas of boats fishing the Loire estuary with fine-meshed nets for the tiny *civelles* (elvers, or baby eels) that are today sold for incredibly high prices to Spain or Japan. ● *Tourist office: Tues-Sat, 10am-noon & 2-5pm. Quai Sadi-Carnot, Paimboeuf (tel: 02 40 27 53 82).*

LA GRANDE BRIERE

ⓘ tel: 02 40 66 85 01 fax: 02 40 53 91 15
www.parc-naturel-briere.fr
tourisme@parc-naturel-briere.fr

A marshy, secretive landscape of peat bog, wildfowl habitat and thatched cottages lies just to the north of St-Nazaire. The Grande Brière, a national park of 40,000 hectares (half the size of Dartmoor) with a 6,700-hectare marsh at its heart, is surprisingly difficult to get to by car. To reach the eastern edge of it from the St-Nazaire bridge, first follow Nantes signs onto the eastbound N171, then turn off after 4km, at Montoir-de-Bretagne. For the west side of the reserve, take the N171 westward towards Guérande, and then follow signs for St-André-des-Eaux and St-Lyphard.

Using their flat-bottomed boats known as *blins* or *chalands*, the locals paddle along the 130km of canals to catch fish and eels, and to cut reeds for thatching their low, whitewashed cottages. Guided tours of the wildlife-rich marshes—said to be the second-

BRIERE EXTRAS

Market: Thurs (1 July-31 Aug). Kerhinet.

Specialities: Eels. Frogs' legs. Freshwater fish.

Restaurant: Auberge de Kerhinet. Logis hotel in a pretty, thatched cottage. Menus from 20€. Kerhinet (tel: 02 40 61 91 46).

Festivals:

Fête des Métais. Day of old crafts & customs. Kerhinet. July.

Fête des Chalands Fleuris. Decorated boats. St-André-des-Eaux, 8km SE of Kerhinet. Aug.

Kerhinet: typical village of the Grande Brière.

largest in Europe—are available by boat, by horsedrawn cart, on foot or on horseback. The prettiest spots (and the most crowded in peak tourist season) are the village of Kerhinet on the west side of the reserve, and the Ile de Fédrun, a small "island" on the east.

❯**Kerhinet**. This picturesque village on the west side of the park, 4km south-west of St-Lyphard and roughly half-way between that village and the town of Guérande, is hard to locate as it's completely invisible from the road. A discreet car park is sited behind a hedge on the north side of the lane linking the D51 and the D47, midway between Kerbourg and Breca. From here you can walk 100 metres or so into Kerhinet, where some 20 thatched, stone-built cottages have been beautifully restored. Several are now exhibition centres and craft workshops; one is a museum showing a typical Brière interior and another—the Auberge de Kerhinet—is a hotel. ◑ *Musée de Kerhinet: Easter-30 Sept, daily 2.30-6.30pm (1 July-31 Aug, daily 10.30am-1pm & 2.30-6.30pm). Kerhinet (tel: 02 40 66 85 01). 5€, children 2.50€.*

❯**Ile de Fédrun**. The island of Fédrun, on the east side of the park, lies a couple of kilometres south-west of the village of St-Joachim. You can drive to the island across the marsh, along a raised causeway; look out as you go for kingfishers and other wetland birds. Lining Fédrun's roughly circular road system is a collection of typical dwellings—mostly thatched. These include the Maison de la Mariée, full of wedding souvenirs. (Nearby St-Joachim was renowned throughout Europe a century ago for the manufacture of artificial orange-blossom, an essential part of every bride's head-dress.) Another thatched cottage, La Chaumière Briéronne, has been furnished to show the way of marshland life in days gone by. ◑ *Museums: early May-31 Aug (for 2004, open only from 1 July), daily 10.30am-1pm & 2.30-6.30pm; 1-30 Sept, daily 2-6pm. Ile de Fédrun (tel: 02 40 66 85 01). 5€ (admits to both), children 2.50€.*

GUÉRANDE

ⓘ **tel: 02 40 24 96 71 fax: 02 40 62 04 24**
www.ot-guerande.fr
contact@ot-guerande.fr

Sturdy stone ramparts still completely encircle this beautifully-preserved medieval town, 20km west of St-Nazaire. Park outside the town walls before exploring the maze of picturesque streets full of restaurants, *crêperies* and shops, and the ancient collegiate church with Romanesque decorations carved on its stone pillars.

Guérande's fortune was founded on the salt-producing industry at Saillé, just to the west. This business declined in the 19th century after Frenchman Nicolas Appert discovered that canning was a more convenient way of preserving food. However, salt-making is now enjoying a revival, and *sel de Guérande* is again in demand.

GUÉRANDE EXTRAS

Market: Wed & Sat. Mon (1 July-31 Aug, 6-10pm), crafts, books & postcards.
Specialities: Sea salt.
Festivals:
Fête Médiévale. Juggling, fire-eating & other medieval entertainment throughout the streets. Mid May.
Festival Celtique. Breton music & song, games & activities. Aug.

❯**Musée du Château**. The museum of local history is housed on three floors in one of the town's massive, 15th-century stone gatehouses. Furnished interiors illustrate domestic life on the Guérande peninsula, with *coiffes* (lace head-dresses) and costumes, decorative porcelain from nearby Le Croisic, paintings, pottery and crafts, plus information on the region's traditional salt-making and linen-weaving industries. ◑ *1 Apr-30 Sept, daily 10am-12.30pm & 2.30-7pm; 1-31 Oct, daily 10am-noon & 2-6pm. Porte St-Michel (tel: 02 40 42 96 52). 3.50€, students 2.50€, children 1.70€; family (2+3 or more) 9€.*

> **Musée de la Poupée et des Jouets Anciens**. A charming collection of dolls and toys from 1830 to the 1930s, presented in glass-fronted cabinets in one large room of a converted chapel in the town centre. They are grouped by theme—baptism, wedding, the schoolroom, the milliner's shop and so on—and are shown alongside beautifully-made miniature furniture, crockery and utensils. ● *Tues-Sun 2-6.30pm (1 May-31 Oct, daily 10.30am-12.30pm & 2.30-6.30pm). Closed 8 Jan-8 Feb. Chapelle St-Jean, 23 Rue de Saillé (tel: 02 40 15 69 13). 3.50€, children 2€.* ㅤ

> **Maison des Paludiers.** The back-breaking work of a *paludier* (salt-maker) is explained in this village 3km south of Guérande, which is surrounded in summer by hundreds of dazzling salt-pans. Inside the visitor centre, a film and a large model help to explain how sea-water taken into the intricate circuit of *oeillets* (a series of shallow basins), is gradually evaporated by wind and sun to leave the fine crystals that are raked off and gathered for sale. ◑ *1 Feb-31 Oct, plus Nov & Dec school holidays, daily 10am-12.30pm & 2-5pm (1 July-31 Aug, daily 10am-12.30pm & 2-6.30pm). 18 Rue des Prés-Garnier, Saillé (tel: 02 40 62 21 96). 4€, children 2.60€. Guided tour of a salt-marsh, 1 July-30 Sept on reservation; 5.60€, children 4€.* ㅤ

MACHECOUL

ⓘ tel: 02 40 31 42 87 fax: 02 40 02 31 28
www.machecoul.com
otm4@wanadoo.fr

This attractive market town on the edge of the Marais Breton (see page 42), near the border of the Vendée and Loire-Atlantique and 40km south-west of Nantes, is dominated by the twin spires of its large 19th-century church. At the start of the Vendée Wars, Machecoul saw one of the first risings against the Republicans, on 11 March 1793, when 3,000 Vendeans massacred those whose sympathies lay with the new régime (see page 31). Today, the town is quiet—especially on Mondays—and, apart from the enjoyable Wednesday market, there is strangely little to visit.

The jagged silhouette of a ruined castle that once belonged to the sadistic Gilles de Rais, or Bluebeard (see pages 149 and 164), can be glimpsed among the trees bordering the old Nantes road. The locals use the sinister theme as the background to a series of medieval dinners in May and for an excellent *son-et-lumière* acted out against the château ruins in July.

Rue du Marché, leading from the picturesque market-hall, is lined with interesting shops (as well as some paintwork-scraping concrete bollards). The tourist office will organise guided tours in English on request. Staff can also provide details of canoe-hire at St-Même-le-Tenu, 4km to the north-east, and advise on local footpaths and cycle trails, on riding and fishing facilities, and on wine-producers to visit in the surrounding Pays de Retz. There is horse-racing between September and June at the town's racetrack.

Try and make a trip around the marshes to the west by car, bike or on foot; it's particularly beautiful towards sunset when herons flap languidly across the landscape and keen-eyed hawks hover above unsuspecting smaller wildlife on the ground.

> **Église de St-Étienne**. In the picturesque village of St-Étienne-de-Mer-Morte, 9km south-east of Machecoul, is a free-standing bell-tower with a pointed spire. It is the remains of an ancient church into which stormed

MACHECOUL EXTRAS

Market: *Wed (throughout streets). Sat (food hall only).*

Specialities: *Le Machecoulais cheese & other dairy products from Fromagerie Beillevaire. Mâche (corn salad). Muguet (lily-of-the-valley, a traditional French gift for 1 May).*

Restaurant: Les Voyageurs. *Gastronomic restaurant, known for pike, lobster & quail. Menus from 14.50€. Place de l'Église, Paulx, 4km SE of Machecoul (tel: 02 40 26 02 76).*

Brocante: Broc'Ouest. *Large old barn in centre of a village 16km SE of Machecoul. Tues-Sat 10am-12.30pm & 2.30-7pm; Sun 2.30-7pm. 44 Rue Nationale, Falleron (tel: 02 51 68 45 45).*

Factory shop: Micmo. *Gitane & Micmo bicycles on sale. Follow "vélos déclassés" signs to shop at back of factory. Mon-Fri 9am-noon & 2-5pm. Rue Marcel-Brunelière, W of D95 Challans road (tel: 02 40 78 23 23).*

■ **St-Étienne church:
Gilles de Rais' downfall.**

MACHECOUL EXTRAS
Festivals:
Soirées médiévales.
Middle-Ages-style meals
in the market-hall. May.
Fête des Fous. Dancing
& theatrical shows
around the castle. July.
Sur les Chemins de
Gilles de Rais. Son-et-
lumière presentation
about notorious local
resident, Bluebeard. July.

Gilles de Rais on Whit Sunday 1440, at the head of a band of men. In the middle of High Mass, he seized Jean le Ferron, one of the congregation, and dragged him to his nearby castle at Machecoul. For this act of sacrilege, Gilles de Rais was later arrested and taken to Nantes, where he at last confessed to his many horrible crimes before he was hanged on 26 October 1440 and his body burnt at the stake. ●

➤**Moulin à Eau.** Just outside St-Étienne (see above), on the banks of the Falleron river, is a pretty litttle stone watermill recently restored to working order. Alongside it is a small playground—though children need close supervision so near to the water. ● *Site open all year.* ○ *Interior: 1 July-31 Aug, Sat, Sun afternoons (times not available at time of writing). St-Étienne-de-Mer-Morte, on D72, 500m W of village (tel: 02 40 31 42 87). Free.*

➤**Maison du Paysan.** The little museum at Touvois, 15km south-east of Machecoul, contains agricultural implements, a reconstructed classroom, and a delightful reconstitution of a general store, full of period buttons and other items of haberdashery. ○ *1 June-31 Oct, Sat, Sun 3-7pm (1 July-31 Aug, Wed, Sat, Sun 3-7pm). On D65, SW of church (tel: 02 40 26 30 49). 2.30€, children 0.80€.*

➤**Chapelle de Fréligné.** The delicate spire visible across a field 2km south of Touvois (see above) tempts you to stop and explore this charming 17th-century chapel in the hamlet of Fréligné. Said to have been built by English sea-captains returning from the Crusades, it was severely damaged during the Wars of the Vendée and has been much restored. ●

LES MOUTIERS-EN-RETZ

ⓘ tel: 02 40 82 74 00 fax: 02 40 64 77 07
www.mairie-lesmoutiersenretz.fr
tourisme@mairie-lesmoutiersenretz.fr

■ **Gone fishing: perfect
peace in a pêcherie.**

Some intriguing ecclesiastical features (see page 158) may be found in this appealing old village 7km south-east of Pornic.

Fishing is a popular pastime here. On the beach at low tide, locals root among the rockpools or push giant shrimping-nets through the shallows. Others retreat to quaint, spider-legged *pêcheries*, the wooden huts on stilts that are strung along the coast from Bourgneuf to the Pont de St-Nazaire. Rather in the same way as the UK's pigeon-lofts or allotment sheds, these isolated structures provide an escape for the menfolk—somewhere to sit and dream, away from the obligations of home. As the tide rises the occupants let down into the water the large square nets that dangle in front, hoping to winch them back up loaded with mullet, plaice and other small fish to take home for supper.

Some 3km north of Les Moutiers, the family resort of La Bernerie-en-Retz has a sandy beach with the added attraction of a captive sea-water pool, so that children can bathe whatever the state of the tide. From La Bernerie, a signposted "Route de l'Huître Vendée-Atlantique" (oyster route) follows the region's oyster-raising industry southwards to Fromentine and the island of Noirmoutier. Local tourist offices along the way have leaflets showing locations of oyster-growers that welcome visitors for a guided tour, followed by a tasting of half a dozen oysters and a glass of wine.

LES MOUTIERS EXTRAS
Market: Thurs (mid June-
mid Sept) & Sat. Tues
(15 June-15 Sept) & Fri, at
La Bernerie, 3km N of
Les Moutiers.
Specialities: Oysters.
Shop: La Fraiseraie.
Delicious strawberry
sorbet, jams & liqueurs
made from locally-grown
fruit. 2 Rue Georges-
Clemenceau, La Bernerie,
3km N of Les Moutiers
(tel: 02 40 64 64 82).

➤**Église St-Pierre**. In the cool interior of Les Moutiers church, a handsome model sailing ship hangs below a wooden ceiling shaped like the upturned hull of a boat. A coin dropped in the box behind the pulpit will start a light show about the unexpectedly magnificent 17th-century altarpiece. For some more recent history, if you understand French, you can also read a document about the sinking of the *Lancastria* (see page 165), bombed in 1940 while evacuating

■ La Bernerie-en-Retz: sand, sea, sun—and oysters.

Allied servicemen. Around 60 of those who drowned are commemorated in the local cemetery. ●

➤**Lanterne des Morts**. In the shady square outside Les Moutiers church stands a stone column dating from the 11th century, a rare structure known as a "lantern of the dead". Whenever a death occurs in the parish, a lamp (electric today, of course) is lit inside; the light glows through the slit windows day and night until the burial has taken place. ●

➤**Chapelle de Prigny**. Guided tours are given of a tiny 11th-century chapel built in primitive Romanesque style, though with the addition of some colourful baroque altarpieces. The church's pretty slate-roofed bell-tower was added as a lookout point in the 12th or 13th century by the Knights Templar. ○ *1 May-30 Sept, Sat-Sun 3-5pm (1 July-31 Aug, Fri-Sun 3-6pm). 1.5km E of Les Moutiers (tel: 02 40 82 74 00). Admission charges not available at time of writing.*

NANTES

ⓘ tel: 02 40 20 60 00 fax: 02 40 89 11 99
www.nantes-tourisme.com
office@nantes-tourisme.com

Shipbuilding, biscuit-making, sugar-refining and food-canning are the traditional livelihoods of this pleasant river port of more than half a million inhabitants. Straddling the Loire, Nantes is regularly voted by readers of the influential French national weekly magazine *Le Point* as the town in which they would most like to live.

■ Nantes trams: ultra-modern city transport.

The city grew rich in the 17th and 18th centuries on proceeds of the sugar and slave trades. During the Wars of the Vendée it was the site of a ferocious battle in which the Vendean leader Cathelineau was mortally wounded. It was later the headquarters for the notorious Republican General Carrier who instituted wholesale drownings of prisoners in the Loire (see page 38). Though you would not guess it from the profusion of old buildings, some dating back to the Middle Ages, the town was heavily bombed by the Allies in September 1943.

To get the best out of a day trip, try and visit Nantes between Wednesday and Saturday. (Most shops are closed on Mondays, and museums on Tuesdays as well as on public holidays.) The big-city smartness and brisk pace of life make a big contrast to the relaxed climate of the Vendée, so you probably need to snap out of holiday mood as you arrive in town and make an effort to be a bit more streetwise and security-conscious.

Driving around the confusing one-way system can be tricky, so abandon the car as soon as possible and visit on foot, or by tram and bus. There is a large underground car park beneath the Tour de Bretagne—a skyscraper visible from almost anywhere in town—and a multi-storey one near the railway station; or try the pay-&-display parking on the streets north of the station. Alternatively, travel in by train; if you leave the station by the north exit, (*sortie nord*) you will be right opposite the tram stop and the Jardin des Plantes (see page 161), ready to start exploring. The city's easy-to-understand tram system has three lines, intersecting near Place du Commerce; trams run east-west or

NANTES EXTRAS

Markets: Tues-Sun, Rue Talensac, N of Tour de Bretagne; Place du Bouffay, NE of main tourist office. Sat, Place de la Petite-Hollande, S of Place du Commerce.

Brocante: Marché aux Puces. Flea market. Sat, Place Viarme, W of Talensac market hall.

Specialities: Beurre-blanc (a rich, buttery sauce). Berlingots (pyramid-shaped boiled sweets). Canard nantais (duck). Biscuits (BN & Belin brands). Sugar. Market-gardening: carrots, leeks, & lily-of-the-valley (see page 156).

Restaurant: La Cigale. Fabulous décor in the famous Art-Nouveau brasserie. Open daily 7.30am-12.30am. Menus from 16€; also breakfast, brunch & tea served. 4 Place Graslin (tel: 02 51 84 94 94).

Le Pescadou. Fishy dishes served for almost every course at a smart restaurant, S of the castle. Menus from 20€. 8 Allée Baco, off Square Elisa-Mercoeur (tel: 02 40 35 29 50).

Festivals:

Les Folles Journées. Prestigious five-day festival of classical music, each year on a different theme. Jan.

Carnaval. Large street carnival. Mar.

Les Rendezvous de l'Erdre. Family fun & music on & beside the River Erdre. Early Sept.

north-south and have the name of the terminus clearly shown on the front. Tickets, including good-value 24-hour ones (3.30€ at time of writing) that are also valid on the town's buses, must be bought from slot machines at tram stops before boarding. The ticket has to be punched, or *composté*, to validate it on entering the tram. (For an all-day ticket, you do this just on the first trip.)

A good first stop is the main tourist office, south-east of the Commerce tram station, at the junction of Cours Olivier-de-Clisson and Rue Kervégan, where you can pick up a free town plan and brochures, and ask for information. Rue Kervégan is the central street of the "Ile Feydeau" ("Feydeau Island") district, formerly surrounded by the Loire, but now landlocked in a tide of swirling traffic. Narrow and cobbled, and at present rather run-down, the street was the preserve of wealthy 18th-century shipowners. Still visible today, their houses feature ornate balconies and decorative carved stone faces, called *mascarons*, over doors and windows.

Nantes has two distinct characters, divided by the Cours des 50 Otages—the central north-south boulevard that runs north of the tourist office. To the east is the old town, a series of narrow pedestrianised streets around the château and the Ste-Croix church containing 15th- and 16th-century houses, many unusual shops, and a second tourist office in Place St-Pierre, near the cathedral.

To the west lies the busy Place du Commerce. Behind one corner of the square, look for Passage Pommeraye, an unusual 19th-century arcade on different levels linked by steps that climb steeply to finish at Rue Crébillon—the town's smartest shopping street. Turn left for Place Graslin, with its opera house and beautiful turn-of-the-century brasserie, La Cigale. Just south of Place Graslin lies an elegant, traffic-free avenue of 18th-century houses called Cours Cambronne. Alternatively, if you cross Rue Crébillon and continue north you come to Rue du Calvaire, with the Nantes branch of the Galeries Lafayette department store.

More mundane shopping centres are available on the fringes of town. South of the station, on a large island that lies between two

■ Nantes: the imposing ramparts of the Château des Ducs de Bretagne.

branches of the river Loire, is a huge modern *centre commercial*, or shopping mall, the Centre Beaulieu, which has a hypermarket and many French high-street clothes shops.

Nantes is well served for transport. The city has an international airport on the south-west side, with several flights a day from London. It also has a regular TGV rail service from Paris and from Lille-Europe, the latter linking with Eurostar trains from London. Be warned, though, if you arrange to meet anyone at Nantes railway station: make sure you specify the north or the south exit (*sortie nord* or *sortie sud*), or you might have a long and frustrating wait.

➤**Musée du Château des Ducs de Bretagne**. The majestic 15th-century castle lying between the Ile Feydeau and the railway station, formerly the residence of the dukes of Brittany and kings of France, is undergoing a vast renovation programme. At present, one building houses a changing series of temporary exhibitions, but once restoration is complete, in 2006, you can expect state-of-the-art presentations of the city's archaeological, commercial and industrial heritage. ● *Wed-Mon 10am-6pm (1 July-31 Aug, daily 10am-7pm). 4 Place Marc-Elder (tel: 02 40 41 56 56). 3.10€, students 1.60€, children free.*

➤**Cathédrale St-Pierre et St-Paul**. Within the lofty, white stone interior of the city's flamboyant-gothic cathedral is the spectacularly-decorated tomb of Duke François II of Brittany and his wife, commissioned in 1502 by their daughter Anne, Duchess of Brittany and Queen of France (see also Musée Dobrée, page 161). ● *Daily 8.30am-7pm. Place St-Pierre. Free.*

➤**Musée des Beaux-Arts**. Western painting from the 13th century to the present, featuring some fine works by Georges de la Tour, a strong showing of 19th-century French artists and a large collection of contemporary art that includes 11 paintings by the pioneer of abstract art, Wassily Kandinsky. Don't miss the unusual sight of an immense Rubens hanging above the museum's subterranean lavatories. ● *Wed-Mon 10am-6pm (Fri until 8pm). Closed 1 Jan, 1 & 11 Nov & 25 Dec. 10 Rue Georges-Clemenceau (tel: 02 51 17 45 00). 3.10€, children free.* ♿

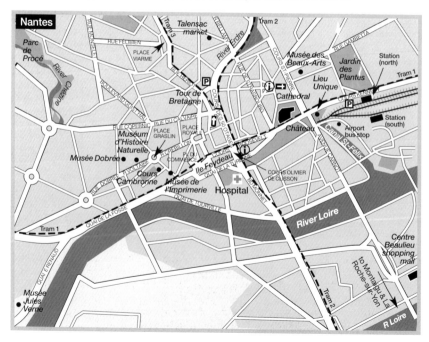

Jardin des Plantes: a green oasis near the station.

>**Jardin des Plantes**. Birdsong drowns the hum of traffic once you step inside the city's delightful botanical gardens, modelled by their founder upon those of Kew. Opposite the north exit of the railway station, the garden makes a marvellous open-air "waiting room" if you have time to kill between trains. There are wonderful spring magnolias, rhododendrons and camellias, plus green lawns and summer colour. Good entertainment for children, too, with roundabout, climbing frame and sandy play area. ● *Daily 8am-dusk (greenhouses closed Tues). Free.*

>**Le Lieu Unique**. One of the most conspicuous buildings in Nantes stands just south of the railway line, near the station's *sortie sud*, or south exit. Exuberantly decorated and magnificently restored, this 1905 domed tower—once the glory of the city's LU biscuit factory—is now an avant-garde arts centre, with café, bookshop and other facilities. ● *Tues-Sat 3-9pm; Sun 3-7pm. Quai Ferdinand-Favre, off Avenue Carnot (tel: 02 40 12 14 34). Admission free; ticket prices vary.* &

>**Musée de l'Imprimerie**. Interesting displays on the history of printing, showing the materials needed for illumination, woodcuts and other techniques. A two-hour tour is given daily at 2.30pm (except Sunday), during which the guide explains how the machines in the adjacent printshop work, and even puts a few of them in motion—though what you are shown depends on whether the main tour party visiting at the time consists of primary-school children, or of knowledgeable students about to embark on a printing career. ● *Mon-Sat 10am-noon & 2-5.30pm (1 Oct-30 Apr, Mon-Sat 10am-noon & 2-5.30pm; Sun 2-5pm). 24 Quai de la Fosse (tel: 02 40 73 26 55). 4.60€ (Sun 3.05€), students & children 3.05€.* &

>**Ile de Versailles**. Tranquil, pretty Japanese-style gardens on an island in the river Erdre, north of the city centre, and easily accessible by tram. Camellias, azaleas, rhododendrons and cherry trees flower in spring; all year you will find bamboos, reeds, cloud-pruned pines and, in the little museum called the Maison de l'Erdre, aquariums full of freshwater fish. ● *Gardens: Daily, 8.30am-dusk (1 Apr-22 Oct, daily 8.30am-8pm). Museum: Wed-Mon 11.30am-5.45pm; Sat, Sun & public holidays 10am-noon & 3-5.15pm. Quai de Versailles (tel: 02 40 29 41 11). Free.* &

>**Muséum d'Histoire Naturelle**. Comprehensive natural-history museum, full of stuffed animals and skeletons of every description. Among its more unusual features are an excellent vivarium housing live snakes—from adders and grass-snakes to anacondas and pythons—and, between the mummies and the monkeys on the first floor, the grisly sight of a tanned human skin. Its original owner, an 18th-century-soldier, desired it to be used after his death to cover a military drum but its resonating quality proved inadequate for his wish to be realised. ● *Wed-Mon 10am-6pm. 12 Rue Voltaire; entrance in small park behind building (tel: 02 40 99 26 20). 3.10€, students & everybody after 4.30pm 1.60€, children free. Free to all on third Sunday of the month.*

>**Musée Dobrée**. Thomas Dobrée (1810-95), son of a rich Nantes shipowner, built this granite palace to house his collections of furniture, prints, porcelain, sculpture and curiosities. They include the heart of Anne de Bretagne (1477-1514), the duchess of Brittany who became twice queen of France—by marrying first Charles VIII and, later, Louis XII. ● *Tues-Fri 9.45am-5.30pm; Sat, Sun, 2.30-5.30pm. Closed public holidays. Rue Voltaire (tel: 02 40 71 03 50). 3€, children 1.50€.*

>**Musée Jules Verne**. Although he was born in Nantes, the great visionary writer (1828-1905) never actually lived in this elegant, late-19th-century house on a clifftop site overlooking the river. Serious students of Verne's large output will appreciate the film posters, theatre reviews and the many editions of *20,000 Leagues Under the Sea* and other titles on display over three floors of the house, but the collection has a distinctly "glass-case" feel that may not appeal to children. In a small room-setting near the entrance is some of Verne's own furniture; in another room you come across his much-fingered globe. On the lowest floor a half-hour film on Verne's life and works is

screened, and children can try and work out the rules of a board game based on *Around the World in 80 Days*. Museum notes available in English. ● *Wed-Sat, & Mon, 10am-noon & 2-5pm; Sun 2-5pm. 3 Rue de l'Hermitage (tel: 02 40 69 72 52). 1.50€, children 0.70€.*

➤**L'Erdre et ses Châteaux.** Hidden away to the north of Nantes, the Erdre is a breathtakingly beautiful river, fringed with green fields and bordered by several country mansions dating from Renaissance times. You can take enjoyable cruises, with commentary, along this peaceful water-way aboard glass-sided boats—though rather ugly from the outside, they're comfortable enough within. Prices for the three-hour lunch or dinner cruises include a meal. ◗ *1 Apr-31 Oct (detailed timetable from tourist offices). Sightseeing cruises from 9€, students 5€, children 4€; family (2+2), 25€. Lunch cruises noon; dinner cruises 8pm (advance booking essential). Bateaux Nantais, Quai de la Motte-Rouge, Place Waldeck-Rousseau (tel: 02 40 14 51 14). Lunch cruise from 50€, dinner cruise from 57€; children from 18€. www.bateaux-nantais.fr/*

PASSAY

ⓘ tel: 02 40 13 30 00 fax: 02 40 31 34 98
www.mairie-lachevroliere.fr
commune@mairie-lachevroliere.fr

This pretty fishing village 20km south-west of Nantes and 3km west of La Chevrolière provides the closest view of a mysterious wetland nature reserve, the Lac de Grand-Lieu. The vastness of Grand-Lieu lake—which can extend to as much as 6,300 hectares (24 square miles) in winter—can be truly appreciated only by visitors arriving by plane at Nantes-Atlantique airport, who might be lucky enough to have a bird's-eye view of it dur-ing their approach. With its floating forests, peat bog and many rare plants, this wildlife haven has been chosen as a breeding site by a colony of white spoonbills as well as by 1,000 nesting pairs of grey herons.

Passay gives the best access to the lake of anywhere, so walk down to the water's edge and—if you are there in wet weather—notice how the peaty ground feels like a damp sponge. The pretty, single-storey cottages are still home to the dozen or so local fishermen who are authorised to net tench, pike and other river fish. They also catch eels in long, black-netting traps, keeping them alive afterwards in the sinister-looking tarred boxes, resembling miniature wartime landing-craft, that you see floating semi-submerged in the shallows. Visitors are allowed to join the fishermen on a couple of days a year, during the summer fishing festival, when they can take a trip into the interior by *plate* (a flat-bottomed boat) and watch the fish being pulled in, to be sold off later in aid of fishermen's charities.

PASSAY EXTRAS

Market: *Wed at La Chevrolière, 3km E of Passay.*

Specialities: *Eels & freshwater fish.*

Restaurant: Restaurant des Pêcheurs. *Eels, frogs' legs & other freshwater delicacies; menus from 19€.
11 Rue du Port (tel: 02 40 04 31 94).*

Festivals:
Fête des Anguilles. *Eel festival. Apr.*
Fête de la Pêche. *Fishing day, using traditional nets. 15 Aug, & following Sun.*

➤**Maison du Pêcheur.** A lighthouse-like observatory looms 11 metres above the roofs of the vil-lage, marking the position of this museum of local life among the low-built stone cottages. After watching a video about the wildlife of the lake, you can climb to the top of the observatory tower and look through telescopes to try and spot some real birds. A fascinating museum at the far end of the garden features wall-panels explaining the fragile ecosystem of this watery environment, displays of local fishing equipment and, as a grand finale, a wonderful aquarium of eels, carp, pike and other freshwater fish. ◗ *1 Apr-31 Oct, Wed, Fri, Sat, Sun, 2.30-6.30pm (1 June-31 Aug, Tues-Sun 2.30-7.30pm). 16 Rue Yves-Brisson, Passay (tel: 02 40 31 36 46). 2.50€, children 1.50€.*

Apart from Passay, here are a few other points around the perimeter that give either a fleeting glimpse or some further information about the wildlife of the Lac de Grand-Lieu:

St-Aignan-de-Grand-Lieu. Take an anti-clockwise route around the lake from La Chevrolière, 3km east of Passay, and look for signs to St-Aignan off the D11 on the north side of the lake. The route to the lakeside is indicated from the village centre, finishing at a large car park from which a shady footpath leads down to the shore.

St-Lumine-de-Coutais. At a village south-west of Passay, 19km by road but a lot less as the heron flies, you can carry your binoculars up the 173 steps of the church tower for an excellent view across the lake. *If closed, key available from St-Lumine mairie (tel: 02 40 02 90 25).*

St-Philbert-de-Grand-Lieu. You can't see the lake from here, but this little town near its southern edge has a good museum about the area's bird and animal life. (See pages 167-168.)

LE PELLERIN

ⓘ tel: 02 40 04 56 00 fax: 02 40 04 69 02
www.mairie-lepellerin.fr
sg@mairie-lepellerin.fr

Something of a seaside atmosphere pervades this small town on the south bank of the Loire, 18km west of Nantes. Its name comes from the *pèlerins*, or pilgrims (see page 31), from countries farther north who arrived here in large numbers by cargo boat during the Middle Ages to start their long walk to Santiago de Compostela, in north-west Spain.

A car-ferry service runs across the fast-flowing river to Couëron on the north shore, a 10-minute trip costing *2.90€* per vehicle that saves a long drive via St-Nazaire or Nantes. A similar ferry runs between Indre and Basse-Indre, 7km farther east.

➤★ **Planète Sauvage**. Lions, tigers, giraffes and zebras are among the 2,000 animal residents of this excellent drive-through safari park 10km south of Le Pellerin, which can easily provide a whole day's entertainment. The trail winds for 10km and takes about two hours, so on a hot day it's wise to take something with you to drink. (If you'd rather let someone else do the driving, there is a circuit by coach at 10.30am & 2.30pm.) Later, on foot, you can look at reptiles in a reconstructed African village, watch sealion and falconry shows, and embark on an amazing treetop ramble across swaying, jungle-style bridges watching monkeys cavort below you. This last part is great fun but you do need both hands free, to hold on, so it might be difficult for toddlers, for people shaky on their feet or anyone carrying a small child. ◑ *Mid March-11 Nov, daily 10am-6pm; last admission 4pm (1 June-31 Aug, 10am-7.30pm; last admission 5.30pm). Port-St-Père (tel: 02 40 04 82 82). 16€, children 10€; supplement for coach trip 6€, children 4€.* ♿ *except jungle walkway.*

➤ **Le Labyrinthe**. A large maze, 8km east of Le Pellerin, delineated by 13.5km of green privet hedges, which the owners claim makes it the world's largest permanent hedge maze. It's pretty challenging trying to find the site in the first place; look for signs to "La Mouchonnerie" off the busy Nantes-to-St-Nazaire road along the south side of the Loire. Allow a good hour to find your way through the whole maze; as you work towards the centre you come across four elegant mini-marquees with different family entertainments going on inside. Open for evening visits on nights with a full moon; take a torch, though, in case the sky is cloudy. ◑ *Early Apr-31 Aug, daily 9am-7pm (full-moon nights, also open 9-11pm); 1-30 Sept, Wed, Sat, Sun 10am-7pm. Chemin des Réservoirs, Bougenais; exit C5 from D723, signposted "La Mouchonnerie" (tel: 02 51 70 60 99). 6€, children less than 1.10 metres in height 3€.* ♿

■ Planète Sauvage: step out on the jungle walkway.

PORNIC

ⓘ tel: 02 40 82 04 40 fax: 02 40 82 90 12
www.ot-pornic.fr
contact@ot-pornic.fr

There is a real Breton flavour to this chic seaside resort full of narrow lanes and steep steps, which was a favourite of Gustave Flaubert, George Sand and other 19th-century literary celebrities. Some 18km south of the St-Nazaire bridge, Pornic has a rocky coastline dominated by a fairy-tale castle with pointed slate roof, whose prettiness belies the fact that it once belonged to the infamous Gilles de Rais (see pages 149 and 157). The clifftop Sentier des Douaniers (Customs path), on either side of town, provides fantastic views over the sea. Sandiest beach is the Plage de la Noëveillard, just beyond the marina. Farther west, some exquisite villas look over the sea in the smart Ste-Marie district.

The most extensive beach in the area is that of Tharon-Plage, 8km north-west of Pornic, lying to the west of the D213. This fast road leading up to the St-Nazaire bridge links many seaside resorts. Fluttering flags along its length officially proclaim it to holidaymakers as the "Route Bleue," or "Blue Route".

Farther north, you might notice a wonderful smell of baking as you come abreast of St-Michel-Chef-Chef, 8km north of Pornic. The town is the home of Bahlsen's St-Michel biscuit factory, whose products you will find laid out on the shelves of every supermarket.

➤ **Faïencerie de Pornic**. Inside this factory shop you can pick up half-price bargains of some of France's favourite pottery designs. Look out for the ingeniously-designed flat, round dishes for pizzas or tarts, with painted numbers around the edge to help you divide up the slices fairly among different numbers of people. You can view a half-hour video about the industry, watch an expert at work decorating plates, or even have a go yourself at painting anything from ramekins to tankards (collect the finished product a few days later, after firing). ● *Mon-Sat 10am-12.30pm & 2-6pm (1 July-31 Aug, until 7pm). Closed public holidays. Chemin du Cracaud, NW of Pornic town centre (tel: 02 51 74 19 10). Admission free; plate painting from 6.95€, according to the size of object chosen.*

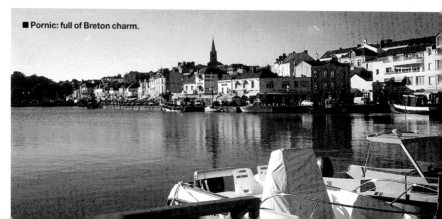

■ Pornic: full of Breton charm.

➤ **Cimetière Anglais**. Some 400 victims of the World War II sinking of the *Lancastria* (see below) are among the British and Commonwealth servicemen and -women buried in this beautifully-kept cemetery north-west of the town's main bridge, near a large school building. ● *Place Joseph-Girard, off Rue du Val-St-Martin.*

➤ **Exposition Cerfs-Volants**. Dangling from the ceiling of a century-old general store in the tranquil resort of Préfailles is a collection of historic kites (*cerfs-volants*), including hundred-year-old examples that carried advertisements, cameras, and wireless and meteorological equipment. Among the fish-hooks, pottery, stationery and household items on sale beneath them, you can also buy more modern kites to fly on the headlands nearby. ● *Mon-Sat 9am-12.30pm & 2.30-7pm (school-holiday periods, Mon-Sat 9am-12.30pm & 2.30-7pm, Sun 9.30am-12.30pm). Grand Bazar, 31 Grande Rue, Préfailles, 11km W of Pornic (tel: 02 40 21 61 22). Free.*

ST-BRÉVIN-LES-PINS

ⓘ tel: 02 40 27 24 32 fax: 02 40 39 10 34
www.mairie-saint-brevin.fr
office.tourisme@mairie-saint-brevin.fr

The most popular holiday centre on this part of the coast, 2km south of the St-Nazaire bridge, St-Brévin is divided into two districts: a northern part full of shady pine trees, and a more open, south-west-facing beach area known as St-Brévin-l'Océan.

With mini-golf and casino, street entertainment and forest walks, there is something for all ages at St-Brévin besides the obvious attractions of its 8km of sand. If you are wondering about the purpose of the bizarre-looking wooden structures on stilts that are dotted along the shore, you will find the explanation on page 157.

Just off Mindin, at the mouth of the river Loire, occurred one of the greatest maritime disasters in history. At least 3,000 Allied troops and civilians (some estimates put the number as high as 6,000) were drowned on 17 June 1940 when the *Lancastria*, a merchant ship evacuating them to Britain following the fall of France, was sunk by enemy bombing in just 24 minutes. Commonwealth War Graves Commission headstones in many town and village cemeteries up and down the coast mark the places where the unfortunate victims were washed ashore and, later, buried—many of them at Les Moutiers-en-Retz (see page 158) and in the Allied war cemetery at Pornic (see above).

➤ **Musée de la Marine**. Inside a 19th-century fort almost under the south approach road to the St-Nazaire bridge is an interesting museum of the sea. The rooms are full of model boats of all scales and types, deep-sea diving gear, stories of local nautical disasters and informative displays about the slave trade that enriched the city of Nantes in the 18th century. ○ *Mid June-mid Sept, Tues-Sun 3-7pm. Fort de Mindin, Place Bougainville (tel: 02 40 27 00 64). 3€, children under 12 free.*

ST-BRÉVIN EXTRAS
Market: Thurs & Sun, St-Brévin-les-Pins. Sat, St-Brévin-l'Océan. Mon (1 July-31 Aug), Mindin, 2km N of St-Brévin.
Festivals:
Grands-Mères Automobiles. Parade of vintage cars. Early May.
Rencontres de Cerfs-volants. Festival of kite-flying. Late Aug.

ST-NAZAIRE

ⓘ tel: 08 20 01 40 15 fax: 02 40 22 19 80
www.saint-nazaire-tourisme.com
contact@saint-nazaire-tourisme.com

As you cross the Loire heading north from the Pays de Retz over the Pont de St-Nazaire, the rooftops below change from rounded Roman tiles, with their Mediterranean feel, to the more businesslike slate of Brittany. (Though the beautiful, curved 3.35km bridge, 61m above the mouth of the estuary, is well signposted for drivers going north, it is harder to find from the other side. If heading south, look for signs to Noirmoutier or to St-Brévin.)

As an important U-boat port during World War II, St-Nazaire suffered so much Allied bombing that 85 per cent of its buildings were flattened. The heavily-fortified German submarine base was the target of an audacious Anglo-Canadian raid on 24 March 1942, when the destroyer *Campbeltown*, crammed with explosives, was rammed into the gates of the huge lock and blown up, disabling the dock for the remainder of the war. After the D-Day landings in Normandy, in June 1944, many German troops in Brittany continued to hold out in St-Nazaire, Lorient, Brest and other large ports. The Allies chose to leave these "pockets" while they continued their advance on other fronts, and so St-Nazaire was not liberated until 11 May 1945, three days after VE Day.

Today entirely rebuilt, St-Nazaire has a bright, modern face. The smart shopping centre is focused on the semi-pedestrianised Avenue de la République and on nearby Rue de la Paix. The shipbuilding industry that launched such great ocean liners as the *Normandie*, in 1935, the *France*, in 1962, and more recently the *Queen Mary 2* still dominates the northern shore of the estuary.

To the west, the town claims to have at least 20 beaches, starting from just south of the Escal'Atlantic centre (see page 167) and stretching westward—including that of St-Marc-sur-Mer, the setting for the Jacques Tati film *Monsieur Hulot's Holiday*. St-Nazaire has also featured in literature, as the backdrop to Tintin's adventure *The Seven Crystal Balls*. The town's Tintin fans have installed comic-strip panels at certain points to remind you where the fictional boy detective and his faithful dog, Snowy, are reputed to have passed.

The latest tourist attraction, to the east of the town centre, is a brilliant concept that re-uses the indestructible German submarine base to show aspects of St-Nazaire's maritime history. Following colourful little signs for the "Ville-Port" brings you to a huge car park beside the giant World War II buildings. Here you can enjoy the ocean-liner "experience", Escal'Atlantic, and a tour of a real French submarine (see below). The port's visitor centre also offers bus and walking tours of the shipyards (*chantiers navals*) where the vast liners are built, and visits to l'Aérospatiale where parts of the Airbus plane are assembled. (These tours need to be booked well in advance, and you have to show a passport for the Airbus visit.) In summer, there are also night-time boat trips around the docks, past the enormous cranes and artistically-illuminated quays.

■ Maritime heritage: step aboard a submarine at St-Nazaire.

> ★ Sous-marin *Espadon*. As you enter the concrete-roofed, German-built submarine dock that lies across the water from the Escal'Atlantic base, you cannot refrain from giving a shudder when you first glimpse the sinister silhouette of the 1950s

ST-NAZAIRE EXTRAS

Market: Tues, Fri & Sun, Place du Commerce, W of Rue de la République.

Restaurant: Le France. Popular beach bar & restaurant just beneath the statue of film-maker Jacques Tati; menus from 10€. St-Marc-sur-Mer, 11km SW of St-Nazaire (tel: 02 40 91 96 13).

Shop: Pâtisserie Boulay. If you can't wait to try the delicious pastries on sale, pop into the tea-room at the back of this chic city-centre cake shop. 57 Avenue de la République (tel: 02 40 22 48 92).

Monsieur Hulot: on holiday at St-Marc-sur-Mer.

French submarine *Espadon* ("Swordfish"). During a 30-minute tour up and down the narrow companionways and steep ladders, a recorded commentary (available in English) describes life aboard when there were bunks for only two-thirds of the crew (the other third was on duty), and just two lavatories for 65 men. Afterwards you can climb to a viewing platform on the top of the dock for a much-needed breath of fresh air, and to look down on the Forme-Écluse Joubert, the large lock that was attacked by Allied commandos in 1942 (see page 166). ● *Contact details & opening times as Escal'Atlantic, below. 6€, including Écomusée; children 4.50€; family (2+2 children under 12) 17.85€ (1 Apr-31 Oct, 8€, children 5.50€; family 22.95€). Advance booking recommended.*

➤★ **Escal'Atlantic: L'Aventure des Paquebots.** *Paquebot* is the French for ocean liner and, as soon as you have climbed the gangway and entered the chic, wood-panelled foyer within, you forget you are inside a massive, reinforced-concrete structure and feel you really have stepped aboard a luxurious 1930s' floating palace. At times you emerge during your tour of corridors and cabins, saloons and engine-room—all newly created inside the monolithic World War II building—to find yourself on "deck", with the (fake) wind in your hair and (real) salt water lapping below. It takes a good hour and a half to see it all. A big surprise is in store at the end. ● *1 Feb-31 Dec, Wed-Sun 10am-12.30pm & 2-6pm (1 Apr-31 Oct, daily 9.30am-12.30pm & 1.30-6pm; 1 July-31 Aug, daily 9.30am-7pm). Last admission 90 minutes before closing-time. Closed 1-31 Jan. Base Sous-Marine, Ville-Port, Boulevard de la Légion-d'Honneur (tel: 08 10 88 84 44). 9€, including Écomusée; children 6€; family (2+2 children under 12) 25.50€ (1 Apr-31 Oct, 12€, children 8€; family 34€). &*

➤ **Écomusée.** After the submarine visit and the liner experience, the rather traditional town museum is inevitably a bit of an anticlimax. It contains information on local birdlife, St-Nazaire's shipbuilding industry (including some splendid models), prisms from a lighthouse, and photographs of the wartime devastation of the town and its reconstruction. As in British cities after the war, many inhabitants lived for up to 30 years in "temporary" pre-fabricated houses. ● *Opening times as Escal'Atlantic, above. Admission included with tickets for Escal'Atlantic or submarine.*

➤ **La Plage de Monsieur Hulot.** Devotees of Jacques Tati's classic 1953 film *Les Vacances de Monsieur Hulot* can have fun trying to spot the locations used in the movie at this seaside village, now a suburb of St-Nazaire. St-Marc is 11km south-west of the town centre, but can be hard to find—if you don't see signs to it, try aiming for the better-marked resort of Ste-Marguerite which lies farther west. And be prepared for a bit of walking: the village is incredibly busy on summer weekends, and parking can be a problem. The beachside Hôtel de la Plage is still in action, and a bronze statue of the gawky Monsieur Hulot now stands for ever gazing down onto the sands, which have been re-named in his honour. Strangely, the French seem baffled by the British reverence for Tati's engaging fictional character—for really side-splitting entertainment they usually prefer re-runs of old Benny Hill shows! ●

ST-PHILBERT-DE-GRAND-LIEU
ⓘ tel: 02 40 78 73 88 fax: 02 40 78 83 42
http://st.philbert.gd.lieu.online.fr
st.philbert.gd.lieu@online.fr

Near the southern limit of the great wetland known as the Lac de Grand-Lieu (see page 162), stands one of the oldest churches in France. In this pretty village 23km south of Nantes, you can rent boats or fish in the calm waters of the Boulogne. Opposite the

campsite to the north of the river is a cheery playground equipped with bouncy castles, mini-golf and other delights; you can also learn to play swin-golf (see page 16) on a 14-hole course.

➤**Abbatiale St-Philbert.** More than 20,000 visitors flock each year to this ancient church built in 815 by monks from St Philbert's Abbey, on the island of Noirmoutier (see page 51), to preserve the relics of their founder from repeated Norman invasions. Though continuing raids by the Norsemen meant that the saint's remains had eventually to be carried eastward again for safety as far as Tournus, in Burgundy (where they are venerated to this day), you can still see his empty sarcophagus in the crypt. The chunky columns of the church's interior are built from alternating bands of white stone and warm brick, creating a surprising chequerboard effect. Concerts, theatrical performances and exhibitions are held in the church during the summer; a medieval garden has been laid out behind it. ● *Mon-Sat 10am-noon & 2-5.30pm, Sun 2-5.30pm (1 Apr-30 Sept, daily 10am-12.30pm & 2.30-6.30pm). Place de l'Abbatiale (tel: 02 40 78 73 88). Entrance via tourist office. 2.50€ (includes garden & bird museum, see below), children 1.50€.*

■ St Philbert-de-Grand-Lieu: country pursuits.

ST-PHILBERT EXTRAS

Market: Sun.
Specialities: Muscadet & Gros-Plant wines.
Brocante: St-Philbert *Brocante. Furniture & collectors' items. Fri-Tues 10am-1pm & 2.30-7pm. La Chaussée; on N edge of village, off the roundabout, just before D117 (tel: 02 40 78 72 16).*

➤**Maison de l'Avifaune du Lac.** Pass through the tourist office to visit this museum devoted to the more than 200 types of bird that live near, or pass through, the great wetland to the north of the village. As well as an audio-visual presentation about the flora and fauna of the Lac de Grand-Lieu you can see, beautifully displayed in large glass cases, stuffed spoonbills, kingfishers, curlews, coots and herons. Pressing buttons to try to identify the different species by lighting up their names is an excellent way of extending one's French vocabulary. ● *Admission details as for church, above.* ♿

VALLET
ⓘ tel: 02 40 36 35 87 fax: 02 40 36 29 13
www.cc-vallet.fr
tourisme-vallet@wanadoo.fr

This little town 20km south-east of Nantes is the epicentre of Muscadet production, and everything in Vallet (the final t is sounded, making the pronounciation Val-ett) seems to proclaim its connection with the celebrated dry white wine. The cinema is called "Le Cep" ("The Vine"), a restaurant on the main square is called "Les Tonneaux" ("The Wine-Barrels"), the wonderful Sunday-morning market features a number of wine-growers, and the tourist office produces a calendar detailing a vineyard to visit for almost every day of the year. Called *Bienvenue dans nos Caves en Muscadet*, this leaflet lists 60 of the area's top wine-producers who have arranged a rota between them covering each day from March to December. Maps are also available of the signposted "Route Touristique du Vignoble Nantais" (see page 133). If you have no time to embark on either, you can taste and buy a selection from 35 growers presented at the Maison du Muscadet, on the Ancenis road. Before too much tippling, though, keep in mind the strict French drink-drive laws (see page 20).

Try and make a detour to visit Vallet's cemetery in Rue de Bazoges (off the main square). Among the time-worn traditional gravestones is the unexpected sight of some large decorative memorials, constructed and devotedly maintained by some of France's gypsy community. You cannot fail to be moved by the masses of flowers and pictures inside the glass enclosures, and by the reverence with which the travelling families remember their dead. They do ask, however, that visitors do not take photographs.

➤**Labyrinthe des Vignes**. A novelty in the world of mazes is this one made from vines, artfully trained to form passageways in the fields. In the little building containing the ticket-office, the owners offer tastings of their wine and grape juice, sell packs of wine, and invite you to go down into their 14th-century cellars to enjoy an amusingly laid-out trail and quiz (available in English) on how wine is made. ○ *15-30 June, Sat, Sun 10am-6pm; 1 July-31 Aug, daily 10am-6pm. Château de Fromenteau, 1km W of Vallet on D106 (tel: 02 40 36 23 75). 5€, children 4€.*

➤**Musée du Vignoble**. Superb presentation (including a wine-tasting) of everything to do with Muscadet production, displayed in a modern building on the southern edge of Le Pallet, 7km south-west of Vallet. As the village was the birthplace of the philosopher and theologian Pierre Abélard (1079-1142), the museum also tells the story of Abélard and of his scandalous love-affair with, and marriage to, his young pupil Héloïse. After suffering intense persecution, he became a monk, then a hermit, and finally took up the post of abbot at a monastery in Brittany. Héloïse entered a convent from which she wrote him a series of celebrated love-letters. She died in 1164, 22 years after Abélard, and was buried beside him. ◑ *1 Mar-11 Nov, Mon-Fri 1-6pm; Sat, Sun & public holidays 2-6pm (1 July-31 Aug, Mon-Fri 11am-6pm; Sat, Sun & public holidays 10am-noon & 1-6pm). Closed 1 Nov. Le Pallet (tel: 02 40 80 90 13). 4€ (includes a glass of Muscadet), students & children 2.50€; children under 12 free.* ♿

➤**Maison des Vins de Nantes**. Serious connoisseurs can compare and contrast the wines of the Nantes area at this excellent *centre oenologique* (wine-specialist centre) 10km west of Vallet. Amid fantastic views across vineyards that produce 85 million bottles a year, you can learn about the local wines and try a few from among the 150 different labels on display. These range from local red Gamays and sharp, white Gros-Plants, through the light wines of the Coteaux d'Ancenis, to Muscadets of the Coteaux de la Loire and Sèvre-et-Maine. ● *Mon-Fri 8.30am-12.30pm & 2-5.45pm (1 June-31 Aug, Mon-Sat 10am-12.30pm & 2-6pm). Bellevue, near La Haie-Fouassière, 10km W of Vallet (tel: 02 40 36 90 10). Free.*

VALLET EXTRAS

Market: Sun.

Speciality: Muscadet.

Restaurant: Les Tonneaux. Popular bar on main square; menus from 9.50€. 2 Rue de Bazoges (tel: 02 40 33 92 77).

Festivals:

Expo-Vall'. Three-day wine fair & charity auction. Mid Mar.

Le Motor Show. Parade of old cars around local villages, ending with a rally in Vallet. Apr.

Jazz-sur-Lie. Wine-tastings & open-air concerts. Le Pé-de-Sèvre, near Le Pallet, 7km SW of Vallet. Late Aug.

VERTOU

ⓘ tel: 02 40 34 12 22 fax: 02 40 34 06 86
otsivertou@oceanet.fr

Pretty village on the Sèvre Nantaise river, 7km south-east of Nantes and just off the south-east side of the expressway that hurtles around the city (leave it at junction 47). Beside the cruises (see below), attractions at this peaceful spot include several smart waterside restaurants, plus hire of canoes or small electric boats.

➤**La Sèvre au fil de l'eau**. Travel in a glass-roofed boat along the picturesque river Sèvre, sipping a complimentary glass of wine. During the 90-minute cruise through Muscadet vineyards, a French commentary points out 18th-century waterside mansions known as *"folies nantaises"*, reputed to have been built for their mistresses by rich Nantes shipowners. The ticket office opens 30 minutes before departure, though it's best to book places by phone first. Follow road signs to the Parc de la Sèvre car park, then walk from there to the right along the river until you reach the Bateaux Nantais landing-stage. ○ *Mid Apr-mid Sept, usually Sun & public holidays (full timetable available from tourist offices), 4pm. Bateaux Nantais, Parc de la Sèvre (tel: 02 40 14 51 14). 9€, students 5€, children 4€. www.bateaux-nantais.fr/*

VERTOU EXTRAS

Market: Sat, Sun.

Restaurants: Le Monté Cristo. Gastronomic dishes served in a beautiful waterside setting overlooking the River Sèvre. Menus from 14€. 11 Quai de la Chaussée-aux-Moines (tel: 02 40 34 40 36).

Festival: Salon des Antiquaires. Antiques fair. Mid Mar.

Bibliography

PHRASE BOOKS
Dorling Kindersley "Eyewitness": French Phrase Book. Covers menus, travel, health, pronounciation and everyday phrases. Helpful sections such as "Things you will see", including pictures of street-signs, and "Things you will hear", with questions that you might be asked at a garage, a hotel or when shopping.
Eat Your Words in France, by Erica Morris and Terry Morris. Slim, pocket-sized book that is invaluable for deciphering menus. It lists cuts of meat, various cooking methods and many different desserts.
Collins Gem: 5,000 French Words, by Barbara Christie. Compact book to keep in the handbag. Useful phrases, plus categories of vocabulary for shopping, garages, banks etc.

HISTORY
In addition to books mentioned on page 38:
Maillezais: The Story of a French Abbey, written and illustrated by Edwin Apps. Entertaining history of the now-ruined Vendean abbey. Obtainable from bookshops in the Maillezais area, and from ww.amazon.fr/

ACCOMMODATION
In addition to the suggestions for guidebooks on hotels and bed-and breakfasts, provided on pages 11, 12 and 16:
Vendée: Art de Vivre et Patrimoine. Free brochure of country-house hotels, obtainable on request from the Vendée Tourist Board (address on page 11).
Good Camps Guide, by Alan Rogers. Detailed descriptions and appraisals of hundreds of campsites throughout France.

MAPS
In addition to maps mentioned on page 17:
Michelin map 989 *France*. Single-sheet map of the whole country, on a scale of 1:1,000,000. Useful for route-planning.
Michelin France: Tourist and Motoring Atlas. Large spiral-bound book, on a scale of 1:200,000, makes an excellent navigational tool for use in the car.

Unless otherwise stated, the above are available from UK bookshops, and from www.amazon.co.uk/

Glossary

The phrase books listed above should help you through most situations. However, here are a few more unusual French words that you may read, hear or need to use during your time in the Vendée:

arobase	The @ sign in an email address.
biologique, or *bio*	Organic.
bocage	Undulating wooded areas of central and eastern Vendée.
brocante	Furniture and objects at the cheaper end of the antiques market.
coefficient	Figure in tide-tables indicating magnitude of tide on a particular day. The higher (or lower) the *coefficient*, the higher (or lower) the high and low tides on that date.
dégustation	Tasting—for example a free tasting of wine (though the provider obviously hopes you will make a purchase).
dépôt-vente	Second-hand shop—usually old furniture and assorted objects that could be classified as *brocante*, or junk.
dolmen	Giant stone "table" built by neolithic man as a tomb, and originally covered with earth.
donjon	Castle keep or central tower. (Frequently mistranslated. Despite similarity in sound, it is *not* a dungeon!)
hôtel de ville	Council offices in a town; *not* a hotel! (See also *mairie*.)
interdit	Forbidden. (*Pêche interdite* means "No fishing".)
Je suis allergique à...	I am allergic to...
location	Rental. (As in *location de vélos*, cycle rental.)
mairie	Council offices in village. (See also *hôtel de ville*.)
marais	Marsh, fens, marshland.
menhir	Large standing-stone erected by neolithic man.
mogette/mojette	White haricot bean, a favourite Vendean vegetable.
occasion	Second-hand (usually *d'occasion*); can also mean bargain.
respectez	Keep off. (*Respectez les pelouses* means "keep off the grass".)
touche étoile/dièse	Telephone star/hash button.
VTT	Mountain bike. (Pronounced "vay-tay-tay"; short for *vélo tout-terrain*.)

Index

Picture credits

All photographs in this book are © Angela Bird, except the following:

pages 14, 33 (dolmen), 61, 67, 105, back cover ("Green Venice"): Jean Lesage/ Comité de Tourisme de la Vendée.
page 16: Rob Busby.
page 18: Adrian Hulf.
pages 20, 34 (Neptune), 163, back cover (beach): Justine Hulf.
pages 23, 34 (Les Sables), 35 (Green Venice), 45, 46, 52, 53, 84, 134, 141 (oak chapel): John Bird.
page 33 (farmhouses): Michael Julien.
pages 34 (Apremont), 152: David Darlow.
pages 35 (Puy-du-Fou), 142, 143, back cover (Puy du Fou): Jean-Eric Pasquier/Rapho—Puy-du-Fou.
page 36 (Charette): Comité de Tourisme de la Vendée.

page 59: Carolyn Boakes.
page 64: Engraving from Le Rouleau d'Apremont: Château d'Apremont au XVIe siècle d'après Jehan-Baptiste le Florentin.
page 93: Brenda Wilson.
page 95 (both pictures): Office de Tourisme de Luçon.
page 113 (lime kilns): Josette Ahuir.
page 122: Bruno Derbord/Ville de Niort.
page 144: René Golder.
pages 158 (tram), 159, 161: Office de Tourisme Nantes Atlantique/ A.Delaporte.
page 166: Dominique Macel/Mairie de Saint-Nazaire.

Shell pictures on pages 34 and 82 reproduced by kind permission of their creator, Danielle Aubin.
Engravings on pages 64, 131 and 149 reproduced with the authorisation of the attractions concerned.
Pictures on pages 99, 103 and 118 reproduced by kind permission of the properties' owners.

Achevé d'imprimer en mai 2004 sur les presses de
l'Imprimerie Graphique de l'Ouest au Poiré-sur-Vie (Vendée)
Dépôt légal : mai 2004 – Imprimé en France